PLEASE MAY I LE

PLEASE MAY I LEAVE THE ROOM?

By

KEN GRIFFIN

All illustrations by Ken Griffin

© Ken Griffin, 2014

Published by Wendy Griffin

All rights reserved. No part of this book may be reproduced, adapted, stored in a retrieval system or transmitted by any means, electronic, mechanical, photocopying, or otherwise without the prior written permission of the author.

The rights of Ken Griffin to be identified as the author of this work have been asserted in accordance with the Copyright, Designs and Patents Act 1988.

A CIP catalogue record for this book is available from the British Library.

ISBN 978-0-9930766-0-2

Book layout and cover design by Clare Brayshaw
Cover image © Demachy l Dreamstime.com

Prepared and printed by:

York Publishing Services Ltd
64 Hallfield Road
Layerthorpe
York YO31 7ZQ

Tel: 01904 431213

Website: www.yps-publishing.co.uk

BY WORD OF EXPLANATION

This is a glance at the lighter side of the education process as seen during several years on the West Riding County Supply Staff before Mr Baker and subsequent Education Ministers started their "improvements".

There are many things that happened both in school and in my private life which I have not included. To compensate I have written at some length about a flat which exists only in my imagination but which gives some continuity to what would otherwise be a disconnected discourse. My 'flat-mate', Peter, is on the other hand very real as are the other characters, young and old, and the stories of what happened to them. I may, it is true, have embellished them a little here and there, but that can be put down to an ageing memory or just artistic licence.

Teaching and learning are very serious matters and there are libraries of portentous tomes to prove it. After around 35 years on the shop floor I feel that I have neither the knowledge nor the desire to add to this sea of speculation and heavy-handed advice. If there is anything at all to be learned from what I have written it is that anyone unable to see the funny side of almost any situation would be well advised to forget teaching as a career. They would almost certainly go stark staring mad and end up in a nursing home ..... Or, of course they could write another book on how to teach.

There is no reason why 'Frontown' in the book should not be given its proper name of Leeds, but for obvious reasons the names of other places and people must remain anonymous.

CHAPTER ONE

It was all Hitler's fault. If he'd only stuck to painting houses instead of going on about master races and lebensraum I would never have become embroiled in classroom brawls with Delius Potter – a sobering sequence of cause and effect which should make all would-be dictators pause and reflect. It was because of the aforesaid Hitler that I ceased slaving in the lower echelons of the photographic trade and became what might roughly be described as a soldier. It was not my natural metier. Unlike my old school friend Peter (of whom more anon) who rocketed to a well-deserved Majority, it took me six years of determined ineptitude to struggle from signalman to corporal. My attempt to explain to him that it was more difficult in our lot was received with a loud guffaw and a coarse military expression. I enjoyed certain aspects of the life, like riding the firm's motorcycles in competition over rough terrain and playing saxophone in the unit dance band but, for the rest, anyone who wanted it only needed to ask as far as I was concerned.

When the end of hostilities became more than just a wishful dream, some people who had the imagination to see beyond the 1918 "home fit for heroes" philosophy, inaugurated the idea of rehabilitation training courses and my interest in the future, moribund since 1939, started to perk up again.

Rejecting pre-war ambitions of being either a speedway star or the leader of the band at the Dorchester Hotel (they didn't seem to have courses on those, anyway), I began to consider the teaching profession. In the days when I left school such notion would have seemed the height of conceit. Teachers, like ministers of religion and bank managers, were superior beings to whom respect was due and who lived on a higher plane than we mere workers. Six years of rubbing shoulders with a broad cross section of the community reduced to mediocrity by the donning of the uniform had modified these traditional values and I decided to give the academic world the benefit of my experience.

In the fullness of time the army and I parted without regrets on either side and I embarked on what was called and "Emergency Training Course for Teachers". The college must have been a disappointment to anyone looking forward to oak panelled halls and shady cloisters, being situated in a hotch-potch of huts adapted from some redundant military usage in a nondescript small township in Lancashire. Nevertheless I found it much to my liking. The principal and staff contrived to make it feel like a serious educational establishment, the work was intensive and purposeful and the students were a companiable collection of ex-servicemen.

After thirteen months of this I was adjudged competent to instruct the young and started doing so in a rough, down-town school in one of the least desirable areas of a large West Riding City. After a short but illuminating stay I moved to a smaller and less exciting establishment catering for mixed infants and mixed juniors in a semi-rural district just outside town. Here I really began to learn the finer points of my craft to the stage where I felt that the status of "Qualified Teacher" was not altogether unjustified. I started to live in a sort of woolly cloud-cuckoo land, happy after the wartime alarms and excursions to be ticking over unadventurously from nine to four each Monday to Friday and receiving enough money to escape serious debt. If not deliriously happy, I was contented in a bovine sort of way and never gave serious thought to the possibility of change.

The Head, a nondescript sort of person who demonstrated his superiority each morning by giving a perfunctory wave from his car as he passed me at the bus stop, appeared only rarely from his office and then usually to apologise to some member of staff for not being able to take a lesson due to something urgent having just cropped up. This was so much normal procedure that alternative arrangements were automatically put into operation and there was an absence of either surprise or resentment.

He was also head of the Local Evening Institute, a task which, according to popular rumour, consisted almost entirely in chatting up the members of the Ladies Keep Fit, Dressmaking and Flower Arranging classes between seven and nine each evening. The administrative part of his duties he found could be more conveniently carried out during the daytime when the school secretary was available.

The other members of staff were a pleasant enough lot with whom one could share a joke or do a crossword at break times without ever creating the desire for any deeper friendship. Only the efforts of odd children such as Delius Potter, who would have stood out as exceptional in a gang of Corsican bandits, ruffled the calm of our existence. Then, one day, into this life of comfortable mediocrity, stepped Mr J.W. Garland, County Council Inspector.

I understand that nowadays Inspectors are called Joe or Stan or maybe Deirdre, but at the time of which I write there was no such familiarity. The distinctions in the educational hierarchy were strictly observed and the news that an Inspector was to pay a visit was sufficient to cause the head to rush around in a frenzied sort of way exhorting his staff to get their hair cut, wear sober clothing and cover the walls with children's work of unblemished perfection.

This hysteria naturally had its effect, particularly on the younger female teachers who would probably be reduced to tears, and even those of us who had experienced worse things in foreign parts were not unimpressed. My own sang, for example, became considerably less froid when I was told that this Mr Garland was coming to see me personally. No explanations being forthcoming as to the reasons for this recognition of my presence by the top brass, I made such preparations as I thought necessary and laughed nervously when other members of staff volunteered predictably pessimistic opinions.

As is so often the case, the reality was a bit of a let-down, the fearsome Mr Garland turning out to be a smallish man, mild tending to vague in manner and not, it seemed, the sort to go throwing his weight about at the expense of young and nervous teachers. Would I mind, he asked apologetically, if he sat in for a while on my lesson? I minded a great deal. Very few teachers, however confident when they have a class to themselves, take kindly to working under the eye of critical authority and can, if a trifle unsure of themselves, degenerate into gibbering idiots. So I said I had been looking forward to the opportunity ever since I had heard he was coming.

I went on to intimate that he was welcome to stay for the rest of the week if he felt so inclined and that it needed only this to make my cup of happiness overflow. No snake, tracking its prey through the long grass, could have crawled more effectively.

"Where", I asked, "would you care to sit?"

I was a bit smug about this, as an important part of my pre-planning had been to leave only one place available at our double desks, next to Dolores Finch who could be guaranteed to behave reasonably well and whose exercise books were a delight to behold. At least this should have been the only place but I hadn't allowed for the last minute absence of Fred Billings who, as his mother explained, had had to go to the hospital for his eyes. Needless to say it was Fred's place in the far corner of the room which appealed to Mr Garland. That put him next to Ginger Thomas who couldn't be guaranteed to do anything normal and whose books looked as though they had come off the compost heap.

Mr Garland took out a notebook and pen and gave Ginger a bright smile. Ginger looked at him as he did everything else, slowly and unwinkingly. Not rating what he saw very highly, he scowled and relapsed into his normal learning attitude – chin on the desk and arms wrapped round his head like an orang-utan.

The rest of the class, after a few preliminary skirmishes, went into the comatose state, which indicated that, in accordance with Standing Orders for Visits by Important Personages, they were on their best behaviour.

"This", I thought, looking at the faces turned politely in my direction, "is going to be murder."

And so it proved to be. The first ten minutes might have been taken from the text book illustrating everything a good modern school should not be. Lecturing the exhibits at a waxworks would, I felt, have been more profitable. In an attempt to establish some of that rapport which was highly spoken of in education circles at the time I trotted out one or two of the feeble witticisms which usually had them rolling in the aisles. The children had apparently got it into their heads, however, that Best Behaviour in front of Important Personages must not include any kind of levity and the only response was a solitary giggle, instantly repressed and culminating in a death rattle. I could hear my voice becoming hysterically shrill and I all but thumped a small perfectly innocent boy on the front row just for the reassurance of hearing another human voice.

The situation was saved by, of all people, Delius Potter who, unaccustomed to the quiet, fell asleep. As his chair was tipped back at an angle of 45 degrees, the hollow clang as his head struck the heating pipes caused considerable merriment. There was some argument as to whether the sound came from the pipes or from Potter's head, Potter saying one thing and everyone else another. A final decision on the matter was postponed until playtime when as Summerbridge, a lad of considerable intellect, pointed out, banging Potter's head against a netball post and listening carefully in the manner of a scientific experiment would set the matter beyond doubt. This fair solution to a worrying problem clearly satisfied the majority of the class and they returned to something more like their normal listening pattern.

I stole a quick glance at the back of the room in time to see our Important Personage picking himself up out of the corner. It seemed he had been deposited there when Ginger, the realisation that something interesting was afoot in another part of the room filtering through to his consciousness, had leapt into frenzied action leaving a trail of books, overturned desks and County Council Inspectors behind him. Having returned Ginger to base the lesson restarted.

Specially prepared lessons of this sort are rarely a riotous success ignoring, as they do, the inspiration of the moment, and this was no exception. It was not such as to warrant a standing ovation but at least the children became involved and there were no further alarms until the bell went for playtime.

I managed to get the class to leave in some semblance of order, only Jane Crump with her spotless school uniform, dimpled cheeks, bubbly blonde hair and simpering smile, lingering near Mr Garland and gazing at him wistfully.

"Please Sir," she whispered coyly, "the next time you come will you sit next to me, sir?"

"How nice of you, my dear," said Mr Garland, as easily fooled as any ordinary mortal who wasn't to know that she ran the class protection racket,

I will remember that when I come again."

The only other one to show any reluctance to go out was, not surprisingly, Delius

Potter who found himself cast in the unusual role of victim.

"It isn't fair sir," he protested as I prized his fingers one by one from the door handle, "there's a load of 'em and they're going to bang me 'ead. I shall get bashed in, sir, and you know what you've told me about bashing people in."

"That was a different situation, Delius, as you well know. You were doing the bashing and the bashee was a harmless little first year," I said, "now get out and face the music like a man. If it hurts, come back after playtime and let me know. I can't say fairer than that."

Some fond goodbyes in the background indicated that the other tete-a-tete was ending and, as Jane smirked past me, I managed to propel Potter towards the outer door.

"That's it, Delius!" I called after him, "you get some fresh air. It will make your head feel better."

I turned to give my attention to Mr Garland.

"Ah, well," I said, "that's that for a few minutes. Nice children – a bit rough, some of them, but nice. Er..... can I take you to the staff room for a cup of coffee, or would you rather have it with the Head?"

"Thank you, Mr Curtis. I will go in and have a word with the Head before I leave. Just so, just so. Before I do that, I wonder whether you could spare me a few minutes of your time? There are one or two things I would like to talk over with you and this seems as good a time and place as any."

"Of course, sir," I lied, "I'll be delighted. Please sit down, I'm sure we shan't be disturbed here."

With the possible exception of a visit from a bloody Potter, this was no more than the truth. Certainly no member of the staff would dream of disturbing the holy ritual coffee drinking for anything less than a full-scale conflagration and even then only when the flames started licking round the staff room door.

Mr Garland sat on the edge of a desk and looked thoughtfully at his note book and then over the top of his glasses at me.

"Now then, Mr Curtis. How long have you been teaching?" "Just over five years," I said.

"Just so, just so. They're a lively little lot you have here. You coped with them competently – yes, most competently."

He appeared to go off in some little interior world of his own for a few minutes, his eyes gazing blankly out of the window. When he did speak again, his words came like a bombshell.

"You will, no doubt, be thinking in terms of promotion. Deputy Headship; a small Headship even. You are not too young, particularly with your army experience and it is only natural to wish to progress – to have ambition – yes, indeed, just so."

I was never more surprised in my life. Had he said I was a disgrace to forward thinking educationists and ought to consider something more suitable to my talents, like a lavatory assistant or going into a monastery, I would have been hurt but able to follow the reasoning. To be accused of having ambition was something quite different. The notion was so new to me that for a moment I was quite dazzled by it. I could almost see myself as the chap at the top with an office in which to hide and a blonde secretary to share the loneliness that comes with power.

"Of course, sir," I heard myself saying, "the desire for an opportunity to use my experience to greater advantage is rarely out of mind. Ambition," I added by way of clarification, "is the spur."

The last bit didn't sound quite right, but for an off-the-cuff effort I was quite pleased with the general effect.

"Just so, just so," said Mr Garland, looking at me over his spectacles in that disconcerting way and, I noted with surprise, with a quite definite twinkle.

"Now, in my experience," he continued, "the first step up the ladder is always the hardest. There are hundreds of applications for every advertised Headship, you know, particularly in good areas. Good people, most of them. It's hard to turn them down, but that's the way it is at the moment. What a young fellow like you needs is something that makes you stand out from the rest. You need to widen your experience. The best way to do this is to get on to the County Permanent Supply Staff. The elite of the profession I call them and a first class stepping stone to promotion. Have you ever thought about that?"

As I hadn't the faintest idea what he was talking about I was able to admit that no such thought had occurred to me. As far as I knew, the Supply Staff were men who came round in large green vans delivering chalk and exercise books and suchlike when required to do so by the Head. I could see this being a way of widening experience but hardly as a trump card when apply for Headships. I decided to play along and try to sort the thing out without too great a show of ignorance.

"Obviously," he went on, "it is essential that you should be prepared to Travel. Travel is necessary and unavoidable. You have, I take it, not objection to Travel?"

We seemed to be back with those chaps in the green vans except that he undoubtedly said Travel with a capital 'T' which seemed to suggest something more exotic and executive-type. However, I thought it safe to indicate that Travel had no fears for me, that I did quite a lot of it, that I had always been accustomed to it and that it was, perhaps, better to travel hopefully than to arrive.

"Just so, just so. You do realise that this means the whole of the West Riding? That means from Doncaster in the south to Sedbergh in the north – a very large area indeed. However it is only fair to tell you that Mr Elsworth, who sorts all these things out from County Hall, does try to keep people at schools within twenty miles from their homes if at all possible. That raises the second point I wish to make. It may be necessary to send you – that is a member of the Supply Staff – to any type of school. Anything at all, you understand, from Special Schools for handicapped children to Grammar schools or Infants or anywhere, in fact, where the need is greatest. This is why I regard the Supply Staff as the elite of the profession. Just so, just so. The elite of the profession."

At last the picture was clearing. I was aware in a vague sort of way that there were teachers available in case of staffing emergencies but had never stopped to wonder how they were recruited or organised. It seemed I was about to find out. "The salary would be an immediate improvement, of course. Group Nought Headship to begin with plus travelling allowance from school to school and regular promotion up to Group Two, subject to approval or course."

Here was temptation indeed. What a Group Nought Headship allowance might be I had no idea, but it would obviously be a step up from what I was now beginning to see as a miserable pittance. The idea of moving around had its attractions too. I might even be able to afford a car – something small and second hand, but adequate for travel. What really made me see the attractiveness of the proposition was the thought of handing over Delius Potter to drive someone else mad. I had sufficient common sense to know that every school had its Delius Potters, but just at that time I'd had about enough of this particular one.

"I must admit that I hadn't given serious thought to the Supply Staff," I said, "but now you mention it I can see that it has its attractions. How long do Supply Teachers usually stay at one school?"

"Could be two days or two years. There are no limits laid down, but to be of much use to a school educationally, rather than as a temporary child-minder, one term is about the shortest period and we much prefer it to be two or three terms. It's the demand that dictates the Supply, as it were. Just so, just so.

I sniggered politely and proceeded to the serious business.

"I find this all most interesting," I said, "and I would like to give it serious thought. What is the procedure for appointing people on to this supply staff?"

"There are two vacancies at the moment, so you are not going to have too much time for deliberation, I'm afraid. If you like I'll get the office to send you a form straight away along with a screed telling you more about what's entailed. Fill it in immediately and send it to me at County Hall. You'll be called for interview within a few weeks. I have a feeling you might well be accepted, you know, though I can't promise anything, of course. Just so. Well, good luck Mr Curtis. I'll just pop in and see the Head before I go. Don't forget – the elite of the profession. Just so, just so. Goodbye then, and thank you for your hospitality."

I sat in a daze for a while. I had left for school that morning with few worries and no ambition, content that each day should come and go without the necessity for leaping in and out of slit trenches or obeying orders which could result in discomfort or pain or worse. I had, I admitted to myself, dug a pretty comfortable slit trench in civilian life, but was it not time to start looking a little further? You feel secure in a trench but the view is a bit restricted and you don't get very far. And now this man Garland had come along and awakened the ogres of greed and dissatisfaction. It seemed that the time for decision had been thrust upon me. Was I to be found wanting?

"Not so, just so, just so!" I proclaimed loudly, to the astonishment of Delius Potter who had crept in unseen and was doing his best to hide behind the glass-panelled door.

"Potter," I said, "if you do not go out this very moment and have your head banged against a netball post I will not be responsible for my actions. I am feeling very excited and in this condition I am likely to do nameless things to you for which my picture would appear in the Sunday papers. OUT!"

I swept into the staff room thinking that, for once, I could claim to have earned my cup of coffee. I needn't have bothered. The lesson bell went the moment I crossed the threshold and there wasn't any coffee left anyway.

During the next few days I went through the procedures of trying to think of devastatingly original things to say about myself on the forms which arrived, and of telling the Head that I was doing my best to leave him. He didn't seem as heartbroken as I expected. There followed a period of requesting that I attend for interview at County Hall at 10am on the following Tuesday. The Head was more put out at my asking for the day off than he had been at the prospect of losing me altogether. I did think of suggesting he should send for a member of the Supply Staff but thought better of it. He hadn't much sense of humour.

Although I had lived within twenty miles of it for most of my life, I had never been to the county town, so gave myself plenty of time to find my way around when the day arrived. It was still only just after 9 o'clock when I came out of the bus station and found that County Hall was just around the corner. Most impressive it was, too, massively constructed in typical provincial classical style calculated to induce a sense of awe in a prospective interviewee rather than put him at his ease. After walking around it once with a purposeful air, which took about one minute, I toyed with the idea of finding somewhere where I could get a cup of tea. This I eventually rejected on practical grounds. I could envisage that the consequences of a pint or so of liquid on top of what I was alarmed to recognise as symptoms of acute nervousness could be inconvenient at a crucial stage in our negotiations.

I lit a cigarette, smiled jauntily at the Ruritanian Admiral on duty at the main entrance to show him how much at ease I was and stumbled off for another voyage round the block at reduced speed. I rehearsed to myself the clever answers I had worked out in reply to the questions I thought I might be asked. Modelling my style on that of Mr Garland, I mentally inspected myself over the top of a pair of steel-rimmed glasses.

"Now, Mr Curtis," I asked myself, "Why do you wish to join the West Riding County Permanent Supply Staff"?

With a tricky bit of mental adjustment I looked myself fearlessly in the eye. "The reasons", I answered firmly yet thoughtfully, "are essentially twofold.

Firstly I have a natural ambition to improve my status in my chosen profession and I believe this to be a stepping stone towards that end, not only by reason of its immediate financial advantages, but also because, as a member of the Supply Staff, generally acknowledged by the leaders of educational thought to be the elite of the profession, I shall be in a most favourable position to accumulate a much wider and deeper fund of experience than would be possible under more orthodox teaching circumstances. Secondly, such expertise and experience and understanding of children as I already possess would, I believe, be used to the greater benefit of the teaching service and thus to the children of this county, in the wider sphere of activities which would present themselves on the County Supply Staff".

The first part of this, I had to admit to myself, might have gone a bit out of hand and I doubted whether I could do it all in one breath. In general, though, I was favourably impressed by the obviously sincerity and scholarship which had gone into the reply and was about to offer myself the job without further ado when I got that funny feeling that someone was watching me.

Bringing myself rapidly out of the interview room and back to the pavement I saw that two large policemen were, indeed, regarding me with mild curiosity. Further down the road two more appeared to be pointing me out to a person in plain clothes and large boots, and from the edge of the kerb an unwinking official eye was inspecting me from inside a police car. It dawned on me that my harangue had probably not been as silent as I intended, and furthermore, that I had unwittingly extended my perambulations to include the headquarters of the County Constabulary. Even now I could envisage messages speeding to neighbouring mental homes enquiring whether they had mislaid anyone.

"Good morning officer", I said brightly to the nearest policemen and, feeling this to be somewhat inadequate as an explanation, added "ha ha ha! Interview you know never been here before not much to do before ten o'clock seem to be a bit early just wasting time really going over things you know Ha ha ha! Interview you know I'm all

right really can you tell me where there's a toilet?"

I couldn't help feeling that this lacked something in clarity and was all set for a quick dive back to the bus station before I was arrested when the larger and more rubicund of the two smiled.

"Not to worry sir," he said, "It's happening all the time round here. We can always tell when its Tuesday, can't we Bill?"

"Aye," replied Bill, "We can allus tell when it's Tuesday right enough. We see all these young chaps in their Sunday suits going up and down muttering to 'emselves and my mate says to me 'Tuesday again, Bill – interview day'. Aye we can allus tell when it's Tuesday".

"If you don't mind young feller, I'll give you a bit of advice," said the first policeman, "Given it to many a one, I 'ave, and they've come back and thanked me for it. It's just to put you at your ease a bit when you go into that there room and you see all them big wigs all tarted up and lah-de-dah and looking down their noses at you. You just think on; most of 'em know nowt about t'job and they're nowt special underneath. They're nobbut human beings like you. They all eat and sup and fart like anyone else. That's right, isn't it Bill?"

"Aye, that's right enough. All except Obediah of course".

"Oh, aye, except for Obediah. But there you are. You just think on that, young feller".

"I will," I said, "and thanks very much. I know you're right but I'm not sure it's going to get rid of these butterflies. Who is this Obediah by the way?"

"There you are Bill – what did I say to you? This young feller's up for t'first time, I said. Even then most of 'em know about Obediah. Well, now, Obediah is chairman of your selection lot. Been at it for years 'e 'as. He's also King of Coalstone and he's cute as a barrowload o' monkey's. Retired miner, 'e is, and red hot Labour of course. I reckon he's about two hundred years old, but he's mustard, is Obediah.

"Aye," concurred Bill, "He's mustard, is Obediah. And talk of the devil – this is him coming now. You'd better get a move on, lad."

A small, wizened, crooked figure was alighting from an old Ford van which had pulled up outside the main door. Supported by a stick, he walked jerkily across the wide pavement to where the admiral was managing to salute, smile ingratiatingly and hold the door open all at once. As he passed where I was standing he suddenly lifted his head and looked straight at me. It was with a sense of shock that I saw a pair of the bluest, alertest eyes I had ever seen, shining out of the crinkled walnut of a face. For a couple of seconds he looked me up and down.

"I've never seen thee afore," he said, "but I reckon tha's for interview. Doant worry ovver much, lad. Thi time'll come if tha's patient and if tha's worth it. Now get on inside or tha'll be late and that'd be a bad start.

Before I could think of anything to say, Obediah had gone. "Undoubtedly," I thought, "Obediah is mustard."

"Interviews; waiting room sixteen upstairs," said the admiral with a quick return to his superior manner, so setting in motion what I came to suspect was a carefully managed pre-interview softening up process.

Having stormed the outer defences, the next obstacle to overcome was the staircase. On the face of it this should present no problems, but this was no ordinary flight of stairs with the utilitarian purpose of getting from one level to another. It was superb, opulent, curving creation in marble, wrought iron and polished wood straight out of a Hollywood musical. Ginger and Fred would have looked well on it; a bewigged flunkey announcing the nobility and gentry would not have been out of place. I fell up it; only a little of the blood from my chin despoiling the white shirt which I had spent hours ironing the night before.

It seemed that the architect, having let himself run riot with the staircase, had run out of ideas or space or money, for the corridors to which it led were quite narrow and gloomy. This only served to emphasise the immensity of the door to room sixteen when I eventually found it, but even this was no preparation for the room itself. It was roughly the size of St Pancras Station, an impression heightened by the wreathing tobacco smoke which hid the further walls and ceiling. Looking down from the nearer walls were dark likenesses in oils of past civic dignitaries wearing ermine robes and expressions of disapproval. Neither they, nor the artists who had painted them seemed particularly distinguished, but en masse they had considerable impact, frowningly suggesting the futility of human ambition. The remainder of the furnishings consisted of a table of about the same surface area as a tennis court, masses of chairs of severely upright character and thick, dusty brown curtains which effectively kept out any stray beams of natural light. Sitting around, either silently or muttering quietly together in groups were about twenty men in interview suits, and a dozen women, half of whom had clearly spent a considerable time emphasising their feminine charms and the other half who seemed equally determined to conceal them. Most of them looked dedicated; a few looked as though they would like to go home; they were almost all smoking like mill chimneys and they were all looking at me.

As befitted one being considered for the elite of the profession, I assumed what I thought was a casually dedicated expression and murmured a firm yet dignified, "Good morning."

Without exception they turned their backs on me and resumed whatever it was they had been doing before I made my entry. Some sat on the extreme edge of their chairs and studied the floor, some adopted a couldn't-care-less posture, which fooled nobody and some, whom I took to be the more seasoned campaigners, looked almost normal. Snatches of talk rose above the general level.

"So I said to my boss, 'It's no good my going for anything under a Group 5 – I should be losing money."

"Of course, our exam results have improved so much since I took over a couple of years ago that old Filigree insisted on me applying for this new place ...."

"I hope we're out here before 2 o'clock; I've fixed up a date for this afternoon. There's no point in going back to school, is there?"

"They'll be down in the second division unless they get rid of that silly prat they've got at centre half ...."

I turned to the man sitting nearest to me, one of those who seemed reasonably at ease and even, I suspected from his expression, taking some sort of delight in studying the panorama of humanity before him.

"Have you any idea how long we are likely to be here?" I asked

"You know, I thought you were a first timer," he said. "They make you sweat it out for an hour or two beforehand and then again afterwards until everybody's been in.

In some ways that's worse, because it gives you time to think of the silly bloody answers

you gave and all the clever things you should have said. I should say we'll be lucky to be away by two o'clock. Do you mind my asking which school you're up for?

"Well, actually it's not a specific school. I'm on interview for the Supply Staff."

"I didn't know they interviewed here for that lot. Anyway, you won't get one of the main committees so it shouldn't be too harrowing."

"How many are there on the committee?"

"It seems like the hordes of the Philistines when you see 'em sitting there staring at you, but only one or two are capable of speech. Half are local and half are county and then there's all the inspectorate in fancy suits and bow ties, lined up to proffer advice. The rest usually follow it, too, because most of them know as much about education as I do about the love life of the gooley bird."

The door opened and a sad, clerical looking person came in bearing a single sheet of paper which he consulted thoughtfully.

"Is Mr Gronfield here," he asked.

"Ah, yes of course. I didn't notice you at first. Will you come this way please, Mr Gronfield?"

They left with something of the gaiety of a funeral cortege, leaving others to put out the fire.

"Well, there's number one to the slaughter," said my companion. "Poor old Gronfield. He gets full marks for persistence but I'm afraid he never gets over the final hurdle. He teaches at the school next to mine and, unfortunately for him, word has got around that he is conscientious, reliable and unbelievably dull. Pity really because in many ways he's a dam' good teacher. But I shouldn't be telling you all this; it's a failing of mine."

"Not a bit of it. I'm finding out how little I seem to know. For instance, a friendly neighbourhood policeman was telling me just before I came in about someone called Obediah. How does he fit into the scheme of things?"

"You really are new aren't you? You're not by any chance a southerner or anything like that? No, I thought you didn't sound like one. Well, you are obviously from the north of the Riding if you don't know Obediah. He's bloody mustard, is Obediah. He's been mayor of Coalstone so often they're thinking of giving him the place and then, of course, he's chairman of the selection committee, so you can say that any Head appointed to the Riding since William the Conqueror has Obediah to thank.

I'll tell you one thing though. It'll probably be him chairing one committee this morning and Mrs Spencer-Hyphen-Tonks the other, and give me Obediah every time. That's more than you can say for that other toffee-nosed bitch. I really do talk too much.

She's not a relation of yours by any chance, is she?"

I disclaimed all knowledge of any of the officiating parties.

"Perhaps it's just as well. You never know who you're going to meet on this game, though. Nepotism tends to be a bit rife, so one should be careful."

"But surely," I said, "Even if a committee member happens to be your uncle or something, you still have to know what you're talking about and be able to show some evidence of having done something worthwhile. I mean, the real criterion must surely be merit?"

"My dear naïve young man. When did you last meet a Head who had been, or gave any evidence of having been, appointed on merit? You see, it works like this.

You may get on the short list on the recommendation of the local people and that means the councillors in that area have got to know you and that means if you live in Barnsley you become an active socialist and if you come from Harrogate you join the Conservative party. That's method one. Now, you may be picked up by the County people and that means the Inspectors, so you go where they go, attend the courses they run, and trot out the latest educational jargon from some book or other and make sure they know your name. That's method two. If you have the stamina to get on both lists, you're home and dry. Then there's the surefire, foolproof way – get yourself in Obediah's good books. They just pick a couple of monkeys from the local zoo to oppose anyone that Obediah wants on."

Even allowing for a degree of exaggeration, I was feeling uncomfortable at these revelations. Any ideas I might have had about British fair play, democracy and let the best man win, were beginning to seem childish. I told my companion that if even some of what he said were true, I would have expected outcries from all sorts of interested parties.

"It's not really as bad as it seems," he said. "You see, look at it this way. There could be hundred applications for the Headship of a school in the right sort of area.

Somehow they have to make a start at whittling this lot down to a manageable size, so they chuck out all those over a certain age add those with the wrong qualifications. You still have fifty or so left, so what are you going to do about it? Look down the list and see if there are any names that you recognise. And that's where we came in."

"Do you mind if I ask how you stand in all this?"

"Not at all. I'm Head of a small Junior school not all that far from here and there's a lot of reorganisation and building and so forth going on. I'm in for the new place, which will be a lot bigger. It's a technicality really but the motions have to be gone through."

"You mean that the other applicants are wasting their time here?" "I'm afraid so."

"Are you, by any chance, a relation of this Obediah person?"

He gave a broad smile, "No," he said "but we get on pretty well."

Any further revelations were cut short by the re-entry of the clerky person. "Is there a Mr Curtis here?" he asked.

"Er.. yes," I replied, surprised at being so high on the list.

"Will you follow me please, Mr Curtis. I am afraid you are in the wrong room. Applicants for the Permanent Supply Staff meet in Another Place".

I stumbled after him with as much dignity as I could muster and, after a circuitous journey, was led into a room somewhat smaller than the one I had just left but equally imposing in a dark, depressing sort of way. There were only two men sitting at a table; one was Mr Garland, the other a cheerfully rubicund individual smoking a large pipe.

"Come on in, Mr Curtis," said Mr Garland. "Sorry about the confusion over rooms, but no matter, we can get on now."

The pipe smoker was introduced to me as the Mr Elsworth who controlled the comings and goings of Supply Staff members. I liked the look of him. He was casual to the Inspector and gave me a grin which verged on the conspiratorial.

I was pleased to notice that the butterflies which had been playing havoc with my internal workings had apparently flown elsewhere; I found I was beginning to think as coherently as was my normal practice and the feeling of being about to have several teeth extracted without anaesthetic was rapidly diminishing. I thought it possible that, if asked to give tongue, I might be able to string together one or two comprehensible phrases. So great was the relief that I all but started on the peroration I had performed earlier for the benefit of the police force without bothering to wait for the questions.

"I have, of course, spoken to Mr Elsworth about our conversation the other day," said Mr Garland. "We have, in fact, discussed your case at some length. Our only real doubt is whether you have had quite enough experience. You have, I believe, been at only two school?"

"That is so, sir," I replied, seeing an opening at last and diving for it like a rabbit into its hole, "It is true that I have only been at two schools but, during that time I have taught every age group except the reception class and every subject on the timetable with the exception of girls' biology. I feel, therefore, that to a large extent.... "

"Just so, just so," interrupted Mr Garland, looking at his watch. "I think that Mr Elsworth and I have a pretty fair idea of the depth and breadth of your experience, Mr

Curtis. Mr Elsworth, have you any questions you would like to ask Mr Curtis? No.

Well, in that case, I have pleasure in offering you a place on the Permanent Supply Staff, to take effect from the beginning of the next term. May I take it that you accept?"

"Oh, er.... yes, of course. That is, thank you very much.... " I began.

"Just so, just so. We shall require formal acceptance in writing, but Mr Elsworth will fill you in with all the details. Would you mind waiting outside for a moment?"

He held out his hand. "Congratulations, Mr Curtis. The elite of the profession, remember – something to live up to, eh? Just so, just so."

I leaned against a window ledge in the corridor outside and tried to collect my thoughts. I was, officially, a Headmaster Group Nought, which sounded pretty important; I was a member of an elite corps; because of this I would, in a year or two, be an established and permanent Headmaster; as a bonus I would shortly be saying goodbye to Delius Potter forever.

There were only one or two things I didn't know as I stood gazing out of the window at the dustbins in the well below. One was that I was to remain on the County Supply Staff for the next twenty years. The other I discovered a few days later as I was reading the evening paper. A local children's home was to close, it reported, and as a result my present school would have fewer children and therefore be overstaffed. It was understood, the article went on, that the one teacher concerned had been appointed to the County Permanent Supply Staff. Even to my trusting mind there could be no doubt about it, I had been courteously but most effectively conned.

CHAPTER TWO

I was at this time, sharing a flat with Peter Lee, the old school friend mentioned earlier in this chronicle. As recounted, during the Hitler conflict he had spent four years reaching the heady heights of Major, while I took rather longer clambering to Corporal. Anyone with army experience will appreciate the immense gulf that this created, but I think I may say without boasting that I treated him perfectly normally on those rare occasions when we were on leave together, and when the army finished with us and gave us our striped suits and pork-pie hats it was as though there had been no war. That is not quite accurate because Peter, having been an officer and a gentleman, thought it behoved him to wear a large moustache and converse in a mixture of superlative and strange oaths. Come to think of it he was like that at school, anyway apart from the moustache. He had always been a very positive sort of person with the comfortable facility for seeing all things in terms of black and white. Anything receiving his approval was the subject of unbounded enthusiasm and classed as 'super'; all other things were 'diabolical'. Two factors could make this outlook disconcerting. One was that he could change allegiance, without batting an eyelid, in the middle of a sentence. The other was that some of his friends found difficulty in matching his excessive adulation of what seemed to us to be pretty humdrum sorts of things. I remember on one occasion being invited to take part in a gastronomic feast, the like of which had never been experienced by anyone less than the gods. It turned out to be toasted brown bread with a bit of mousetrap cheese on top.

As representative for a firm making rather exclusive and absolutely super something-or-others in the furniture trade, Peter was entitled to a car, albeit the most basic of small Fords which must have been a bit of a come down after chauffeur-driven staff cars. No one would have known. Because it didn't actually fall apart when you pressed the knobs, this vehicle came in the 'super' category and came in useful for ferrying a constantly changing supply of girl friends to remote destinations in the early hours of the morning. Peter's girl friends I hasten to add. For various reasons I had come to an irrevocable decision to avoid amorous connections for the rest of my life and deplored the way in which Peter collected these glamorous blondes, brunettes and red-heads.

According to him they used to queue up to get at him and he had to swat them off like flies. There were many times when he would depart for a week or so, ostensibly calling on valued clients in the Midlands or the North East, two appropriately ill-defined areas where, I suspected, it would have been difficult to track him down until mid-morning because, as he explained, he was seeing someone locally and the best way to get business was to treat his prospective customer to a lunch time drink. There was always some good reason for having a drink whether at lunch, tea, breakfast or any other time. If the ability to imbibe large qualities of alcohol in any known form were the key to business success, Peter's firm wouldn't have been able to cope with the rush.

Towards the end of the Easter holiday Peter was on one of these local runs and we were, unusually, having a modest breakfast of bacon, sausage, eggs and tomato together when the postman called. For me there was a printed card which ran as follows:-

"You will," it said, "report for duty as assistant teacher at Pitdale Secondary Modern School; Headmaster, J H Crabtree Esq, BA, at 9.0 am on Tuesday.... etc." "Pete," I said, "where the blazes is Pitdale?"

"God knows. It's one of those bloody little mining places. Near Wakefield or Barnsley or Coalstone or somewhere. Nobody goes there anyway. Why do you want to know?"

"Because come next Tuesday, it's where I go to work. Look at this."

I threw the card over to him and, with that perverted sense of humour which people of his type seem to possess, he found it amusing.

"Bloody hell fire!" he roared, "you're going to have to work for a living at last, young Curtis!"

With a characteristic switch of mood, he was suddenly dead serious.

"You know what these places are like, don't you?" he asked. "Bloody diabolical. Tough as Hell. Don't' you remember that time a year or two back when some of those youngsters – school kids they were – from Coalstone started coming into Frontown for a Saturday night out, bloody chaos it was. Nobody dared to go out on the streets for fear of having their teeth kicked in and all the police applied for transfers to Glasgow. It was in all the papers. You must remember!"

"I remember nothing of the sort, and neither do you. I suppose it was that fortnight at Sandhurst that turned you into a sadist though, come to think of it, you always did take an unhealthy delight in other people's misfortunes. I haven't forgotten that time when I'd promised to take

Winnie Shaw for a fast lap of the playground on my bike, she on the saddle and me pedalling in front. You never did convince me that the saddle fell off by accident, especially as you were standing laughing your silly head off. She never spoke to me again."

"You were lucky, – saved from a fate worse than death. But that's not the point. I'm trying to help by putting you in the picture. I can't help it if my memory's better than yours. It's a well known fact that mothers down there eat their young. You're going to have a hell of a time, take my word for it. That's if ever you manage to get there. I shouldn't think the bus services are all that bright."

"Lord, yes. It's going to mean getting up at crack of dawn. I suppose public transport does operate at that time in the morning."

The thought of rising with the birds began to prey on my mind even more than the prospect of finding out at first hand whether the legendary toughness of mining communities came under the heading of fact or fiction. I had never been one for leaping out of bed with a merry song and had doubts about the sanity of those who did. What I needed was less fiction and more factual information, and the thought occurred to me that the landlord of our local hostelry was apt to boast, when in his cups, of having been born and bred in Pitdale.

"Tell you what, Pete," I said, "old Wilf Harker comes from Pitdale. He'll be able to tell me something about it."

"Of course," said Peter, "we'll go down for a pint the moment they open. Yes, Wilf will know all about it. The only difficulty will be shutting him up. Super idea."

You could see that, for him, the day had suddenly become alive with glorious opportunities.

Promptly at eleven o'clock we presented ourselves at

the Dog and Goose and I explained the position to the landlord.

"Tha's nivver been to Pitdale!" he explained in astonishment, dropping into the vernacular the moment the place was mentioned, "then I shouldn't bother. You've missed nowt."

And not another word could we get out of him.

In the afternoon I went into town and tried the bus people. They were more helpful and I eventually came up with the following timetable:-

7:00 am	leave home for ten minutes walk to the bus stop
7:10 am	catch bus to Frontown
7:35 am	arrive Frontown and walk to central bus station
7:50 am	leave for Coalstone
8:20 am	arrive Coalstone and change for bus to Pitdale
8:25 am	leave Coalstone
8:35 am	arrive Pitdale and walk to the school

This itinerary combined with a full day teaching coal-blackened savages, an even slower journey back home and a merry evening marking and preparing for the following day held no prospects of joy. As an aged aunt of mine was wont to remark on occasions such as this, I was beginning to wonder whether I had sold my birthright for a mess of potash.

Rarely, however, do things turn out as badly as our imaginations and our so- called friends lead us to expect.

In the present instance I made several unexpected and agreeable discoveries.

The first one was that the bus never arrived until at least 10 minutes after its scheduled time. This was due to a combination of circumstances such as the shortage of snooping inspectors at that time in the morning, and the necessity for the crew to perform the daily opening ceremony at Ted's Terminus Caff in the nearby market town before setting sail. To a man, the crew members shared an exaggerated belief in their ability to make up the lost time on the journey. The fact that they never did, in no way discouraged them. The only way of getting anywhere near it was to put the thing in top gear, jam the accelerator to the floorboards and pretend that nothing was in the way. Then, by cornering on the hubcaps and only stopping for those prospective passengers brave enough to stand in the middle of the road waving their umbrellas, it was possible to arrive about five minutes late.

As I could never be absolutely sure that some eccentric new driver might not be appointed who would insist on leaving on time, I always arrived at the bus stop with plenty of time to spare. They were moments of pure magic. For a start, with the exception of my friends the birds, it was completely quiet, with the incredible quietness of a normally busy place. From where I stood I could see over the lower valley of the River Wharfe and every morning was wonderfully different. Sometimes the change was so subtle as to be almost unnoticeable; sometimes it was difficult to believe that this was the same place as the day before. There were mornings of brilliant luminous blue when, looking up towards the head of the valley, the hills twenty five miles away were sharp against the sky; there were misty mornings when the whole valley was a pearly grey sea with only the crag on the other side showing above it, a pink sail in the morning glow. And always the air, before the fumes from a thousand exhausts had got at it, was clear and fresh, and always there was the warm nettle smell, and hawthorn and grass. I began to wonder why I had never done this before.

Then the bus came and, on the first morning, feeling clean and fresh after my purifying experience, I went upstairs to a swaying hellhole of tobacco reek and choking, retching men. From then on I went downstairs and left the hawking and spitting to those who enjoyed it. There was also the additional advantage that our local Stirling moss's efforts to fling us into outer space as he went like the clappers through the many roundabouts were slightly less awe-inspiring. I even found after a while that I was able

to forget the journey altogether in the pages of a book. It came as quite a disappointment when, years later, I travelled by car and had to save my reading for when I got home.

Another curiously enjoyable part of the journey was the walk through the big covered market in Frontown to the bus station. At the time I was there the wholesalers were just packing up and the retailers were finishing arranging the displays on their stalls with much good-natured banter, and there was the sight and smell of mountains of fruit and vegetables and the funny little café with its steaming tea urns and plates of bacon and eggs. Last of all came Fish Row with its characteristic smell that had me, for a few minutes, standing on the quayside at Whitby and the boats are coming in.

And then, of course, there was Pitdale itself. After my first glimpse I thought that it couldn't possibly be as completely devoid of any redeeming feature as it seemed. My walk from the bus to the school showed that I hadn't seen the worst bits. The main street stretched flatly away to a level crossing in the distance with, in between, a hotch- potch of terraced houses, half-empty corner shops, two pubs, a Co-op and a larger building of angular gauntness which proclaimed itself to be in the Miners' Welfare. Years of being bathed in coal dust had reduced everything – bricks, paintwork, road, even the few people about to a universal cheerless grey. Rising over the roof tops were the symbols of Pitdale's reason for being there – the smoking mountains of pit waste and the functional towers and whirling wheels of the winding gear. And everywhere was the sulphurous smell of the pit.

I was glad to find in the weeks that followed that there were – there had to be – compensations. The people who lived out their lives in this place were tough, uncompromising, hard-drinking, hard-swearing, hard-gambling characters with a sense of humour all their own. They had the sort of community spirit which seems to be found only where men are engaged together in hard, dangerous work and which is expressed, not in flower words or self-congratulatory committees, but by practical help when it is most needed. They had never had any help from 'outside' and didn't expect it now, though conditions had improved since the war. They would help themselves and help each other, and if someone tried to convey their thanks for a service rendered it was likely to be greeted with, "Nay, thee 'od thi noise, Martha, and stop thi' bloody fussing. Tha'll 'appen ' ave to do t'same for me some day."

I didn't know any of this on that first morning as I found my way to the school. Through uniform rows of back-to-back houses I went where the 'slag heaps' really were threatening to slither their way through the doors past a Public Baths and Wash House, round a corner by yet another dingy pub, and there it was. It was both bigger and newer than I had expected. There was a lot of glass, the bricks were still noticeably brick-colour and behind were extensive playing fields. Immediately in front of me was the boys' playground and it was filled with a bubbling, boiling, yelling turmoil of teenagers. The boys, looking incredibly large after my spell in a junior school, were all engaged in an activity which appeared to consist of hurling as many people as possible on to the floor and then jumping on them. Every so often one, braver or more stupid than the rest, would lower his head and fling himself like a charging bull at a wall of other boys who would seize him and, inevitably, crash him to the ground. It was only later that the explanation for this masochistic behaviour occurred to me. I was now in the heart of Rugby League Country.

At the expense of no more than a few superficial bruises I crossed the yard and approached a medium sized youth with over developed muscles and a glum expression. Having apparently run out of people who wished to be bashed against the wall, he seemed to be at a loose end and showed a flicker of interest as I prepared for speech. It has always been at moments such as this that my memory has deserted me so, of course, I completely forgot the name of the Headmaster.

"Take me," I said, "to your leader."

"What's 'e want, Albert?" asked a small child with blond, curly hair, steel rimmed spectacles and an unbelievably angelic countenance.

"Nay, I doant know," replied Albert, "I reckon 'e's a foreigner or summat." "Course 'e's not a bloody foreigner, tha daft bugger," said the angel, "e'll be one one of them 'at comes round selling books and stuff."

"Nay, e'll none be one o' them, Curly. If 'e were one o' them 'e'd 'ave a proper suit on. I reckon 'e's a foreigner."

I could see the reasoning behind this argument but, having had a chance to look at my card, I thought it time to clear things up.

"I wish to see Mr Crabtree," I said, "will you please take me to his office?"

"Thee see to 'im, Curly," said Albert, "I can't make out 'alf of what 'e's saying." "Nay, he nobbut wants John Henry's room. Thee take 'im thi sen."

"Why should I go? He's nowt to do wi' me. And any road, ah'm not right keen on seeing John Henry this morning. I tell thee what," he added, seeing that some generous gesture was called for, "I'll bray thee if that dooan't."

It seemed to me that the time had come to point out that I was neither a deaf mute nor a half-witted foreigner, but a teacher who could understand what they wsere saying and who would appreciate some show of obedience. I took hold of Albert's ear gently but firmly.

"Now then, Albert," I said, 'we'd better start again. First, I know you haven't seem me before but I'm a teacher at this school. Second, I asked you and not your mate to show me to Mr Crabtree's room. Third, if tha dooan't get on wi' it right sharp, I'll pull thi' lug 'oil off. Now, lead on!"

They looked at me with what might have been dawning respect. Curly grinned. "Why didn't tha say so before, sir?" he asked. "Cum on, we'll both show thi." When we eventually arrived at the office the Head greeted me with a great display of warmth. He was a large man who would, I could see, be the life and soul of any party.

"Ah, yes, Mr Curtis. The office said you would be coming. Good to see you. Excuse me just a minute will you? Shan't keep you long."

He turned towards the door where my two guides could be seen attempting an invisible departure.

"Moggs! Come here!" he bellowed.

Albert skidded to a halt and retraced his steps with little evidence of pleasure.

"Now, then, Albert, you know I never forget, even after a holiday. Where is it, lad?"

"Please, sir, I 'aven't got it sir."

"Haven't got it lad. What do you mean, you haven't got it? Where is it?"

"Please sir, I forgot, sir."

"Albert, Albert – do not mess me about. You know very well you didn't forget it and you know that I know you didn't forget. You've spent it, haven't you lad? Probably on cigarettes if my information is correct. Really, I would have thought that even you would have been in this school long enough to know me better than that. You know you can't fool me don't you lad?"

"Yes sir," mumbled Albert who seemed to have come to the conclusion that trying to do a Canute against this verbal tide was going to get him nowhere.

"Yes sir, yes sir!" echoed the Head. "You will bring it to me at five minutes to nine tomorrow morning without fail."

He put his mouth within about six inches of Albert's ear, and his voice rose to a crescendo.

"Tomorrow morning, remember, and no more feeble excuses. If you don't', I shall probably beat the daylights out of you and then dance on the remains. Have you got that, Albert Moggs?"

Albert winced, turned a shade paler and made noises indicative of having got it whereupon the Head, with a startling change of voice said conversationally, "Right – run along, lad. Thank you for bringing Mr Curtis along."

"What exactly was his crime?" I asked.

"Broken window. It's happening all the time in this greenhouse of a building but I'm certainly not going to stop them playing football or cricket at play times. There's a standard charge of sixpence and usually they bring it along without being asked. It does little towards the cost, of course, but it touches them where it hurts. He's not a bad lad, our Albert. Not the world's greatest brain, but a useful footballer. No cricketer, though. Are you a cricketer by any chance, Mr Curtis?"

I admitted that, although I had some enthusiasm for the game, it was strictly as a spectator. It was generally acknowledged by anyone who had seen me play that I was the world's worst performer, being quite incapable of holding a catch, bowling a length or keeping a straight bat.

"Now that's interesting," said the Head thoughtfully. "There must be some logical reason for this. You are obviously reasonably intelligent and you look in very fair physical shape. How about eyesight? Do you ever wear glasses?"

I said that I had never found the need to do so.

"I'll bet that's your problem! If you'll take my advice you'll go and see an optician at the first opportunity. Better still go and see your doctor. There are all sorts of reasons why eyesight might be a bit sub-standard, you know. No need to be ashamed of it. There are plenty of players at County or even Test standard who wear glasses. But, there we are. We'd better get down to business. I can't have you talking about cricket all morning can I?"

I said there were a few other things I would like to discuss, such as which classes I would be teaching, which subjects I would take, the organisation of the school and so on.

"Of course, of course. Now, you will be in charge of Form 4L. They live in the Nissen hut near the canteen. The best thing you can do is have a word with John Edmonds. He had last term's 4L until his illness. Come on, I'll take you along to the staff room."

Such confidence as I had to start with was rapidly evaporating. Form 4 I could understand. That would be the top age group, fourteen to fifteen year-olds. But what on earth did the 'L' signify? Surely not and indication of their ability? And why, for heaven's sake, in a Nissen hut? And what about Mr Edmond's illness which had been touched upon rather too lightly for my liking? I began to have a horrible feeling that I was being got at. People had told me that Supply Staff were used for the jobs that nobody else wanted and if ever I smelt a job that nobody else wanted, this was it.

The staff room turned out to be a noisy, laughing, smoky place with a confusion of chairs, tables, books, teacups and people. With one exception the men seemed to be built on the same generous lines as Mr Crabtree and with the same sort of extrovert behaviour. Apart from being less obviously muscular, the females were much the same so that there was the sort of din that greets you when arriving late at a particularly large and boozy party.

The one exception was a pale and unsmiling individual who sat silently in a corner unravelling his tie and twitching.

Apart from a few "Good mornings", no one took any notice of our arrival until the Head, seizing on a brief lull in the cacophony, called out, "Ladies and Gentlemen!"

Silence fell and I was introduced.

"Welcome back everybody. I hope you've all had a good holiday and that your loins are well girded for the new term. This is Mr Curtis who has come to help us out until we get a replacement for Jimmy. He will be taking 4L this term. I know you will look after him until he gets to know the place. Nice to see you back John. You're looking much better. You will be taking 1C as we arranged, of course. Have a word with Mr Curtis about 4L before you go over there will you? Put him in the picture. The rest of you will no doubt introduce yourselves in due course. See you later, Mr Curtis. If there's anything you need, don't hesitate to ask."

It came as no great surprise to find that the sad looking person in the corner was the John on whom I was to rely for my information about 4L. That he was suffering from some sort of nervous disorder only confirmed my suspicions about the hazards ahead and I couldn't help thinking that if, as the Head had said, he was looking much better, doctors must have queued up to study him before his improvement. I was not encouraged.

"There's not much time to tell you anything, Mr er....," said my predecessor in a querulous voice. "I've got to prepare for my new class, you know. I should be there now. Really, John Henry had them after I did. I do think he might have put you in the picture himself."

"Don't worry about the details, Mr Edmonds. If you can just give me a few basic facts about who they are and where I can find them, that will do for the time being."

We were interrupted by a man who, amongst a large and cheerful lot, could have taken the prize for being the loudest and most cheerful of them all.

"I'm Grinton," he said, "Deputy Head. It's all right, John, you get along and see about your new lot. I'll brief Mr Curtis.

With mumbled thanks, John departed.

"A broken reed, I'm afraid, our John," said Mr Grinton,

"and, as you will find, John Henry hasn't really the time to see to details like giving you a guided tour or dishing out books. I'd better explain to start with that this class of ours is all this term's leavers bundled together in the Nissen Hut. You know, of course, that they leave at the end of the term in which they are fifteen, so there are three lots of leavers each year. It's a damned stupid idea, of course, but we're stuck with it, so John Henry had this notion of putting them all together in one group — A, B and C streamers. The administrative reason is pretty obvious; the educational reason is to prepare 'e m for life in the great outdoors. Most of them know more about the great outdoors than we do, but that's what we say if anybody asks. Come on, I'll show you where the hut is."

Nissen huts are Nissen huts and this one was no different from many in which I had spent dreary hours in the army. The interior was painted in a deep shade of mud and the furnishings consisted of a number of trestle tables, various types of chair, a blackboard which, in the absence of an easel, was propped up on a large wooden box and three immense cupboards, all of different colours and evidently the relics of some previous civilisation.

"Not much to look at, I suppose," said Grinton, "but it's all yours. Other than setting fire to it you can do what you like with it, and pretty much the same goes for 4L."

"But what about a timetable?" I asked.

"Make your own. You just have 4L all the time, so it's up to you. Give yourself time to think about it and then let me have some idea what you intend to do. They are assumed to have completed their academic syllabus so there's no more specialised teaching for them. Actually you'll find that some are pretty bright and others still think a times table is something you put the clock on. Anyway, with your experience, John Henry is hoping you will come up with something or other that will occupy their last few weeks here gainfully.

They rather got on top of poor old John last term, I'm afraid. We first suspected something was wrong when Arnold played the introduction to "Onward Christian Soldiers" in the assembly one morning and John saluted and started inspecting the ranks. Talking of assemblies, they'll be going straight into the hall this morning for John Henry's beginning of term harangue, so you won't see 4L until at least half past nine.

Have a look round and make out a list of anything you need. Let me have it at break time and I'll see what I can do for you.

Harking back to poor old John.... sounds like a Negro spiritual doesn't it? Anyway, as I was saying, the kids round here tend to be a bit tough, but they're a good lot underneath. It's up to you to see that if anyone's going to have a nervous breakdown around here, it's one of them and not you. See you later."

The next half hour I spent in trying to find something of value in the cupboards. After crawling around in their cavernous interiors and discarding as surplus to requirements a collection of assorted cardboard boxes, egg containers, bristleless brushes and other junk, I came up with the following inventory of materials with which to start my Experiment in Education:-

Item One: One maths text book, minus several pages and apparently mainly concerned with the timing of steam driven locomotives on the newly inaugurated Stockton to Darlington railway.

Item Two:	An assortment of odd bits of exercise paper torn out of partially used books and mostly in a state of disintegration.
Item Three:	Twelve bottles of castor oil.
Item Four:	A small cardboard box containing dust and three pieces of chalk, all of a strange khaki colour.
Item Five:	Sixty three copies of 'The Water Babies' by Charles Kingsley. Item Six: One mouse, dead, presumably of a surfeit of (2) above.
Item Seven:	Eight bulb bowls containing bulbs, also dead.
Item Eight:	One brand new unused leather-working outfit, presumably requisitioned by someone after being on a course or reading a book.

With the possible exception of the sixty three copies of 'The Water Babies' by Charles Kingsley, which had the appearance of being first editions, I could see little of value.

I was beginning to feel light-headed. Too much had happened too quickly and all of it bad. In another two minutes or so I would be faced with the task of gainfully occupying thirty or so teenagers until 4 o'clock. I cursed Mr J W Garland with a slow, solemn and comprehensive curse of which even Peter would have been proud. I thought of Delius Potter with something of the emotion of a fond parent. Then there was the noise made by a large number of large adolescents recovering from a Head Teacher's harangue, and 4L had arrived. I was again struck by their size but, to my relief, they sat down quietly enough and looked at me with interest. They were it seemed to me, weighing me up as a heavyweight boxer might weigh up his opponent before leaping up and plastering him all over the floor.

The first move was going to be mine and, at this stage in our relationship, I had to let them know who was boss. The next five minutes were going to be crucial and I was determined that they were going to be spent in stamping my authority on the proceedings.

"Right 4L!" I roared in a voice like that of a sergeant major recalling a squad of marching men from the edge of a cliff, realised I was probably overdoing it a bit and started again.

"Right 4L!" I said in a quieter but firmly determined manner, "My name is Mr Curtis and I'd better let you all know straight away that I like things mooing dye.. that is to say, doing my way. That is the way I like and, of course, expect; my way, that is. So we'll do the register. My way is to call out your name and because I don't' know you yet, although I will before the day is out, you will see, I want you to answer "Yes, sir" or "No, sir" as the case may be and at the same time you will put up your hand so I can see who you are. And I shall not forget."

"Please, sir, Mr Curtis, sir, can I ask a question, sir?" enquired an innocent, apologetic voice that spelt trouble as surely as anything I ever heard.

"Yes, lad, but hurry up. We have a lot to do."

"Please, sir," said the voice, "if we answer, 'No, Sir,' do we have to put us hands up, sir?"

"Good lad, good lad," I said, stifling the giggle which had started before it had wondered who might be the first. You have to be on your toes in my class. Now let's get on with the register."

I cast a keen glance in the direction of each voice as it answered, more to impress the class than in the expectation of remembering a single name. I knew they weren't taken in by this, any more than they were by my 'deliberate mistake', but they regarded it as all part of the act. So far I reckoned we were about breaking even. They were not going to eat out of my hand, but neither, it seemed, had they any immediate plans to tear me limb from limb.

One recognisable face did surface amidst the general anonymity, that of my erstwhile guide, Albert Moggs.

"Ah, Albert," I said, "I'm pleased to see you are one of us." "Aye," said Albert.

This exchange, lacking in sparkle though it did, created some interest amongst the other members of the class who suddenly broke their silence to enquire of Albert where and how he had met me before.

"It were nowt," protested Albert, embarrassed at the idea of being on speaking terms with the Establishment," I nobbut showed 'im to Johnny Henry's room. An' I wish I 'adn't bothered an' all. I got a right rollocking.

"Right, come on 4L, let's get on," I said and, to my gratification something like a more normal atmosphere seemed to prevail, rather like the case when Delius Potter's

head heralded a return to normality during Mr Garland's visit in the halcyon days of long ago.

Eventually all the names were called and I bent over the register, partly to fill in noughts and opposite the names of those who hadn't thought it worth their while getting out of bed, and partly to give me time to consider my next move.

"Right!" I said loudly with my customary originality.

There was a noise and a rushing wind, such as is made by a train on the London Underground emerging from a tunnel. I looked up and found that the room was empty. Well, not quite empty, because closer inspection of the darker recesses revealed Albert Moggs and an excessively well-developed girl holding hands and conversing in low tones. Any ideas I might have entertained that what I considered my sophisticated but authoritative approach had won the day, quickly disappeared.

"Hey! You two!" I bellowed.

They looked up and around the room with a glance that had in it more of surprise than alarm.

"Hey, sithee, Sylvia, they've gone," said Albert.

"Aye. We'd better go us-selves, hadn't we? See you later Al," said the fair Sylvia adding, as an afterthought, "Ta Ta Sir."

"Oh no you don't," I said, "come here you two and explain to me slowly and simply just what has happened and where everyone has disappeared to."

"They're on jobs, sir," said Sylvia. "Jobs – what do you mean, jobs?"

Sylvia gave me a look full of female compassion. It was clear to her that this new teacher was half-witted and that it was her role in life to do what she could for him by patience and understanding.

"Jobs mean work, sir," she explained.

"That's right, sir," chipped in Albert, determined to show that he, too was capable of a thought. "Jobs is work – you know, like painting and cleaning up and er... er..."

He was saved from the necessity of taxing his brain any further by the entrance of a young man in sports coat and flannels.

"Now then, Mr Curtis," said the newcomer, "I'm free 'til break-time so I thought I'd just pop along and see how you were getting on. It's a bit confusing to start with, I dare say."

He turned to Albert and his friend.

"You two. You know where you're supposed to be. Stop mooning at each other like a couple of love sick cows and get there, quick. Hop it!"

He perched on the end of one of the safer looking tables.

"Hope you didn't mind that," he said "somebody will be chasing 'em if they don't get a move on."

I flopped on to a chair.

"Please feel free to do anything you think fit. I am surrounded by happenings which I do not understand and over which I have no control. Five minutes ago I had a class – a real, all talking, all singing, all moving class. Now it seems I've imagined it all.

If you can give me one or two clues it might stop me from thinking I'm going potty."

"Obviously John Henry hasn't given you the complete picture. Have a cigarette and relax. You've nothing to worry about until break time and then only whether you will survive in that snake pit of a staff room. If you are sure I won't be boring you I will reveal all in a manner of speaking. My name is Ted Dunning, by the way, and we tend to use Christian names round here, so what shall I call you?"

I told him my name and assured him that I would certainly not be bored by any revelations which would throw light on the present dark confusion.

"Well, it's quite simple, really. Every term, as you've probably been told, we shove all the leavers into this one lot; the brainy ones – and there are some, you know, in spite of all you may hear to the contrary – to the dunderheads. God knows, there's no secret about those. Well, last terms' lot were a bit lively. First they sent poor old John, who tends to take his sorrows a bit too seriously, to the loony bin, so we got one of you supply blokes in and he disappeared under mysterious circumstances one Thursday morning. Some say he joined the Foreign Legion, and others hint that the kids who were doing gardening spend an unusually long time on the rockery that day. Anyway, the upshot was that John Henry stormed up and down and said he's sort 'em out himself.

Actually what he did was to get all the staff to say what non-teaching jobs they could do with a bit of help on – cleaning cupboards out, painting the shed, weeding and that sort of thing. Then he made a list out and as soon as the register was called each morning, all the kids dispersed to the far corners of the school and, in one or two cases, beyond.

Now, this new lot you've got – he had them all together the day before we broke up and told them exactly what they would be doing today and what would happened to them if they forgot. Hence the exodus. He calls it Forward Planning and, to be really honest, he did it because he didn't trust County to send us anyone else.

"I see," I said, "that does make it a bit more comprehensible. Thanks, by the way, for giving up your free period like this. It's helped a lot."

"Think nothing of it. In any case I'm not being entirely selfless as I may have led you to believe. You may have noticed that John Henry likes an audience. He has a habit of collaring anyone who hasn't the wits to keep out of the way and doing to them what he calls discussing education. Actually it means listening to John Henry doing a monologue and, whatever it starts with, you can guarantee it will finish with cricket. He's a cricket nut. Don't get me wrong, he's a good Head as Head's go, and he's a decent bloke, but that doesn't mean I want to spend my free period listening to him. So, I can either go and sit in the bog for an hour or I can come here, which is off his main route round the school. So truth will out. And here I am talking about John Henry hogging the conversation and I haven't give you a chance to get a word in edgeways. Sorry!"

I protested again that I was grateful for any information he could give me.

"But it won't do, will it? This set up, I mean, I can't just come in the morning, say 'one, two, three, go' and then wander round the place like a slave or something."

"I'm sure you're right. I know it would bore me silly, but it was only a stop-gap arrangement, you know. Have you any bright alternatives, bearing in mind that you've got 'em all day and that most of them would rather not be here, anyway?"

"At the moment, not a thing. Not surprising really when, up to half an hour ago I imagined I was just and ordinary class teacher. It might not have been a bad idea to drop me a hint beforehand. Anyway, I'll think of something. It's all right being jocular about phases like, 'preparing them for the world outside school' but there is something in it, isn't there"

"That's true, in a way, but I reckon less so than in most places. All the boys will be going down the pit like their dads and granddads, you know. The only difference is they'll be a bit older when they start, but I doubt if that means they'll be any more mature than their parents were at 13 or 14. The girls haven't much more choice. There's a newish clothing factory. They'll maybe take half a dozen or so; a handful will go as clerks or shop assistants in Coalstone and that's about it. Most of them will get pregnant and marry a miner by the time they're twenty and so the tradition is perpetuated."

"That's not a cheerful outlook, is it?" All the more reason why someone should try to do something about it, don't you think? Do I sound big-headed? I know nothing about the area and I'm not pretending I can shake the foundations of a local culture, but it's worth a try, isn't it?

"It won't do any harm. But I think it would be a mistake to get too carried away by the idea. The local culture is mighty powerful. How many people have you ever met who wanted to move here from some other place? To most people we are just a name on the side of coal trucks in the station yard. Yet there are still enough people to work the pits. It's just that something or other keeps 'em here, generation after generation, even those who have the chance to move out."

He threw his cigarette on the floor and ground it in with his heel.

"There are some who got the chance. Me, for example my dad was a miner and my two brothers still are. They were prepared to sacrifice some beer, baccy and betting money so that I could have the clothes and books and things I needed to go to college. So, you see, I escaped."

"And yet you still live here?"

"Yes, stupid, isn't it? I went to teach in Blackpool when I left college. Thought it would be heaven on earth. I imagined all the people I knew back home who saved up all year to go to Blackpool for a week – and I was going to be paid to live there! All those birds in thin summer dresses on the look out for a good time, the Tower Ballroom, all the boozers. One long, non-stop holiday, I thought. I stuck it for a year and then applied for this job here. The call of the culture or some such thing. I know it's a hole, but it's my sort of life and they're my sort of people and I like it."

"I can understand that, all right. But at least you got away from the pit. I can't see you wanting to work there. The sad part, to me, seems to be the lack of choice, from what you've just told me. Maybe a lot of the lads will want to go mining, simply because it's always been the thing to do, and their dads do it and all their mates. But surely, if they hate the very thought of working down a hole in the ground – and it would frighten me to death – they should have some alternative. That goes for those who are not bright enough to go to college, too."

"Well, there's one thing, Ken. If you can think of giving 4L an element of choice, we'll back you up as much as we can – and that will go for John Henry too. But be warned, old boy. Don't hold out too great hopes that it's going to make a lot of difference to anybody's future. Come on, let's see if there's any coffee ready. It's nearly break time."

For the rest of the day I wandered around the school checking up on my charges, learning the geography of the place, and meeting most of the staff on a more personal basis than was possible in the crowded confines of the staff room. Surprisingly, most of 4L were actually working, though it would be stretching the truth to say that they were likely to qualify for productivity bonus. The first exceptions I found were friend Moggs, to whom I was becoming quite attached, and his outsized girl friend. They were skulking in slightly compromising circumstances in a dark corner of the P.E. store, and were quite unabashed by their discovery.

"I'm only 'elping Sylvia to sort out these netball posts and things, sir," protested Albert when I suggested he should be elsewhere, "you can't expect a girl to carry those, sir. It's too heavy work for a girl, sir."

As Sylvia was clearly capable of bending iron bars with her teeth, the remarks lacked conviction.

"Mr Dewey is looking for you on the field, Albert," I told him. "He seems anxious to know why, when painting the rugby posts, you balanced the paint tin, without a lid, on the crossbar and, as you might say, deserted your post.

I suspected that whatever attributes Albert might possess to make him spoken about in the pubs and clubs of Pitdale, speed of thought would not be one of them. He was, you might fairly say, stolidly dim, but on this occasion he was ahead of me.

"Oh, God," he murmured appealingly, "He didn't go and.... he didn't knock... he didn't, did he?"

"He did. Bearing in mind the way he was speaking about you when I saw him last, you are right to call on help from the Almighty. If I were you I'd make my explanations as soon as possible, and they'd better be good. A few moments ago he was collecting sharp stones and calling your name."

"I've got to go, Sylv.," said Albert and charged off looking unhappy. The only other untoward incident was much more sinister.

I went into one classroom where two of my boys were supposed to be doing some tidying up on their own. One of them, a rather scruffy, nervous looking lad, was pretending to sort out some plants on the window ledge and managed to knock several of them over as I opened the door.

The other, a tall, thin youth in narrow trousers, a voluminous jacket and winkle- picker shoes, was taking the lid off a small round tin inside the teacher's desk. The tin, I could see, contained money.

"What are you doing with that tin?" I asked.

"Miss Greenway must have left it out by mistake," said the boy. "I knocked it on't floor when I were cleaning the desk. now I'm putting it back. There's nowt wrong with that, is there?"

"No, there's nothing wrong with that, if that's what happened." "Are you calling me a liar, then?"

No, not yet. The way you are behaving, I might get around to it before long."

I turned to the other boy who was looking as though he had an earnest desire to be elsewhere.

"Is that what happened?" I asked him.

"Yes, sir, that's right sir. Just like 'e said, sir. He were putting it back, sir." "I see. What's your name?"

"Dufton, sir. Derek Dufton." "Thank you. And yours?"

The tall boy stared at me for a moment without speaking and then said, "Fenton."

"Right, Fenton," I said, "when I asked your name I meant your full name. also, when you speak to me I think it only polite that you say either 'Sir' or 'Mr Curtis. Now let's try again. What is your name?"

"Graham Fenton.... Sir," he said deliberately.

"Right, Graham Fenton – and you, Dufton as well. You will never go inside a teacher's desk again for any reason at all. Now give me that tin and I'll see that Miss Greenway gets it back. Mr Dewey is wanting extra help on the field. Report to him – and I shall ask him what time you arrive. Go."

I was worried. There was no doubt that Fenton was lying and that Dufton was supporting him through fear. I felt I could do without problems of this sort on my first day. However, there it was and I would have to do something about it, the first thing being to find out whether any money was missing. It was at this stage that I realised I had been foolish to let the suspects out of my sight, but it was too late to do anything about that now. I set off in search of Miss Greenway.

Not being as experienced or as devious as Ted Dunning, she had been cornered by the Head and I ran them to earth in his office.

"Character building, you know," I heard him say as I approached the open door, "that's what education is all about. How many long divisions are they going to need down the pit? How is it going to help them to get coal if they can recognise a reflexive verb when they see one? No, the thing that's going to see them through difficult times and keep them a step in front of their fellows is character. Take a game like cricket. Play it properly; play it at the right spirit; you are developing character. It's always seemed to me a great pity that girls haven't got a game in any way comparable with cricket. I know there are women's cricket teams which show admirable common sense, but it's not really the genuine article, is it?

"Ah, hello Mr Curtis. Miss Greenway and I were just having an educational discussion. How are things going? Hope you are settling in alright. Is there anything I can do for you?"

I explained that I was really wanting Miss Greenway to check the money in her tin, and told them both what had happened.

"No need to tell me the name of the boy," said John Henry. "I will take a small wager it was our old friend Fenton. The other lad could have been one of a dozen."

I told him he was quite right and that the other boy was one Dufton.

"Yes, it could well have been Dufton. He'd be scared out of his wits, of course, and back Fenton up. He's a harmless individual, but you were quite right to suspect Fenton. He's been a pain in the neck ever since he came to us. Has any money gone, Miss Greenway?"

"No, it's all right. My own fault, of course, for leaving the desk unlocked. But the tin was definitely inside and not on top."

She looked at me gratefully for the interruption and hurried off to check up on the other contents of the desk, or so she said.

"Fenton is one of that fortunately rare breed – a bad clever boy. Not only that, but when Fenton gets angry there isn't a boy in the school – and we've some pretty tough characters twice his weight – who will willingly get in his way. Didn't Kipling write about even the tiger getting out of the way of a mad dog? It's like that with Fenton.

When he gets mad he loses control and he's afraid of nothing. You were fortunate that he didn't go off when you were pointing out the error of his ways. As I say, he's got brains too. Always been in an 'A' form and could be quite a mathematician. His family are agin the establishment, too. His father is a holy terror. So, what with one thing and another, Fenton is the unofficial cock of this particular midden.

Now about other things? Are you managing all right?"

I told him. I said I wanted books, pencils, pens, art materials, a good record player and, if possible, a small sum of money weekly towards the scheme which was starting to take shape in my mind.

I was promised the lot.

By the time I arrived home, Peter was preparing the evening meal. He had sharply defined phases in his attitude towards eating. There were times when he scorned the insularity of the English and condemned with appropriate invective their lack of initiative in sampling the delicacies of other nations . On these occasions he gave the impression, to anyone unaware of his little foibles, that he asked for nothing better than a couple of sheep's eyeballs and unaccountably became the archetypal John Bull, maintaining that what was good enough for his father was good enough for him and refuse with evident loathing anything more exotic than fish and chips followed by spotted dick and custard.

Before I got as far as the door I knew that he was having one of his mystical east spasms. The smoke being generated and billowing out from the kitchen window could have been reported as a hazard to aircraft and the smell would have sickened an inhabitant of the poorer quarters of Bombay.

"I can't identify it from the stench," I said after I had finished wiping the tears from my face, "what do you call it?"

"Oh, hello Ken. Didn't see you come in," said the chef leering through the fog, "I'm doing the meal tonight."

"I rather gathered that. Do you know what it is?"

"Of course I bloody know what it is. It's curried sausages."

"What else would have that delicate aroma? I should have known. Do you do it for the sake of the atmosphere or do we have to eat the things as well?"

"You eat the flaming things, of course. I think they seem just about ready. Get a couple of plates out, will you, and knives and forks and maybe a dash of tomato sauce. This is going to be a rare and uplifting experience for you, young Curtis."

In view of the trauma surrounding its birth it came as a surprise that the yellowish, brownish, blackish concoction which appeared on my plate, was not unpalatable. I even said as much to the creator.

"Super, isn't it?" he agreed modestly. "Now then, how have you survived the day at Pitdale? Is it as lousy as you thought?"

I gave him a resume of the day's events and said that the rest of the evening was going to be given over to mediation on my programme for 4L.

"So, you see," I told him, "I shan't have time to go with you to the Dog and Gun tonight. Sorry, but I really must get things sorted out in my head. I think I've got the general pattern but it all needs putting into some sort of order and I reckon that's going to take until bedtime."

Peter said it didn't really matter as there was a new barmaid at the Dog and Gun who seemed to fancy him and I would only have been in the way.

It was midnight by the time I had set out what seemed to be a workable system. Peter had returned quite early bearing several bottles of beer and the news that he had managed to rebuff the barmaid's advances.

"If you want to know what I think," he had said, "I think that kid who was doing the pinching is only the tip of the iceberg. I'll bet there are dozens of them just as bad, or worse. Everyone knows what miners are like and young 'uns are the worst of the lot. It isn't reasonable to suppose, that on your first day, you just happened to come across the only one who's light-fingered. I'll bet they're a right bloody shower. A year or two in the forces would do them the world of good. If I were you I wouldn't mess about with all that clap-trap you've been doing all night; I'd give 'em nothing but maths and English all day and I'd rattle their teeth if they so much as moved."

"Peter," I yawned, "you know as well as I do that you are talking a load of eyewash. No, old lad, what I have worked out isn't particularly original or clever, but it's a bit more imaginative than your suggestion and I think, it will work. And now I'm going to bed or it will be time to leave for that wretched bus."

As I went to the bathroom I reflected that, whether it was a mess of potash or not, I had certainly left my comfortable little slit trench well and truly behind.

CHAPTER THREE

My master plan, when announced to the Head and selected members of staff, had the explosive effect of a gently bursting bubble. The general feeling seemed to be that it was an improvement on the existing Wackford Squeers type arrangement, but that high hopes should not be entertained. As a sub-normal sheep would have found difficulty in not effecting such an improvement I was not flattered. Nor was I discouraged, however, and suspected that John Henry, at any rate was not displeased when he said he would rearrange the timetable so that Jean Smedley, the Senior Mistress, would be able to give a hand.

The remainder of that first week was spent writing many letters, accumulating much stock from various departments of the school and, as far as the members of 4L were concerned, completing the jobs they had been allocated. I told them that the following Monday would see a change of plan and that wandering around with an empty bucket and an earnest expression would thereafter cease to constitute a days work.

It was gratifying to realise that, by the end of the week, I was seeing 4L as so many individuals who, by an administrative quirk, had been thrown together for this brief period in their lives. Any worthwhile teacher knows in a very short time the good ones and the bad ones in a class – those to trust and those to keep an eye on. I was now recognising the less obvious ones who make up the majority of any group and yet who are individuals in their own right with their own problems and preferences and abilities. In my more optimistic moments I was even beginning to feel accepted and that was good, for without that, a teacher might as well be a child-minder or, worse, a lecturer.

I had kept as close a watch on Graham Fenton as was possible under the circumstances and, as far as I could tell, he had done no positive wrong. He stopped just short of being surly when he spoke to me and carried out any task he was given without cause for complaint. On one or two occasions I saw him glancing at me and making some comment which caused sniggering amongst the few boys who curried his favour, but that was hardly a punishable offence.

There were stories of him beating up one or two of the smaller or more timid children after school time, apparently for the sheer hell of it, but they were never substantiated by the victims. Then one morning the rumour got around that he had, on a previous evening, had a disagreement with another 4L boy, one Gary Gates. The story went on that he had lost his temper, virtually gone berserk, and kicked, bitten, scratched and flailed about in the manner to which the other boys seemed to find both shameful and frightening. Gary Gates was a bright enough lad, by no means cowardly, and well liked by both the staff and his contemporaries. I made an opportunity to see him alone during the morning.

"Good Lord, Gary!" I said to him, "you've got your face in a mess, haven't you? What happened?"

"Oh, it's nothing, sir. Just an accident," he said sheepishly.

"Come off it, Gar. Unless you mean you were run over by a bus, that's no accident. What really happened?"

"Like I said, sir. It's nowt really. It looks worse than it really is. It was just an accident sir".

"I can understand you not wanting to tell tales, Gary, but you know perfectly well that everyone in Pitdale knows what happened and that includes me. It's only a matter of confirming it. Just tell me one thing. Was anyone in 4L concerned?"

"I've nothing else to say, sir – honest, sir. Can I get on with my work now, sir? Mr Charlesworth won't be right pleased if I haven't finished by dinner time."

I left him to it and hoped, without great conviction, that if friend Fenton could not be prevailed upon to mend his ways, he might at least confine his unpleasant behaviour to out-of-school time.

On the Monday I gathered my flock together after registration and announced the new arrangements.

"As from today," I said, "you will be following a timetable which I have pinned up on the wall over there. Although we shall call it a timetable, there won't actually be any set time when we change from one thing to another. It will depend entirely on how each one of you is getting on. Some of you might produce better work if you have the chance to go on and finish it; others would find that sticking at one thing for too long means getting stale and careless. To start with, I am the one who decides, so don't' go away with any ideas that this is some new-fangled system where you can please yourself whether you work or not."

Up to now I had had their attention. To say that they were agog would be stretching a point, but there was a certain air of expectancy. My next announcement would, I felt sure, produce a completely predictable reaction. It did.

"First," I said, " we shall have maths."

Before the communal groan had time to develop, I continued.

"All right, all right! I know you think you have been doing maths since you first started school and that there's nothing left to learn. I'm talking about things you will need to know when you leave here. How many of you could work out how much money you should get in your pay packet at so much an hour? That means taking into account things like income tax and National Insurance. Then there's sick pay or unemployment pay. All these things you will need to know and, what's more, you're going to look a proper Charlie to your work makes if you can't do it. Have you ever thought about how much extra you have to pay if you buy a bike, say, on the never-never, instead of paying cash?

Not only that; you will need to know how to fill in forms of all sorts for all the things I've just been talking about and I've got some of the actual forms for you to have a go at. I suppose you could call that English."

"Sir!" burst in James Hart, a fairly bright boy who was always prepared to chance his arm, "Are you going to show us how to fill in betting slips, sir, 'cos that's the only writing my dad ever does?"

"Ee, d'you know, my dad's the same", agreed a waspish girl whom I suspected of being a milder form of female Fenton. "He never writes owt. He never reads owt either, except t'Sporting Pink. Are you going to learn us how to pick winners, sir?"

"No, Fiona, I am not. There are some things which are beyond a mere schoolmaster. I'll tell you what I will do, though, if we have the time. I'll explain why your dad goes to work on an old pushbike and the bookie has just bought a new Ford Zodiac. What we shall be doing is getting a copy of all the main daily papers – not including the Sporting Pink. We'll spend some time each day looking through them, and the local evening ones, too. That's where you will find all the advertisements for jobs, of course, and we'll have a go at writing applications. Now, are there any questions, so far?"

There were plenty of questions. Some were thoughtful, some were flippant and others demonstrated a lack of understanding, which amounted to genius. The corner where Fenton sat with his acolytes was silent, neither questioning nor commenting.

When the discussion showed signs of degenerating into a free-for-all, I went on to outline the remainder of the scheme. Briefly what it amounted to was that we were going to embark on an instant painless culture session. It centred around a face-lifting operation for the hut, starting with a few coats of arms and displaying these around the room. There would also be music, working from the known to the unknown along well- trodden educational paths. I hoped that other things would be self-generating. All the text books assured me that this would be so, but if I'd been Fiona's dad I wouldn't have put any money on it.

One day weekly would be spent in visiting some commercial undertaking. This, I hoped, would provide the spark for seeking out alternative employment when they left school. As the occupations tended to be of interest to either boys or girls, but rarely to both, the Senior Mistress would take the girls to one place, I the boys to another.

This was greeted with something like enthusiasm. "Hey up! That's a good idea, Sir." "Will we have to go on a bus, Sir?" "How much is it going to cost us, Sir?" "Can we go round a brewery, Sir?"

I told them that we had already received favourable replies from a printers, a chemical works, a glass factory, a brick yard, a multiple store, and the railway. The grand gala opening was to be on the following Wednesday when the boys would be visiting a big printing firm in Frontown, the girls going to the same place a couple of days later.

"We shall be setting off during the morning," I went on to explain, and we shall have our lunch in the works canteen."

"What about us dinner, sir?" Asked Albert

"Sorry, Albert. When I said 'lunch' I really meant 'dinner'. We'll be having our dinner in the works canteen. For some particular reason the management will be paying for it, so you won't need any money for that. Mr Crabtree has generously agreed to foot the bill for the bus fares, so that's taken care of, too."

We went on to discuss the details. There was a general instruction to turn up in respectable clothing and, in some cases, to show a little more enthusiasm with soap, water, brush and comb than was usually evident. They were exhorted to behave in a way which would reflect credit on themselves and on the school, a concept which made me feel like Mr Quelch of Greyfriars. Not quite understanding what I was on about, 4L were prepared to agree readily to all my suggestions.

Later in the day I looked out Jim Dewey who was accustomed to travelling about on Saturday mornings with the quantity of boys, mostly bigger than himself, necessary to make up the school rugby team. I asked him how he got on with them during these visits to the outer world. He seemed puzzled.

"How do you mean?" he asked.

"Well, there are some pretty tough customers amongst them, aren't there? I imagined that when they were out together and away from school, there might be a bit of fooling around and so on. Doesn't it ever get out of hand?"

"Oh, I see. No, there aren't any problems at all. You see, they all want to be in the team and I make it quite clear to them that one step out of line and they are out for two matches. They all understand that and, at the same time they get a clip over the ear 'ole. They don't' mind being walloped if they see the justice of it, but they hate missing out on matches."

"So there you have an unfair advantage. I can't see the threat to stop them visiting a brickyard having the same effect at all."

"Don't be too sure of that. It's getting away from school and from all the other kids who have to go on sweating at their desks that counts as well. Just one thing you need to make sure of, though I'm sure I don't need to tell you. You have to mean what you say. They respect you for it. I always make a point during the first week of catching someone doing something wrong, however trivial, and giving him the full treatment. After that, there's no bother."

On the Tuesday evening I was home before Peter. Some eccentric client out Manchester way had expressed a desire to discuss business with him in that limbo period between opening times. This had puzzled Peter but, partly I suspect, to have an opportunity of getting a closer look at such a strange phenomenon, he had agreed to a meeting and said he would be back latish.

This quite pleased me as I was becoming a little weary of his oriental cooking experiments and fancied something simple and straightforward. I also had a mind to try out a recipe which seemed to answer this description and which had been given out over the radio that morning. On my way through the market I had bought the ingredients. There were two slices of ham, a tin of pineapple, some eggs, Parmesan cheese and a sort of shaker thing containing paprika. The final product, I remembered, was to be served on what they call a 'bed of rice', but I didn't bother to buy any as we had some already. Actually, it turned out to be sago, but I couldn't see it would make much difference.

It dawned on me, as I scraped a coagulant mess from the front of the stove for the third time, that I hadn't paid too much attention to the 'method' bit of the recipe. More than that, I was beginning to have suspicions that, having been bearing in mind two recipes, I may have got them somewhat confused. I was debating with myself whether to write to the BBC about it when Peter came in.

"Don't bother to take your coat off," I said, "We're going down to the Dog and Goose for soup and sandwiches."

"Fat lot of flaming good it is leaving you in charge, isn't it? he complained, peering into the pan in which what was left of the mixture heaved and plopped disgustingly, "What the hell is it?"

"You may well ask," I admitted, "I'm not too sure, but I think I've invented a new sort of ultimate deterrent. We shall probably make our fortune.

"We shall certainly be bloody sick if we stay here much longer. Go and bury it somewhere and then we can get down to that pub."

I washed the two bits of ham under the tap and put them on one side for breakfast.

By the time we had eaten a couple of beef sandwiches with onions and mustard and rinsed them down with a suitable quantity of liquids, Peter had mellowed a little.

"Can't beat good old English food, you know," he said, leering at the new barmaid, who was clearly unaware of his presence. "She fancies me, does that one. But, as I was saying, English food – the best in the world. There's no wonder foreigners are so queer, eating all the muck they do. If you had stuck to something simple tonight, you'd have done a bloody sight better. There are natural laws about this sort of thing, which have been evolved over hundreds of years of experience. Take that stuff you were mucking about with. It's been proved that ham goes with eggs – fried eggs, that is, not those bloody pulped up things. Cheese goes with bread and onions. Rice and sago and such, go with whatever it is they use to make those disgusting sloppy puddings we used to get at school which may not be palatable but are bloody nourishing. I've always said that you can't beat English cooking, haven't I?"

"Yes, Peter," I said. There are times when argument is pointless.

"You know," he went on after recharging his glass, "that was a damned strange chap I saw today. You couldn't tell by looking at him, mind you, and yet I was stuck there all afternoon and he never once so much as mentioned having a drink. I casually worked the subject into our conversation in that subtle way I have and do you know what he said?"

I had to admit that I didn't.

"He said he never touched strong drink and that he preferred not to do business with those who did. Did you ever hear anything like that?"

I said, "no, I had never heard anything like that".

"And neither had I. It shook me a bit, I don't mind telling you. I'm bloody broad minded but there are limits."

"So you didn't get an order, I take it?"

"Of course I got a flaming order, I told him I used to be a slave to the demon drink but I had given it all up. I said I became a reformed character when I was stricken with remorse after coming home in my cups late one night and beating my innocent little lame child within an inch of its bloody life. I may have exaggerated a little."

"You are a liar," I said, "I don't believe a word of it except that you were thirsty, because that's your natural state. You could even have got the order, too, because for some strange reason people do that to you. Heaven only knows why."

"Because I'm a bloody good salesman, that's why. How did you get on with your shower today?"

"I think I'm beginning to get somewhere. I don't expect mind they are all going to finish up fighting for places at Cambridge or anything like that. Some of them have difficulty deciphering the headlines in the Daily Mirror, although they've a pretty good idea what the scantily clad females in the pictures are all about. No, it's just that I feel I'm beginning to understand them and I think they are beginning to accept me. I'm finding out what makes them tick."

"What a load of flaming nonsense. They're having you on, mate. Give 'em an inch and they'll have your guts for garters. I tell you – I wouldn't trust them further than I could throw them. How about that kid who was pinching. Have you sorted him out yet?"

"As a matter of fact I'm feeling a bit rotten about him. Everyone hears about teachers' pets, but there's another side to the coin, too. I'm looking all the time for him to do something wrong and he isn't doing anything. I should treat him just the same as anyone else in the class. We're never likely to be bosom pals, but it's wrong to give a dog a bad name."

"Heaven help me, there are times when I despair of you. There's no wonder this country is going to the flaming dogs with a soft lot like you in charge of the future generation. The reason you give him a bad name is because you caught him bloody nicking something. What he wants is a good hiding."

"Typical layman's attitude," I said, smugly, "all brawn and no brain. I wish I'd had him in the army; send a gunboat; all that claptrap. There's another point I found out today, too. If you touch him he screams for his dad, and his dad comes to school and doesn't bother asking questions and he's twelve feet tall and big with it."

"Probably as soft as butter. Most of these big chaps are. Thump him, too. Or, better still, get him to thump you and then you can sue him for assault."

"You don't really appreciate the situation, do you? According to what I've been told, if this fellow thumps you, you stay thumped. He weighs eighteen stone and it's all muscle. He used to play rugby league for Pitdale Rovers until they sacked him because nobody would play against him. They said he was too rough."

"Yes, well, I can see you might be at some disadvantage there. You never were one for physical violence, were you? In any case, you're not likely to meet him. The main point is that, in my humble opinion, you are being too soft with 'em all."

"You've never been humble in your life you old fraud. You're wrong, too. As I say, I think we are beginning to trust each other. There are the odd one or two, of course, that I don't seem to have been able to get near to yet, but I think it'll come. And now, I'm going to get myself an early night. If you're staying a while, I'll let that barmaid know you are ogling her as I go out."

Next morning I recapitulated on the Rules and Regulations for Behaviour of Children En Route between school and Frontown. I could sense a certain restlessness.

"Nay, sir," said Frank Colley, a boy who, during his ten years at school had succeeded in mastering the reading of one word per year and whose ability to compute ended when he ran out of fingers, "nay, tha's told us all that oft enough, sir. We'll be all right sir."

"Aye, that's right, sir," said Billy Strong, Frank's bosom friend who, though not so advanced academically, was good at being trampled into the ground in the school rugby team, "we shan't let thee down sir."

I felt humbled.

"I know you won't," I said, "and I'm sorry for going on so. Right, then, let's get off."

There was no suggestion that the boys should walk in the crocodile formation to which I had become accustomed at junior school level, but I did insist that they should keep together and behave with decorum. This latter was more difficult than I had anticipated because I had over looked the basic fact that everyone in Pitdale not only knew everyone else, but it also took a keen interest in their affairs. This meant that every man, woman and child passed on the way had to be informed of the reason for our presence on the streets. It reached a climax when we were about to pass, on the other side of the road, a group of men busy waiting for the Red Lion to open.

"Hey up! There's me uncle Jack," said Frank Colley. "Na then, uncle Jack," he roared in a sort of conversational scream.

"Hey up, our Frank," responded a large florid man whose waist line clearly expanded at a rate exceeding that at which he bought new clothes, his waistcoat in particular being held together by the top button only. Our procession had obviously brought some interest in his life until such time as the serious business of the day was legally allowed to start.

"Where are you beggaring off to, then?" he enquired amiably. "We're off to Frontown wi' teacher," screeched Frank.

My murmured protests went unheard amidst the racket of the family conversation which grew even more strident as our party passed on down the road.

"Tha wants to look out for t'birds I' Frontown, then. They're hot stuff tha knows. Don't get thisen caught."

"Nay, we're going to look round summat, or other."

"Make sure tha behaves thisen, then. Hey up, thee – teacher. If he doesn't behave his sen, tan his arse for him. It'll do 'im good, tha knows."

This was apparently some sort of witticism for he laughed uproariously, being joined in the general merriment by his companions, who evidently regarded uncle Jack as a considerable wag.

"That was my uncle Jack," said Frank, who wanted me to be kept in the picture, "everyone knows my uncle Jack."

"He's not exactly the shy, retiring type, is he?" I asked, "I'm not surprised everyone knows him if he speaks at that sort of volume all the time."

Frank, suspecting that my remarks were not altogether favourable, rose to the defence of his kinfolk.

"My uncle Jack can sup more ale than anyone else in Pitdale," he said.

"You must be very proud of him," I said and, turning from Frank to see how the rest were behaving, was surprised to see that they had all turned into gnomes.

"What the blazes do you think you are doing?" I hissed.

"We're waiting for t'bus, sir. This is t'bus stop, sir," said a voice from about knee level.

I could feel control of both myself, and the situation slipping away. With difficulty I stopped my voice from rising a couple of octaves.

"I can see it's the bus stop," I said from between clenched teeth, "Even I can recognise a bus stop when I see one;

especially when I use it every day. What I want to know is why you are all grovelling on the floor."

"Because we're waiting for a bus, sir," said Albert patiently and then, realising that I had still not fully comprehended, added, "t'bus hasn't come yet, sir."

It was only when two clearly respectable men came along and also sank to the pavement, that I realised I was witnessing for the first time the phenomenon known as the 'miners crouch.' Instead of standing up or leaning on a wall when waiting for something to happen, it was the local custom to double up into a position which a camper might adopt when answering a serious call of nature behind a bush. Ever eager for scientific research, I tried it myself later, where nobody could see, and found it both excruciatingly uncomfortable and difficult to stop oneself from falling over.

I was told that miners, accustomed to working in low seams, found it both natural and relaxing.

"For goodness sake, get up," I said "you make me feel like Gulliver. And for crying out loud, don't do that in Frontown or you'll have us all arrested."

Fortunately the bus arrived and we climbed up to the top deck in order. It had been arranged previously that we would cause the least disruption to ordinary passengers, and also enable me to keep an eye on things, if we sat at the front upstairs. I found myself sitting next to Albert and I took it as a minor achievement that he seemed to find this arrangement neither embarrassing nor distasteful.

"Na then, sir," he greeted me cheerily, "it's all right is this." "Better than being at school, eh?"

"Aye, it is that, sir. I don't mind going to school all that much, but I'm not all that keen neither. I'd rather be doing this, anyroad."

"You're not the only one, Albert. I think I would, too. But, just so you don't get rusty, help me work out the fare. There are fourteen of you at fivepence hapenny each and one for me at elevenpence. How much is that going to come to, do you reckon?"

Albert looked at me reproachfully. It was the sort of expression Caesar might have worn as he murmured 'et tu Brutus'.

What Albert said was, "Nay, I haven't any paper, sir. I can't do sums without paper, sir," and then added gloomily, "I couldn't do it anyrooad."

"Of course you could," I said, "It's the sort of thing a bus conductor has to do all day long in his head without making any mistakes."

"Then I'm not going to be a bus conductor," he said, firmly.

"Confidence, Albert, that's what you need. I don't suppose for a minute that the conductor on this bus was any brighter than you when he was at school, but he's practised over and over until he has the confidence to do it and know he'll get it right."

The novel idea that there was someone else in the world no brighter than he and, furthermore, that this person was capable of performing miracles of higher mathematics, struck home.

"Do you really think that, sir, or are you having me on?"

"I'm not having you on at all, Albert. Have more confidence in your own ability and you'll see I'm right."

"Give us it again, sir," said Albert.

By now I was wishing I had never started, but I repeated the problem. "Is it a take away?" he asked.

"No, Albert, not a take away." "A share, then?"

"No, not sharing."

"It's 'appen as well, 'cos I can't do sharing."

He pondered. You could tell he was pondering because his eyes took on a glassy appeareance and his lips moved as though in silent prayer. He was obviously running short on ideas as to what could be done with numbers if you could neither subtract nor divide them. To his relief he was saved from further mental anguish by the arrival of the conductor.

"One elevenpenny and fourteen fivepence ha'pennies, please," I said, "that will be six and ninepence, I believe."

"Then you believe wrong," said the conductor, "It'll be seven and fourpence."

I didn't get angry in spite of the brusque manner and the fact that he had let me down after I had been telling Albert about the infallibility of bus conductors.

"No, I'm sorry, but you have made a mistake," I said quietly, "fourteen sixpences would be seven shillings, less fourteen pence, that's five and tenpence, plus elevenpence, makes six and ninepence."

"Thanks again, Einstein," said the conductor, "twelve fivepence ha'pennies is five and sixpence, plus two more, that's six and fivepence, plus yours, that's seven and fourpence and that's what you're going to have to pay. Of course, you could do it your way if you remembered to knock off fourteen ha'pennies instead of fourteen pence. Q.E. bloody D."

I paid up without a word. The boys, who normally required ten minutes notice before condescending to give part of their attention to what was being said had, of course, followed the exchange minutely. Albert summed it all up in one well turned phrase.

"Yon conductor might not be brighter nor me, sir," he said, " but I reckon he's brighter nor thee!"

For the rest of the journey I thought it prudent to confine my instruction to pointing out things along the way.

We arrived without further incident and reported to the staffing department.

In the presence of many pretty, well-groomed and self-assured girls walking to and fro between the various offices, 4L became embarrassed. They shuffled their feet, looked sheepish and generally behaved like country cousins coming into contact with sophistication for the first time.

Mr Simpkins, the staffing officer, took us into a small room and talked about his company – something of its history, what it did for a living and what bits of it we were going to see. Most of the boys looked as though they were doing their best to follow him, but at some distance behind. I was afraid that the next part of the programme would be to ask the boys whether they had any questions. It was. This came to be the time on all our visits when I wished I could be elsewhere. The pattern hardly varied and I never did think of any way of improving the performance to the point where 4L would appear to be just normal idiots.

First there would be a complete silence giving a strong impression that, without exception, the boys were morons incapable of understanding a word that was spoken to them. That this had some basis in fact did nothing to ease the tenseness of the situation. The speaker would then jolly them along, making a few desperate wise cracks, which would be received with a stony stare from those few who were still paying attention. I would try to smile at him and snarl at the boys at one and the same time, a performance which added to the general effect that we had all escaped from somewhere.

Then a hand would go up and, without fail, it would be the hand of Herbert Hollins. Herbert had an I.Q.

equivalent to that of the average carrot, but he was an earnest enquirer after the truth in his own individual way. The trouble was that he invariably required information on some subject which had not the remotest connection with anything that had gone previously or, just to show he could vary his approach, sometimes seriously volunteered a bit of equally irrelevant information of his own.

Some of his remarks, taken over a number of visits were, "Aren't you too old to work, sir?"

"Why do you have that funny beard, sir?"

"My brother works at the Bessie Pit, sir." "Can I go to the toilet, sir?"

Having allowed Hollins to open the innings, the rest considered it time for anyone else to have a bat and there were usually a few reasonable questions from the intelligentsia, followed by a slow deterioration until Herbert, having had time to rewind himself, put up his hand again. This was my cue to announce that time was getting short and we had better finish there. Unlike the theatrical dictum to 'start well and finish well – they won't remember the bit in between', we invariably started and finished abysmally which made me feel as though I were responsible for bringing a party under false pretences.

On this day, the next event was lunch in the canteen. It had been arranged previously that, rather than offer a choice, a simple meal of sausages, peas and chips, followed by sponge and custard would be adequate. I had pointed out to the boys the desirability of a modicum of good manners, rather than the jungle-like performance evident at school dinners. They had been instructed in the use of the words 'please' and 'thank-you' and in the technique whereby a knife could be used to cut large items into more easily managed units instead of (or as well as) conveying peas and gravy to the mouth. The undesirability of spiking a sausage with a fork and then licking around it like a lollipop had been stressed, as had the lack of need to put the whole of the contents of the place into ones mouth at one go.

What I had failed to say was that, in the refined circles in which we would be moving, it was not acceptable practice to put the whole of ones dinner between two slices of bread and call it a sandwich. Having no specific instructions to the contrary, therefore, everyone did this, having first stuck the individual items together with about a month's supply of tomato sauce.

Trying to hiss instructions through clenched teeth, smile ingratiatingly, eat sausages and peas, and look as though they didn't belong to you really, is a performance not calculated to raise the status of the teaching profession in the minds of the beholders. I was only grateful that the sponge and custard hadn't been served at the same time.

After the meal, the party was divided into two groups and we set off to tour the works. Most works tours are basically similar to all but the uninitiated. We trudged through miles of clattering, machinery-filled rooms and corridors and listened to what our guide had to say. I looked attentive and nodded knowledgeably from time to time. For the most part the boys stood silently, partially comprehending, with just the usual few following the gist.

We lost Herbert Hollins, unfortunately only temporarily, when he was suddenly overcome by the immediate necessity for a visit to the toilet. We saw him disappearing between rows of machines in the direction pointed out by our guide, and then forgot about him.

He was returned to us some time later by a superior sort of female secretary with an expensive hair-do who, we could see, was mentally holding him at arms length between finger and thumb. He had apparently wandered into a high level conference in the board room where he had been sacked and told to go for his cards before managing to explain his presence satisfactorily. The opulence of the directors' toilet which he was allowed to visit before being returned, remained the high spot of the visit and a talking point for the rest of his school career.

When it was all over and we had said our thank-yous and emerged into the open once again, it was agreed by all that it had been well worth-while. The reasons were not all those I would care to have given to a visiting inspector, but I had a feeling that, considering it was the first attempt, everyone had gained something of value. On the bus the conversation continued to be, for the most part, about the way the day had gone. I was pleased, and a little surprised, to notice that the boys of 4L and I were beginning to enjoy each others company.

It was not a local characteristic to give fulsome praise, or even a simple word of thanks unless hard pressed to do so, so I was gratified to the point of smugness when Gary Gates said, as we parted at the school entrance, "It was a good do, sir. We right enjoyed it."

At the flat that evening I told Peter about the success of the day and prepared to bask in his congratulations. I should have known better.

"It's a funny thing," he said, "I was thinking about that kid as I was driving back from Huddersfield this afternoon. You know – the one you imagined you caught pinching something or other."

"The one I _imagined_ I caught?" I queried.

"Yes, that's right. The thought came over me that you'd been hounding the poor little blighter a bit."

"Before we go any further, we are thinking of the same person aren't we? The one who was rifling a teacher's desk and whose father terrorises neighbourhoods like the dragons of old? The one for whom you said the birch was too good, only last night?"

"Yes, that's the one. Well, I'd go easy on him if I were you. We weren't exactly angels when we were at school, were we? I recall, for example, that incident when Harry Pullan and you and I found out by practical experiment what happens when you put zinc and hydrochloric acid together in a sealed container and place the lot in the cupboard of old Sammy Turner's desk. Sammy predicted we would come to a bad end just before he went into his 'This isn't going to hurt me half as much as it's going to hurt you' routine. And he was wrong, you see. Here we are, on the threshold of prosperity and bloody cultured with it. Even Harry Pullan has promised to go straight when they let him out."

"You really ought to give notice when you are going to talk drivel so I could think higher thoughts. Do you know I actually listened to you for a while then? Going back to what I was saying, the only slight cloud on the horizon today has been a suspicion that that lad has been up to something. I can't say what, because I don't know, but teachers get a sixth sense about this sort of thing. Somehow I know there's something wrong and I have a feeling that I am going to find out what it is before very long.

"Rubbish. You are probably killing a proud and adventurous spirit. Think of Winston Churchill. He was a right bloody rogue when he was at Eton or Harrow or wherever it was he went."

"There are times when I could cheerfully bat you one. As far as I can see, all is well apart from this niggling little fear that sooner or later something nasty is going to happen. I hope it's sooner and then we can clear the air."

It happened the following morning.

I had just got 4L started on working out some overtime payments at a time and a half when Ted Dunning came in and told me that John Henry wanted to see me straight away.

"I'll look after this little lot for you," he announced in a voice calculated to reach everybody in the room, "I don't like losing my free periods, so heaven help anyone who breathes too loudly."

He came to the door with me.

"I gather that our revered leader had a telephone call which peeved him a little. You haven't been doing anything you didn't oughter, have you? Seducing the caretaker's wife, or anything like that? Pity. We could do with a bit of scandal round here. Don't bother to hurry back, by the way. I don't really mind being with this shower when I could be having a smoke with my feet on the table.

John Henry was sitting behind his desk as I entered his office. He did not appear unduly perturbed.

"Sit down, Mr Curtis," he said "I'll tell you what's happened without beating about the bush. I've just had two telephone calls concerning your outing with the boys yesterday. The first was from Winnington's the printers. It appears that a rather complicated and expensive block, which they had prepared for an important customer, has gone missing. The last time they saw it was when it was being shown to our lot. The chap who rang me was polite enough to wonder whether it might be possible that one of the boys had taken it for a joke, but we know what he really meant. Do you know anything about it at all?"

My first reaction was one of bitter, humiliating disappointment. Everything that I had done and thought and hoped for had suddenly turned sour, and I could think of nothing at all to say.

"I didn't really expect you to have noticed anything or you would have done something about it. Anyway, give it some thought and let me know as soon as you can. The other call was from the bus company. It took them a bit longer to think we might be involved but they go there in the end. Seats were cut with a knife on two busses yesterday, and they happen to be the two buses our party was travelling on."

"Of course, there's no proof in either case. Someone at the firm may have misplaced the block and the seat cutting may have nothing to do with any of our boys, but it would be stretching coincidence a bit far, wouldn't it?"

My mood changed at this second piece of news.

"Of course it's our responsibility," I exploded. "It's my responsibility. I should have watched them more closely, though I can't think for the life of me how. They've let me down and I've let you down, but to say I'm sorry isn't at all adequate. I'd bet my last penny I know who's responsible, too, but I've no proof and I'm never likely to get any. What do you suggest I should do now?"

"The first thing is to stop blaming yourself. True enough, the responsibility is yours, but that means it's mine, too, and I'm paid to carry the can, so you're not on your own."

"The next thing is that, although you've named no names, I had already thought of Fenton as a possible suspect, but don't go accusing him. For one thing, we may be mistaken, and for another we need proof. If past experience is anything to go by, that's not going to be easy. Sooner or later, I'm going to have to question every boy unless someone spills the beans first. For your own satisfaction and for the sake of your authority, you should have the chance to see them first. What do you think?"

"Yes, you are right, I know. I would appreciate the chance to talk to them. The way I feel at the moment, there won't be many left for you to question when I've finished with them. Unless somebody comes up with a really good story, there's going to be murder done."

"I wouldn't advise you to go as far as that," John Henry smiled. "It's a serious thing and it leaves a nasty taste in the mouth, but it isn't the end of the world."

"Thanks. I do appreciate the way you've taken this. Now, if you don't mind, I'll get off. I have things to do."

I had rarely felt so angry, and when I stormed back into the hut, 4L needed no telling to be quiet and listen. I told the girls to go away into the far recesses of the place and on no account to disturb the proceedings. Ted Dunning I invited to stay to act as a restraining influence, physical if necessary, in case I took it into my head to go for someone with a craft knife.

I normally found getting angry a difficult process requiring a certain amount of histrionic ability, but on this occasion it came naturally. In some of the finest invective I had ever used I told the boys what had happened, going on to add my opinion of people who were so low as to perform such mindless acts and how these sentiments applied equally to those who, through cowardice or misplaced loyalty, shielded the culprits from their just deserts. Mr Dunning listened in open-mouthed admiration as the tirade developed and admitted afterwards in the staff room that he would not have missed it for worlds. I was still at boiling point when, at last, I found I was repeating myself and gave the audience a chance to recover.

"I thought, in my stupid way," I concluded, "that we were getting along pretty well. I thought you had found yesterday's visit useful and enjoyable and that maybe you were looking forward to some more. Well, let me tell you one thing. The way I feel at the moment, there won't <u>be</u> any more. I object to being made a fool of, whether by you lot or anyone else and I don't see why you should have the chance again. First thing this afternoon, unless I have a complete confession from the boy concerned, all future visits are cancelled and it will be maths and English all day and every day until you leave school. Now, if any of you have anything you wish to tell me about what happened, you can start now. I'll ask you one at a time, starting at the back. That means you, Fenton."

He was the only one who had appeared unmoved by my displeasure. Now he stood up, put his hands in his pockets and stared at me.

"No one wants your bloody silly little trips," he said, "and if you're accusing me of.... "

Just what he intended to do remained a mystery because, feeling this to be the final straw, I leapt across the table to grab him by the collar. Seeing me hurtling towards him through the air he, quite reasonably, took evasive action. His winkle-picker shoes slipped from under him, somehow became entangled with the legs of the chair, and he fell as though pole axed out of my range of vision.

By the time I came in to land he was lying on the floor groaning amidst a growing pool of blood.

Whilst I and the class stood transfixed, Ted Dunning moved into action and yanked Fenton to his feet.

"Come on, lad," he said, "there's no need for the dramatics. A bust nose won't kill you. In fact, I rather suspect that you will live, though I won't go so far as to say I would recommend it." Fenton, however, was past the reasonable stage. His sallow face was distorted, not with pain but with anger, as he pushed Ted away from him.

"That's it! That's it" he shouted, "I've had enough. My dad's coming and he'll murder you!" and he ran out of the room.

Ted put his arm up to restrain me as I made to follow him.

"Let him go," he said, "You'll do no good trying to catch him and your dignity will suffer. I'll tell John Henry what's happened. Quite entertaining, really. You must ask me round again some time."

Reaction set in. I felt I had had enough for one day and sat down at the desk to sort out my thoughts. Without a word, 4L went back to their places and started to work.

Everyone on the staff soon found out what had happened, of course, and at break time there was a lively discussion as to what Fenton senior would be likely to do to me when he turned up. That he would turn up, and before very long, there was no doubt. It seemed that he always did turn up, though there was little agreement as to what actually happened from that point onwards. Everyone who had been on the receiving end of one of Fenton senior's little visits had since left, though whether to have a nervous breakdown or to mend a mangled body or from more normal causes was not clear.

Mrs Somers, the secretary, told me not to worry as she has always kept the local hospital telephone number handy in case of emergency. Some of the men exchanged reminiscences of Fenton's prowess on the football field. The accent seemed to be less on skills than on herculean feats of strength, like running for the try line with not only the ball but an opponent under his arm. George Grinton seemed to derive great satisfaction recalling an occasion when Fenton's head collided with the goal posts which promptly broke in two and collapsed all over the players, only Fenton emerging unscathed and scoring a try. I was not reassured.

Charlie Holt, our drama expert, was supposed to be on playground duty but, not wishing to miss any of the real life drama being enacted in the staff room, was doing it by keeping an eye on things through the window.

"One thing I'll say for old man Fenton," he said, "is, that he always turns up on cue. He's just coming into the yard now."

I left the charge to get a glimpse of this living legend and I had to admit that, if anything, the reports had erred on the conservative side.

"We don't really expect you to meet him on your own, Ken," said George Grinton, "John Henry has said that I have to take him straight to the office if and when he appears. He may call for you later, but at the moment it's out of your hands."

"Oh no, it isn't," I said, in the manner of a pantomime audience, "whatever John Henry said, it is me that young Fenton has been getting at and it's up to me to tell his father my side of the story. In fact I'll go and meet him."

I stalked out of the room on to the playground, my real reason for this ostentatious display of bravery being that I considered my chances of flight to be better out in the open than in the confines of the office. The staff, not suspecting my craven motives, were crowding round the windows with the sort of expressions on their faces that are more usually associated with the customers on the front row of an East End wrestling bout.

I could now see my adversary more clearly as he cut a swathe through the throng, his son at his side wearing an expression of smug satisfaction. Without a doubt, this Fenton was the largest man I had ever seen and, even more forbidding, on his broken- nosed, cauliflower-eared face was such an expression of malevolent hatred that I all but made a bolt for safety there and then. I felt rather as David would have done when about to meet Goliath if God had suddenly told him he was on his own.

The boys in the playground, with that uncanny ability to scent a contest probably involving the letting of blood, were tending to form a ring. I felt that it only needed the caretaker to appear with some buckets of sawdust for the picture to be complete.

There was now no one between the man-mountain and myself and I saw Fenton junior point at me and say something to his parent. This person advanced, rubbing one fist in the palm of his other hand and growling, closer and closer. Suddenly he stopped, the growling ceased and the battered face broke into a grin.

"God in heaven," he said, "It's the Corp!" and immediately I knew who he was. "It's Corporal Curtis, 100th Armoured Div., isn't it? You remember me, Corp.,

Frightful Fenton. Bloody Hell, I'll never forget that time you got me off a fizzer down at Aldershot. How are you?"

"Of course I remember you, you old fraud," I said, what in heavens name are you doing in Pitdale, and frightening me to death, at that?"

"Nay, I've allus lived i'Pitdale. By gow, I'm that please to see you. It's right made my day, has this!"

"You've no idea what it's done to mine! Look, Frightful, we've got to meet somewhere and have a real good natter, but don't forget why you came here. You're supposed to be killing me because of this lad of yours, so I'd better tell you what it's all about, hadn't I?"

"Nay, you've no need to bother, Corp. He's not my lad really, you know. His mother was a widow and I married her and they took my name so you see he's nowt to do wi' me, and you can't tell me owt about 'im what I don't know already. T'only reason I come here is to stop 'is mother nattering. Aye, she's a right bloody nagger is his mother. I'd rather have old R.S.M. Gantry going on at me any day, than 'er."

He turned to where his stepson was hovering in the background, evidently displeased with the way things were going.

"Come 'ere, you little sod," he said, gathering him by the ear, "thee come telling me tales about friends of mine and I'll give you what you should have had years ago. And tha can tell this mother I said so."

He gave him a slight push which sent him spinning to the far corner of the playground.

"If you've any more bother wi' that little devil, thump him hard and then give 'im another for me. Now then, let's forget about that. When can you get a bit of time off?"

"There's no time like the present. How about today? Can you be anywhere where we can talk at dinner time – twelve o'clock or thereabouts?"

"You bet I can. Thee get down to t'Railway at twelve o'clock. I'll have you a pint in, and they make some right good beef sandwiches that'll put you on a treat. By gum, I'm right pleased to see thee again. It's fair made my day, has this. Don't forget, then t'Railway at twelve o'clock."

With much playful punching and hand shaking, Frightful took his departure through the crowd, most of whom had not bothered to stay to the end of a disappointing performance.

When I got back inside, the staff were agog to learn how I had contrived to turn the wrath of this fearsome man.

"Just my natural charm," I said, and went off to my hut with a lighter heart.

As 4L busied themselves with whatever it was they were doing, I mused on my first meeting with Frightful Fenton.

We were stationed at Aldershot, and the C.O. had collard me one day and given me the job of drumming up support for a boxing tournament he was organising. In spite of the prevailing boredom, volunteers for this supposedly morale boosting event had been few and he was feeling a bit peeved. It seemed that it was going to be necessary for me to volunteer some names if their owners were not prepared to do so themselves and, in casting around for some suitable candidates, I thought of a new dispatch rider who had just joined us. He was large and ugly and had a much battered face and was a heavyweight boxer if ever I saw one. Not that I had ever seen one, in fact, as boxing was a pastime which held little appeal for me.

I searched out this new man in his barrack room and informed him that he had just agreed to fight for the honour of the D.R.'s in this tournament thing.

He seemed a bit surprised and said he had never been in a boxing ring in his life. "Oh, come on," I said, "you never got a face like that playing ludo."

"No, I got it playing football. Rugby league, tha' knows," he said.

"You must have enjoyed yourself. Seriously, though, there aren't any real boxers in for this thing and all you need to do is go up there and scowl and you're home and dry. Anyway, if you don't, I'm going to cop it from the C.O., so do us a favour and let me put your name down. What is your name, by the way?"

"It's Fenton, Corp. All me mates call me Frightful, though. Look, Corp, if you're sure there's no real boxers in for this thing, I'll have a go. But I know nowt about it. I've never even seen a boxing match."

"That makes two of us, then. Anyway, thanks, Frightful. I'll put your name down, and remember if there's ever anything I can do for you, just come and ask."

It might have been a chance or it might be that the other contestants in the heavyweight division caught a glimpse of Frightful, but so many reported to the M.O. with complaints which caused them to scratch from the contest, that he found himself in the final without ever having stepped into the ring. I was about to join the audience in the packed sports hall to witness his maiden performance when the C.O. called me over.

"Corporal," he said, "this man of yours – what's his name?" "Signalman Fenton, sir," I said.

"That's right, Fenton. Has he got a second?" "A second what, sir?"

"A second, you dummy. Someone to give him advice and er.. er.. see to his needs and so on. Has he bloody well got one or hasn't he?"

I couldn't really see what sort of needs a man in his position could have but thought it wiser not to say so. In any case, now that I thought of it, I had seen on the films of fights at the pictures, a person in a sweater whose job it seemed to be to hold an enamel container for the boxer to spit into, and to wave a towel about during intervals. I assumed that this would be the second.

"No, sir, there's no second as far as I know," I said.

"You can't expect a man to fight without a second, corporal. You will have to do it. Get along there now and see to it."

"Yes, sir, I said, because you don't argue with Commanding Officers. When I arrived in the changing room, Frightful was looking lonely and despondent.

"Cheer up!" I said, "your fortune is now assured. I am your second." "Second what?" he asked.

"Don't you start that. I've been through it once already with the C.O. I am here to advise you and minister to your needs. Have you seen an enamel thing to spit into anywhere around?"

"No, I haven't Corp, but I've seen the chap I'm supposed to be fighting and he's bigger nor me."

I spotted the flaw in this straight away.

"You're wrong, Frightful. There isn't anyone bigger than you."

"Oh yes there is, and in a few minutes I'll be in there with him. You go and have a look. He's in the next room. Then you can tell me what to do."

I went on the pretext of wishing our opponent good luck. There were several people in the room all giving advice, so I assumed they were all seconds or, maybe, thirds and fourths. In spite of this, the room was really filled by one man who, stripped for action, was certainly to within the odd foot or two as big as Frightful, and of hideous countenance. To the exhortation of his comrades, he was dancing up and down and aiming lethal looking punches at a non-existent foe. His face was cold and set in the sort of expression made popular by the more ruthless gangsters in American films. He was a killer if ever I saw one. I mumbled my good wishes and fled.

"Did you see him?" asked Frightful.

"I could hardly miss him, could I? he is a bit on the large side, I suppose. I think we'd better be working out a battle plan. The only trouble is that I don't know of a left hook from a half-nelson."

"Neither do I. I'm not feared of 'im, you know, but I don't want to look daft. I reckon I'll 'ave to think of summat pretty quick." We sat in silence for a few minutes.

"Look, Frightful," I said at last. "We've got to face facts. This chap is at least as big as you, he looks mean and, what's more, he's obviously a boxer. This means you are going to be beaten unless we can think of something unexpected and I can only think of one thing."

"What's that, then, Corp?"

"The moment you get in the ring with him and the chap in charge says 'Go!' or whatever it is they do, you've got to give an almighty swing and cop him with the first punch. With a bit of luck you might knock him out or, at any rate, make him groggy. If it goes any further than that, you've had it. Don't be soft about it. It's him or you and it's got to work first time."

"Aye, you could be right. I don't know if I can do it, mind, but I'll 'ave a go. I can't think of owt else, any rooad."

Shortly afterwards we were told it was our turn and we took our places in and around the ring. I was pleased to see that there was an enamel spittoon thing but hoped fervently that it would not be needed.

The R.S.M. in the role of Master of Ceremonies announced in his normal parade ground voice that the next contest would be the heavyweight championship of the Unit with, in the red corner, Signalman Percy Fenton and, in the blue corner, Private Bill Scraggs. The referee said a few well chosen words about being clean and not holding, there was a blur of light and a whistling sound and Private Bill Scraggs sank to the canvas. One to ten was counted, Frightful's hand was held aloft, there was a great deal of whistling, cheering and booing, and it was all over.

Back in the dressing room, Frightful was both elated and worried.

"By gum, Corp, it worked a treat didn't it?" I thought I were going to get a right pasting, but it worked a real treat. I hope that chap's all right, though. They 'ad to carry him out didn't they? I'll be right sorry if I've hurt 'im. As soon as I've got dressed I'm off in there to see how he is."

By the time we arrived, Private Scraggs was conscious but unhappy. He sat slumped in a chair surrounded by his assistants and managed a wan smile as we approached.

"'Ello," he said, moving his jaw as little as possible as though it were paining him, "didn't last long, did it?"

Frightful grabbed hold of his hand and pumped it up and down.

"Ee, I'm right glad to see thee looking a bit better. I'm right sorry, an' all, if I hurt thee. It were all we could think of, tha sees. I'd never been in a ring before in my life, you see."

"Neither 'ad I," said Private Scraggs.

And that was how I first met Frightful Fenton. Time after time in the next year or so, until the Army decreed that we should go our separate ways, he proved himself to be a good friend, as gentle a man as I ever met, and completely devoid of self interest. I was genuinely delighted to meet him again and eagerly awaited the twelve o'clock bell so that we could catch up on all the news.

When the time arrived I told George Grinton where I was going and hurried through the back streets and down the main road to the Railway Inn next to the marshalling yards where the coal trucks were perpetually clanking and screeching.

I should have known better.

Never having found any pleasure in swilling away such sense as I possessed with excessive amounts of alcohol, and having in mind the miners' legendary prowess in this direction, I should have seen the warning lights flashing bright and clear. Instead I rushed towards my doom like those lemmings one hears about who can't wait to dive into the sea and drown themselves. True to his word Frightful had a pint of the local brew ready for me and lost no time in introducing me to a concourse of his cronies. It became apparent, to my great surprise, that he regarded me as a super strategist to whom he owed a debt of gratitude for having, by low cunning, helped him to escape punishment for one or two minor infringements of Kings Rules and Regulations during our time together.

His mates, having been let into these secrets, clamoured to be allowed to show their gratitude, too, in the only way immediately available.

It was when I found myself telling them that they were the truest and most intelligent fellows I had ever met and that only prejudice had excluded Pitdale from a recent publication on the prettiest towns of England and I intended to do something about it, that it occurred to me that I might have had more than I intended of the innocuous tasting local brew. I was quite sure of it when I looked at my watch and found that afternoon school had been going on for half an hour without me and, moreover, that I was going to die before I got there.

My subsequent incoherent apologies to John Henry were, to my surprise, swept aside.

"News travels fast round here," he said, "We all know where you've been and have followed your progress with interest. Many better men than you have been deceived by that stuff they serve up at the Railway. By the look of you I shouldn't think you'll be doing it too often. In any case you're our local hero at the moment so I suggest you should clear off to the staffroom and I'll get someone to bring you a cup of coffee."

I'd had about enough of being a hero for one day and was mystified at being accused again.

"What do you mean, 'local hero'?" I asked.

"Fenton's father was, without exception, our most obstreperous parent and, quite frankly, he's been a thorn in our sides ever since his lad started here. Now it seems that, by some secret alchemy, you are on drinking terms with him and everyone is overjoyed. We are, indeed, grateful to you."

"Well," I said "I suppose that's right in a way. He's certainly a tough nut, all right, is old Fenton."

The mists and the nausea and the throbbing were diminishing a little. What with that and the glad tidings instead of rocket, I was feeling that I might live after all.

"I would appreciate some coffee if there's any going," I said, "but I'll get back to 4L. I'm all right now – and thanks again."

"Think nothing of it," said John Henry, "but if you could just modify the excitement a bit for a week or two, I think we'd all be grateful. It's been quite a day."

"Yes," I agreed, "it has. It's been quite a day."

CHAPTER FOUR

PITDALE FAREWELL

After my disgusting exhibition at the reunion celebrations with Fenton Senior, things calmed down and there was, for a while, a fairly straightforward carry on. The qualification is necessary because, in a school, nothing is ever completely straightforward. There is always the odd child requiring professional medical attention for instance, the reasons being both varied and, at times, peculiar. Children impaling themselves on railings at playtime or breaking an arm in P.E. or developing symptoms of appendicitis in the middle of a geography lesson are regarded as routine. The boy who got his behind stuck down the toilet in such a position that his knees were touching his ears, or the girl who developed frostbite through being unable to remove her finger from a part of the fridge mechanism were more unusual.

Then of course, there were always parents to contend with. Some were kindly and appreciative, some were unpleasant and abusive, most were just anxious. At Pitdale, the co-operation between home and school was generally very good.

The weather being unusually warm one week, John Henry decided that the time was ripe for a Staff v Pupils cricket match.

This was something I felt I could well do without and I wasted a great deal of ingenuity hiding round corners whenever I saw him approaching. It was a waste of time because, when the team sheet was posted on the staff notice board, my name was on it anyway.

"About this cricket match," said John Henry when he finally cornered me, "what are you?"

"Useless," I said.

"Now, don't expect me to believe that – young fellow like you. I know you told me you ought to wear glasses, but this isn't a county game. I'm trying to get the team sorted out so what shall I put you down as, batsman or bowler?"

"I've never been able to make my mind up which I'm worst at. The safest thing to do would be to put me in at number eleven, and then let me field in some position where the ball isn't likely to go. I'm not bad as twelfth man, but I'm even better in the pavilion making sandwiches."

"Right, I'll mark you in as an all rounder then. What sort of bowler would you describe yourself as?"

"Don't tempt me. Seriously, Mr Crabtree, don't put me on to bowl, please. I'm much more likely to hit the umpire than the wickets – the one standing behind me, I mean."

I never relished the prospect of making a fool of myself and I could see no other outcome in this contest. I was not made any easier in my mind when Jim Grinton told me one day the reason for the Head's addiction to the noble game. It seemed that he had played for his university and, at the same period, been given a trial run in the County team. He had done so well that he had been offered a contract, with the probability of a regular first team place in due course. After a great deal of heart searching he had turned down the offer in favour of a career in education. Although he had never regretted it, there were times when he was tempted to think on what might have been, and the love of the game never left him.

The day of the match dawned bright and clear as they say. I had been praying for rain or snow, so my standing with whoever was in charge up there must have been at a pretty low ebb at that time. I had no whites, so wore the nearest I could muster, a shirt which had been blue but which constant washing had turned into a sort of off-grey, and a pair of flannel trousers which refused to stay up in a seemly manner when I took my braces off.

I felt that the sight of one of his players with trousers slipping round his ankles at the least movement would not please our captain, however much it might have cheered the rest of the team, so I secured them with a bright red tie in lieu of a belt. This gave me a slightly raffish, nineteen twenties, "anyone for tennis" look which went down well with the pupils.

I was pleased to see that I was not the only sartorially incorrect player on our side and that Tim Humphreys, the woodwork man, had made an attempt to lighten the proceedings by appearing in a bowler hat, blue overalls and wellington boots. John Henry was not amused and, had it been anyone other than Tim, would probably have had him arrested. Tim had been at the school since Sherwood Forest reached that far and was said to have known Robin Hood personally. He was bluff and outspoken and treated John Henry as a junior member of staff. It is a curious fact, deserving of deeper research, that woodwork teachers have always been at schools longer than anyone else and are always bluff and outspoken. In general, the same applies to Domestic Science teachers, except that they tend to be much more frightening. However, our captain won the toss and elected to bat, which was another blow. I had hoped that the school would bat first and that, when our turn came, our opening batsman would knock off the required runs without needing to call on my services, but not so. Any other foolish ideas I might have had that our openers would amass such a large score that we would be able to declare, were quickly dispelled during the first over. I had seen so-called fast bowlers at Headingley and Park Avenue playing for teams like Yorkshire and Australia but, seen close to, these large boys of ours were infinitely more awe-inspiring. The professionals, hampered by a tradition of aiming somewhere near the wicket, had sacrificed a certain amount of sheer speed to this end. Our opponents had no such inhibitions. It would not have mattered a great deal, anyway, as the ground was so uneven that the direction in which the ball left the bowler's hand had little relationship to that in which it eventually left the pitch.

John Henry coped admirably. He cut, leg-laced, drove and hooked with such obvious ease that it seemed a shame to have anyone else in the team. Jim Dewey, opening at the other end, was the sort of player whose native ability is not cluttered up by too much orthodox technique. After a razz-ma-tazz sort of innings he skied one too many and, to my delight, Gary Gates, running a considerable distance from behind the wickets, took a spectacular catch.

That was the start of the rot and it became obvious that, before long, I was going to be required to stand at one end whilst John Henry got on with the game at the other. When my turn came, most of the preceding batsmen having cravenly sacrificed their wickets rather than face the barrage from boys only too eager to get a bit of their own back, I walked out nonchalantly twiddling my bat as I had seem some of the great players do. I dropped mine, of course. After calling imperiously for 'leg and middle' I patted the crease and looked round the field in the approved manner, though what I was looking for I would have found it hard to say.

The bowler, one Charlie Cross from 4A who had no cause to bear me any grudge as far as I knew, was tiring a little but there was still enough velocity there for the ball to touch the edge of my defensively outstretched bat and fly through the slips for four.

The next two deliveries were so far off the wicket that I couldn't even see them let alone touch them. The next, and the last of the over, Charlie bowled at full pace. I was lifting my bat backwards to make some kind of stroke when the ball hit it and flew through the air to the boundary. I was already in double figures and very surprised indeed.

It was just as well that I didn't allow any elation to creep in because the next ball I was called upon to receive, due to some aberration of the pitch, actually hit the wicket and I retired thankfully to the pavilion.

During the boys' innings, by judicious hiding behind other players, I managed to miss only one catch. I pretended that this was because I had sprained my ankle and had to remember to hobble for the rest of the game and for a day or two afterwards. I never knew who won, but we chatted and joked a lot afterwards and lied about how much we had enjoyed it.

Meanwhile the ordinary routine carried on. The Nissen hut began to take on something of the air of a medieval banqueting hall and the other classes had trips to come and look at it. One or two quite gifted artists were discovered and encouraged to spend most of their time in the art room where they could work under expert guidance. I had hopes they might use their talents as designers in textiles or in the printing trade when they left school.

Being an enthusiastic, if inept, musician, I was particularly gratified to find a few boys and girls taking an interest in something beyond the then current pop scene.

Some had a leaning towards jazz, in which field I considered myself fairly knowledgeable, others to the classics, which we had the joy of discovering together. Two of them became competent recorder players, by which I meant that they could read music and produce a sound more pleasing to the ear than the bosun's pipe squeal commonly associated with this instrument by parents. One boy, Freddie Jenkins, was exceptionally quick at picking up the rudiments of the trumpet, and was keen enough to talk his parents into buying him a second hand instrument from the local brass band.

Some of the more advanced educational theorists would have been delighted by the apparent chaos which characterised most of our afternoon. Most, or all, of the above activities would be going on at one and the same time, plus a group sprawled on the floor making shields and heraldic devices with gold and silver paint and so on. It was during such a performance, when I was at the top of a ladder supervising the painting of some girders, that John Henry appeared, shepherding none other than the great Obediah.

"Come on down, Mr Curtis," he called out when he had negotiated the various obstacles and located me hanging like a bat from the rafters, "and meet Alderman Smith."

I came down thinking with some surprise that this was the first time I had thought of Obediah as having any other name and, at that, rather an anti-climax.

He looked at me keenly with those incredibly blue eyes.

"I've seen thee before, lad," he said, "nay – don't tell me when. I'll think on. I know – it was outside t'County Hall and then you got yourself into t'wrong room. Now then, how are you liking Pitdale?"

"I'm liking it very well, thank you," I said, "I'm sorry if

it's a bit noisy in here, but we tend to get carried away with what we are doing. I'm so used to it that I don't notice."

"Nay, lad, never apologise. If what you're doing's right, then you can explain it. If it isn't then it's time to pack up and do summat else. I'm told you've been doing all right. Mind, I've been told other things as well. No, no, it's not John Henry as told me. He's pleased with what you've done. But allus think on, lad, there's some on us as keeps our eyes and ears open. You've nowt to worry about. Your chance'll come sooner or later. Good afternoon, then."

They departed as quickly as they had come, leaving me with the uncomfortable feeling that, in five minutes, all my inner thoughts had been read like an open book.

Frightful had managed, by some method into which we thought it better not to delve too deeply, to extract a confession from his step-son, the missing plate had been returned and the bus company placated by some smooth talking from John Henry. That incident was, therefore, treated as closed, and the visits carried on according to plan. We froze on building sites and sweated in a glass bottle works and at most places there were boys sufficiently interested to want further details about employment prospects.

The romance between Albert Moggs and the fair Sylvia foundered when she tried to seduce him one night in the yard at the back of the Miners' Welfare. He ran inside, white and shaking, to enlist the aid of his father who was helping to keep the local brewer in business upstairs. He was given a thick ear and sent home in disgrace. After this he returned to the gentler sport of rugby and it was rumoured that Sylvia found solace in the arms of the barman at the Miners's Arms who was more to her size and weight.

Fenton was no more trouble as far as school was concerned, but there were still reports of bullying and he still had some sort of hold over the other boys, largely because of his reputation of being afraid of nothing. This situation changed unexpectedly during our penultimate visit which was to a chemical works in nearby Coalstone.

It was not the most pleasant of our outings. With the exception of the offices and laboratory which were just bearable, the place was covered in fine powder, varying in colour and smell from one department to another, but uniformly unsavoury. There were men shovelling it, mixing it, putting it into containers, loading it, being covered in it and it all struck me, as a non-chemist, as being rather nasty. I had no reason to disbelieve the man who told us it was destined to become aspirin or washing powder or vanilla flavouring, but it didn't make me like it.

The buildings were gaunt, like giant meccano, full of dirty draughts and eddying yellow clouds. In places it stank so vilely with that acrid chemical stench that is so much more unpleasant than, say, a field of farmyard manure, that even 4L noticed it. Those who had them, held handkerchiefs over their noses; the majority used thumb and forefinger and expressions of anguish.

Our guide seemed surprised and said he couldn't smell anything.

We gradually approached a tall tower with an ironwork staircase spiralling round it and a railed off space at the top. It seemed that this was to be the piece de resistance of our visit and its purpose was explained to us in some detail. I did not understand it at the time and have never felt the need to delve deeper into the mystery since but, as far as I remember, whatever was the raw material was fed in at the bottom and various things were produced as it progressed upwards from level to level. What I did understand was that this was a very tall tower and that we were going to climb it.

The staircase was a skeletal structure with very little to stop the climber from making an unscheduled quick descent, and you could describe the view as unobstructed in every direction including downwards. There was a great deal of unusually loud chattering and laughter as we approached the top, much of it, I suspected, the manifestation of excitement tinged with fear. We all stood at the top in the wind, gripping the railings and picking out well known landmarks.

All, that is, but one.

Suddenly someone said, "Where's Fenton?"

He certainly wasn't on the tower, for it would be impossible to lose anyone up there. I had a momentary vision of him lying in a mangled heap, and then the vision changed and I pictured him doing something dreadful with chemicals at the bottom of the tower and I leapt for the stairway. As I reached the top step I saw him. He was half way up, his eyes closed, his face even paler than usual and his knuckles white as he clung to the railings. He was incapable of moving either up or down.

"Come on Gates and you, Albert. We'd better see to him before he falls off. The rest of you get away from the edge and stay with the guide. He'll tell you when to move."

When we reached him I squeezed under his arm so that I was beneath him on the stairs and then between us we manoeuvred him to ground level.

To seize up like that through sheer terror must be a horrible experience and I felt genuinely sorry for him. There was no gloating, no leg pulling from the other boys, either. There was no need to say anything. They knew, and he knew, that the spell had been broken and that, from that moment, they started on level terms. It was certainly good for him, too. I often wondered how he turned out, but I never got to know.

We still had a few more weeks and one more visit to go before the end of term and it was one to which I had been looking forward with quite ridiculously pleasurable anticipation ever since it had been arranged. Our destination was to be the engine sheds at Southington Junction, not all that far away but an awkward journey necessitating a special bus.

I was like a child before Christmas. This was still the age of steam when a railway engine was a living, breathing thing and every sensible boy wished to spend his life driving one. It is true that some of the boys of 4L expressed a strong preference for such second rate things as cars or buses or aeroplanes, but even they admitted to looking forward to this trip with more than the usual pleasure.

Southington itself seemed nothing very special – just another Pitdale, but with the all-important addition of a junction where trains from the south branched east or west and, of course, the steam train version of a service depot which we had come to see.

We reported to the offices where a cheery, middle aged man in a tidy blue suit introduced himself as Jack Barnett, our guide for the day. There was the usual introductory patter explaining how Southington fitted into the overall railway pattern, the sort of servicing and engine required, and a fascinating description of the types of locomotive, which had to be dealt with. There followed the obligatory question session, opened in typical inane style by Herbert Hollings who informed Mr Barnett that his sister had once been to Blackpool by train, and then we were outside for the really interesting part. It was just as absorbing as I had expected it to be.

We saw the coaling apparatus and the watering apparatus; we went into the sheds and saw the various stages of looking after an engine; we saw all sorts of things which have since been forgotten because we came, at last, to the moment I, at any rate, had been waiting for.

There stood this beautiful monster with its shining paint and metal work and its gently tapering boiler, softly hissing to itself. We walked round it, marvelling at the sheer size and yet, when we stood back, everything was so perfectly proportioned that it looked exactly right. We climbed up on the footplate and the various controls were explained to us. Casually our guide leaned over the side and gave a short toot on the whistle.

"It's a bit crowded, so make sure you hold on," he said "and we'll take her a little way down the line."

Slowly, silently and smoothly we moved away. The metal to metal contact of tyres on rails seemed unexpectedly hard, and forward visibility behind the immense boiler virtually non-existent, but this was it! This was what it felt like to ride on the footplate of a main line express locomotive and, though none of us realised it, the very best and last of its kind. Too soon we slowed and it was explained that we were nearing the turntable where we would swing the engine round and return to the sheds. With fine precision we came to a halt. Most of us climbed down to see how a pipe on the turntable was connected to one on the engine, the vacuum lever was operated and the engine started to turn around of its own volition.

When it had completed the full half circle, Mr Barnett called out to the boys still on the footplate, "Knock off the vacuum lever I showed you."

It was at this point that things started to go wrong. There is an assumption amongst those not accustomed to dealing with young people, that it is only necessary to tell them a thing once for it to be understood. This is a fallacy well known to the teaching profession. I have known students from training college to appear on teaching practice with a large folio of lesson notes which they show you with modest pride.

"That is very good," you say, encouragingly, "but don't expect everyone in the class to get through that lot in the six weeks you are here."

"Oh!" they say in surprise, "that's just the first lesson."

On this occasion the mistake was that, having told my lot once which was the vacuum lever, to assume that they would (a) understand its significance and (b) be able to find it again. As it happened, Billy Strong, who was playing at train drivers, rather than betray his ignorance, had a stab at the first lever that came to hand. It happened to be throttle.

The first intimation we had was a sudden frenzied, pulsating beat from the engine, the wheels spun frantically to find grip, the vacuum pipe parted forcibly and several hundred tons of machinery departed in the general direction of Scotland.

With the exception of our guide who muttered something that was not in the railway manual and galloped off in vain pursuit, we stood transfixed. The idea of Billy Strong in charge of a railway engine after five minutes instruction, not a word of which had he understood, was too frightening to contemplate. The probable route seemed to be into the engine sheds, straight through the wall at the far side and then non-stop to Edinburgh with scenes of carnage at intervals on the way.

Fortunately I had underestimated Billy Strong. After what seemed an hour or so but was, in fact, a few seconds, the engine stopped as suddenly as it had departed. For once in his life Billy had experienced a flash of reasoned thought. It seemed to him, as he explained to me afterwards, that if you pushed a lever one way and something started happening, then to stop it happening you had to push the lever back again to where it was. If it hadn't been liable to misinterpretation I could have hugged him. He leaned out of the cab when the engine came to a halt and beamed at us with self-satisfaction.

"By gum, sir, ah thought ah were a goner then," he said.

We all laughed but, in my case at any rate, there was more relief than humour in it.

When we got back to school there was a message waiting for me to ring Mr Elsworth at County Hall immediately.

"Hello, Mr Curtis," he said when I got through, "I'm sorry to have to do this to you, but an emergency has cropped up so I want you to start on Monday at Carlton Royd school in Shipham. We've managed to arrange for the chap who will be taking your place at Pitdale to start early, so there will be no problem there.

For some reason which at first I could not explain, my heart dropped down to boot level.

"This is a bit sudden, isn't it, Mr Elsworth. I would really prefer to see the end of the term out here. There are only a couple of weeks to go."

"I'm afraid it can't be done. You know we wouldn't move you at a time like this if it could possibly be arranged any other way, but Mr Crabtree has agreed that you can go. It's the old business of going where the need is greatest, I'm afraid, and I've had Mr Charles from Carlton Royd on at me for a couple of days.

"I suppose that's it, then. I would have liked to see this lot through to the end, though. Can you tell me any more about this Carlton Royd Place?"

"Well, it's a special school, of course, for educationally sub-normal children. Not residential, so there's no problem there. Mr Charles did say that he would try to get in touch with you over the weekend to let you know more about it before you start." "But I know nothing of E.S.N.'s. I've never had anything to do with them." "You'll take it all in your stride, Mr Curtis. I'll send you the usual card to confirm the arrangement, but in the meantime you can take it that you will start at Carlton Royd on Monday. Cheerio, then, Mr Curtis."

My feelings were mixed but becoming a little clearer. I had become attached to 4L and wanted to see them through to the end – even to the point of resenting any other person doing it for me.

As it was I wouldn't even be able to say 'goodbye', for this was Friday and they had already gone home. On the other hand Shipham was much nearer home and, after all, this was the sort of thing I would have to expect. E.S.N.'s I wasn't too happy about. It was true that I had never dealt with them en masse but they were, after all, children like any others and I had certainly met plenty who would have qualified if the places had been available for them. On the whole, I decided, I was rather looking forward to a change.

So I said my farewells to John Henry and the few members of staff who were still around, collected my belongings, had a last look round my baronial Nissen hut and departed like the Arab who silently steals away.

Later on, during the holidays, I rang up the Head to find out what sort of employment the boys of 4L had finally opted for. I was confident that, in a period of labour shortage, there would be a fairly wide spread over the industries we had seen.

"Nice of you to ring," said the voice of John Henry, "well, there's Woods. His father wouldn't let him work in the pit at any price, as you know. He's a driver's mate on the lorries. All the others are at the pit, of course. It always happens. Don't forget to call in and see us sometime. Always pleased to see you and hear how you are getting on, you know. It's pleasant to have an educational discussion with someone with lots of bright ideas, and you certainly do have ideas."

"Yes," I agreed, "I do have ideas, don't I?"

CHAPTER FIVE

It was later than usual when I returned to the flat that Friday evening and, although it was really my turn at the stove, I was hoping Peter might have tired of waiting and started to produce something edible. There was, however, neither a welcoming smell of burning nor shouted recriminations at my lateness as I opened the door. Instead, sitting demurely on the edge of our comfortable chair and reading Peter's Daily Express, was a young lady. I just happened to notice that she had a slim figure, nice sort of chestnutty hair and attractive brown eyes. Her general demeanour, combined with the undoubted fact that she was drinking a cup of tea and could apparently read made her, I thought, pretty well unique amongst Peter's girlfriends.

"Hello," I said, "I'm sure we haven't met before. I'm Ken Curtis and I share this establishment with Peter. I'm surprised he isn't looking after you."

"Oh, hello. He was doing but he's just popped out for a moment. He told me you should be arriving at any time."

"That's uncommonly thoughtful of him. He tends not to pay too much attention to me when he's entertaining his lady friends, except to make hints that I might like to go and visit the landlord of our local. Oh dear, there I go, putting my foot in it again. You do realise that There Have Been Others, don't you?"

"Really? To tell you the truth, I hadn't given it much thought. You see...." Whatever it was she saw was interrupted by the crashing of doors as Peter made his usual spectacular entrance.

"Oh, hello Ken, there you are at last," he said, "had to nip round the corner to buy something to eat before they close as it seemed you intended to stay out all night. This is Mrs Worth. She's come to see you – something about starting at a new school on Monday. Mrs Worth – Mr Curtis. And a bloody long time she's had to wait, too."

It is a curious thing, but I have found that the sort of girl Peter tended to bring home, the voluptuous sort who looked as though the chap who was inflating them had forgotten to leave off when he got to the recommended pressure, and whose thought processes were both uncomplicated and predictable, were easy to talk to. You didn't need to actually talk about anything – it was just a matter of stringing together a collection of words which had some sort of vague connecting link and this would pass for conversation. I could keep this up indefinitely, but the moment I met a girl who gave evidence of having a mind, I crumbled. I envied those people – Peter, for example – who, undeterred by glamour and sophistication, could give the impression of being the world's greatest authority on any subject under the sun. Maybe the fact that he thought so too had something to do with it.

My trouble was, as I recognised well enough, that the girl didn't exist who had the same interests and outlook as myself. I blamed nobody for this, but put it down as art of some divine plan over which I had no control. I had to admit to myself that I was a bit odd. After all what girl could be expected to talk about any sort of music, let alone jazz, or to enjoy pottering around in the Dales, or mooning purposelessly through the less fashionable parts of France, or watching cricket or motorcycle trials, or enjoying the simple things of the countryside? In my experience there wasn't a single one. So I tended to keep these things to myself and, not having a great store of intelligent chit-chat,

I dried up. The girls then decided that I was either stuck up or miserable or an idiot and went off to find someone else. On this occasion, realising that I had committed a faux pas, I began to babble. "Oh, I say, I really am sorry. I thought you were... well, it isn't as though you looked a bit like any girl Peter has to do with... I mean, what a stupid mistake. I really do... "

"There's no need at all to apologise," said Mrs Worth with a nice friendly sort of smile, "I should have told you straight away, so it's my fault."

"I don't know what the hell you've been doing in my absence," said Peter, "but I suggest you stop gibbering and let the lady tell you why she's here."

"Yes, well, you see I teach at Carlton Royd School and Mr Charles said you were starting with us on Monday and he asked if I would mind calling to see you as I don't live very far away. I think I'm supposed to tell you what to expect."

"Young lady," said Peter severely, "just answer me one question before you go any further. Tell me, have you eaten since you left school?"

"Well, no, actually I haven't," Mrs Worth replied, "but it really doesn't matter. I had one or two places to call at you see and then I came straight here."

"You mean to say that you have been sitting here waiting for this chap who hasn't the courtesy to arrive on time, without a bit to eat and not a word of complaint?"

"Well, that's dramatising it a bit, but my husband's away on business for the weekend so I have no need to hurry."

"No need to hurry my Aunt Fanny. You must be bloody starving. If only Ken weren't such a lousy cook, we'd ask you to stay for a meal, wouldn't we?"

"Of course, yes. I was just thinking so. But it's our inedible mush I wouldn't want Mrs Worth to risk."

"Take no notice of him, dear lady. You have probably heard people mention my name as a leader of the new experimental approach to cookery. No? Never mind. I would demonstrate to you, but I need time to create and, the way I feel I'd probably die of starvation before it was ready."

"May I make a suggestion?" asked Mrs Worth. We agreed that she may.

"Well, I'm not sure if you are serious or not, but if you are then I can do an omelette or something pretty quickly and then Mr Curtis and I could talk about the school. Oh – I say, I'm sorry. I have no right at all to interfere with your arrangements. I do apologise."

Peter gazed at her with admiration.

"Mrs Worth, you are, if I may say so, a flaming angel – and before you protest at my turn of phrase, young Curtis, I mean that literally. You are an angel with a flaming sword, driving away gloom and despondency, which is pretty good even for my fertile imagination on the spur of the moment. I speak for us both as he appears to be incapable, when I say that we accept your offer with grateful thanks. I've bought some bits of cooked chicken in; we have eggs, butter and possibly one or two other things as well. Come on and I'll lead the way to the stove."

"If you're quite sure I'm not interfering," said Mrs Worth anxiously.

"Mrs Worth," said Peter crudely, "my stomach is already rumbling in bloody anticipation, if you will pardon the expression. Let's not waste any more time in foolish talk. I'll tell you what – as I've been scouring the village for hours looking for food, how about you nipping round to the off-licence, Ken? I reckon we can afford a bottle of his best plonk on an occasion like this."

"Yes, of course," I said, mentally kicking myself for not having thought of it first. "That is, if Mrs Worth feels safe being left with you."

"Don't worry about me, Mr Curtis. I shall have the frying pan and, anyway, from what you told me, I'm not his type."

"When he's that way out, types don't matter. I'll be back in a few minutes anyway."

The meal was a complete success. Mrs Worth had done things with the eggs and chicken which were beyond our amateurish attempts; the plonk, though of no vintage known to man, helped to make my conversation more like that of a normal human being, and the presence of the delightful Mrs Worth herself, combined to turn a simple occasion into a memorable one. I was, indeed, surprised to realise at one point that I was actually doing most of the talking.

"I'm sorry," I said, "I seem to have been talking more than usual."

"Too bloody right you have," agreed Peter, "so I'll tell you what I'm going to do. I have a little business to transact with Wilf down at the Dog and Goose, so I propose to nip down there for half an hour. I shall then return and, if you've finished your chat, I'll run Mrs Worth home and she will not protest because it's the least we can do after the meal. By the way, I can't keep on calling you 'Mrs Worth' after all you've done. Presumably you have another name?"

"This is the moment I always dread," said Mrs Worth, "you have to promise you won't laugh."

"Laugh!" said Peter, "Of course we shan't laugh. What is it?" "Penny," she said.

"Penny!" said Peter with a puzzled frown, "There's

nothing funny about Penny. Oh... I see. Yes, I see what you mean."

"Peter Lee," I said, "If you dare to laugh, I shall dot you with this empty wine bottle. Ms Worth, you can take it as my considered opinion, that it's a very nice name indeed.

"Thanks, Mr Curtis. I feel a lot better about it now."

"Now you are pulling my leg. Do you know, Penny, if I may call you Penny, Mrs Worth, I really think it would be a good idea if I brewed up some coffee before we start talking business. I suppose I really ought to know what I'm letting myself in for on Monday."

Peter, for once, had slipped out un-noticed and, after the coffee, Mrs Worth and I got down to a discussion on what were the most important features of my job, which could be imparted in the next half hour. She was diffident in giving anything in the nature of advice on how to set about the task of educating these rather special children, seeming to be of the opinion that I had some vast store of knowledge and experience on which to draw. This was so flattering and so unusual that I played up to it a bit and so failed to learn anything beyond the physical organisation of the school. It had originally been built as an isolation hospital, I was told, and consisted of a central block with hall, offices, kitchen and so forth, and several separate classrooms connected with each other and the main building by footpaths. All this was amidst playing fields and an outer perimeter of trees. It sounded an improvement on Pitdale to me.

There were only about thirtyfive children altogether, divided into four classes. The class teachers were a Miss Tucker, elderly and amiable, George Gunham who had just finished his course in special education, Mrs Worth and myself. I was in place of the Head's wife who had been on

117

the staff but had contracted some lurgy, which, though not serious, meant that she had to stay at home for at least a term. Mr Charles was most insistent on the continuity of care and attention for his children, which was why I had been sent for in such a hurry.

"I can't see that there's any panic, really," said Mrs worth, "but Mr Charles is a most persuasive sort of person when he gets and idea into his head."

Conversation was becoming more general by the time Peter returned and we clambered into the bit of his car that wasn't already occupied by furnishing catalogues, order books and empty cigarette packets. He drove off in the swashbuckling sort of way he had after discussing business with someone in a pub, so that we arrived shaken but complete.

"Thanks very much for the lift," said Penny, "and it's been a most enjoyable evening."

"Hell's bells, girl, what are you waffling about?" said Peter in the charming way which won him so many friends, "You're the one to be thanked. It's been bloody super."

"Thanks, Penny," I said, see you on Monday."

Pitdale, 4L and the rest, were already a part of the past by the time we returned to the flat. I was looking forward to this new place with something very near to enthusiasm.

The journey turned out to be much easier, there being no need to go through Frontown, and two buses sufficing to set me to within ten minutes walk of the school. It was still only about half past eight, therefore, as I was walking up the long, curving, tree- lined drive, admiring the rose beds and thinking how completely the place was isolated from the surrounding town. This sense of isolation was heightened by the fact that, as far as I could tell, I had it to myself.

I walked round the outsides of the buildings and peered in through the windows. I scanned the distant horizons of the playing fields. I tiptoed through the corridors of the main building, not wishing to break the stillness. There was not a person in sight and the silence was complete. At last, as there had been no response to my tap on the door marked "Headmaster", I cautiously pushed it open and peered inside, half expecting to see a door ajar, and an untouched meal, and an over-toppled chair like the chap on Flannan Isle. There wasn't even that; just a neat office with a desk and a table and a couple of chairs. The only sign of human occupation was a framed picture on the wall which had obviously been painted either by a young and uninhibited child or an eminent modern artist.

By now it was getting on for five to nine and I was beginning to wonder whether I was in the right place, or maybe it was still Sunday, when there was a sudden burst of female laughter. It seemed to come from behind a door at the end of the corridor so, determined to solve the mystery, I walked along, knocked and walked in.

A large, jolly looking lady and a younger girl, both dressed in spotless white overalls were sitting at a table drinking coffee and looking at the Daily Mirror.

"Hello luv", said the large lady, "can I do anything for you?"

"Yes, please," I said, "you can tell me if I'm in the right place. I'm supposed to be starting teaching at Carlton Royds School this morning, but I don't seem to be able to find anybody."

"Nay, you're a bit early, luv. Come in and help yourself to a cup of coffee. There's some cups over there and a jug on the hot plate. Help yourself and then come and have a sit down for a few minutes."

"Thank you very much. I feel as though I could do with something after wandering round this place for half an hour. My name is Curtis, by the way."

"Well, it's nice to meet you, Mr Curtis. I'm the cook, Mrs Patterdale, and this is Elsie, my assistant. You should have come straight in here instead of walking about. Mr Charles is usually first here but we don't see him 'til about ten past nine."

"Ten past nine!" I echoed, "What time does school start, then?"

"Oh, about half past, usually, unless traffic's bad and then it could be later. All the kiddies come by special bus, you see, and it has to go round and pick them all up. The first ones come in a mini bus and that usually gets here at about twenty past. That's right, isn't it Elsie?"

"That's right, Mrs Patterdale," agreed Elsie, who had decided that the Daily Mirror held more attractions for her than my conversation and didn't bother to look up.

There was a sound of a car pulling up outside and then footsteps down the corridor.

"That'll be Mr Charles now," said Mrs Patterdale, pour his coffee out for him, Elsie."

I stood up and moved towards the door.

"Well, thanks very much for the drink. I'd better go and introduce myself."

"Nay, sit yourself down, luv. He'll be coming in here before he does owt else, so you'd best stay where you are."

Sure enough the door opened and a smallish, dapper man with an outdoor look about him came in and, after greeting the cook and her assistant, came over to me, hand outstretched.

"Good morning," he said, "you'll be Mr Curtis. I'm Charles, the supposed Head of this establishment. It's really run by Mrs Patterdale here, so you will do well to keep in with her."

"Ee, you do say some things, Mr Charles," beamed the cook, "one of these days I'll come and sit in your office and you can come down here. That'd cap 'em!"

Mr Charles joined in the roar of laughter. "I know who'd do the better job. I'll tell you what, though – the children wouldn't stand for it. They wouldn't miss me but, by golly, they'd grumble if they didn't get one of your dinners. Seriously, Mr Curtis, you will have better meals here than you would at the Station Hotel and I really mean that."

There was a further sound of a vehicle crunching on the gravel outside and, a moment afterwards, footsteps racing down the corridor. The door burst open and in poured fifteen or so assorted children. They seemed to be aged between nine and thirteen or thereabouts and, looked much like any other school group at first sight. The one characteristic they all had in common was happiness. I thought I had never seen such a comprehensively cheerful looking bunch anywhere. There were noisy greetings.

"Hello, Mr Charles."

"Hello, Mrs Patterdale, I got a hamster on Saturday."

"I say, Elsie, do you know what the bus driver said about you?" "What's for dinner, Mrs Patterdale?"

Two small girls were on the Head's knees and several were vying for the honour of a resounding kiss from the cook. It was all quite extraordinary. In all the schools I had seen previously, the kitchen area was the jealously guarded preserve of the cook and her minions, where even the Head had to have a signed document before crossing the hallowed portals. For anyone else, it was akin to a Christian trying to become first tenor in the choir in Mecca. Yet here everyone was treating the place as the morning meeting ground and, for all I knew, spending the rest of the day there as well.

A boy of about eleven put on a serious face and approached me. For some reason I felt embarrassed which, I reasoned, was quite ridiculous. This was not a monster but a perfectly ordinary boy who happened to find the learning process more difficult than the majority of his contemporaries. I told myself that it was not necessary to shout loudly in baby talk as though addressing a foreigner. It made no difference what I told myself – I still felt illogically uneasy.

"Hello," he said with a directness which I later found to be characteristic. "Who are you?" "I'm a new teacher here. I'm called Mr Curtis. What's your name?" "Barry. Mr Charles told us you were coming. Are you a proper teacher?" "I try to be. Will you be in my class?" "The others are here now," he said, dismissing my question as of no importance and, sure enough, there was a further influx of children, accompanied this time by Mrs Worth and the other two members of staff. Penny came straight over to me.

"Hello, Mr Curtis," she said "do you know, I've been worrying ever since I left you on Friday night. I never told you that we start at half past nine. I do hope you haven't been here too long."

"Only since about seven o'clock, but not a minute has been wasted. I've explored, I've drunk coffee and I've met some of the children. So far I have never seen anything like it."

"I suppose it does seem a bit unusual at first, but you'll get used to it later on. I really am sorry about not telling you the starting time, though. Anyway, come and meet the others."

There was a little more general chat and then Mr Charles shook the children from his knee and stood up.

"Right, come on you lot. It's time you made a start," he said and then, to me, "I'll have a word with you in my office, Mr Curtis, before we go into assembly. Miss Tucker – you will look after Mr Curtis' class until he comes along, won't you?"

Without further prompting the children called out their goodbyes to the cook and her assistant and moved away in animatedly chatting groups. I followed Mr Charles to his office.

"Now, Mr Curtis, I take it that Mrs Worth managed to see you the other evening and put you in the picture about the set up here?"

"Yes, she was most helpful, but I must still profess complete ignorance about teaching these children. I've had no experience with ESN's at all."

"Don't worry about that. You'll find that Mrs Worth and the others here have the two qualities you need more than all the specialist training – sympathy and patience. The book learning and the psychological hoo-hah are all very well, but a bit of common sense goes a long way. The danger lies in allowing sympathy to become sentimentality.

Remember all the time that these are ordinary children and should be treated as such. The fact that they have a disability, is no reason for them getting away with behaviour that you wouldn't accept from a child in a normal school. Believe me, they'll try it on just the same as anyone else."

"I must admit to being a bit staggered by the gathering in the kitchen. I've certainly never come across anything like that before, and they all seem so free and easy and happy."

"Well, you won't get anywhere with these children until you have their complete confidence; until they feel at home with you, in other words. The numbers here are small enough to be able to create something approximating to a family atmosphere. Once a child feels that, we've managed to open the door. Don't expect miracles, though, even then. Progress will seem to be at a standstill for weeks on end, and then you will find that someone is doing something a tiny fraction better than they were last month and you feel over the moon and you send him to me to be praised because that's progress.

Just two things before I take you along to your room. If anyone wants to know what we are trying to do here, forget the educational jargon. We are trying to teach them to read and write and understand simple numbers.

The other thing is, for heaven's sake keep your sense of humour. There is nothing intrinsically funny about being E.S.N and to the parents it can be a tragedy, but laugh with them. Even laugh at them when you're on your own, but let it be kindly laughter. If you don't, you'll finish in the nut house. Now, come on and I'll introduce you to your little lot."

My little lot, in one of the outside classrooms, turned out to be a selection of five boys and four girls of about nine years of age. One boy and a girl had Down Syndrome, one other boy had the loosed mouthed vacant grin usually associated with the weak minded. The others looked like any other group of junior children.

"You will find that the Down Children are extremely affectionate," said the Head. "Charlie there is a bit of a problem. He's really below even our standard, but we don't want to admit defeat with him until we've tried everything. Hello, Charlie! How are you this morning?"

"All right, Mr Charles," grinned Charlie.

He's happy enough. He's never likely to do anyone else out of a place at Cambridge, but he won't do anyone any harm either, and that's more than can be said for some of the clever ones."

We all proceeded into assembly where the singing was of a rudimentary nature, the prayers sincere and easily understood, and where I was introduced to an interested audience who, for some reason, burst into a round of applause. After this moment of glory I returned to the classroom with my nine children for my first attempt at educating at this level. By the end of the morning I doubt whether the pupils were any wiser, but I certainly was. I had discovered that nothing, however apparently self-evident, should be taken for granted. Mrs Worth, had suggested, in her diffident way, that I might start by trying to introduce to them the concept of size, reduced to its simplest terms of 'big and bigger; small and smaller'. I had seized on this idea and done some preparation. Phrases like 'practical experiment' and 'personal involvement' were being bandied about by the cognoscenti at the time so I started by bringing out to the front one Simon Woodhead, the tallest, and Jane Hammond, the shortest in the class.

I stood them next to each other where they beamed triumphantly at the others, evidently under the impression that they had won a prize or, in some other way, achieved a victory. I held one hand flat on the top of Simon's head, the other similarly on Jane's head, thus indicating clearly to my mind that the topic of the day was 'size'. The children, however, whose last teacher had been of a religious turn of mind, evidently thought I was about to pronounce a benediction of some sort and bowed their head reverently.

"We are thinking about size," I announced hurriedly. "Amen," said Charlie.

I rushed on. "Now, what do you notice about these two?" I had asked. "Jane's got fat legs."

"Simon's trousers aren't fastened proper."

"Simon lives near my Auntie Flossie. She says he's daft." "Jane's got spots on her bottom."

"Stop!" I thundered, feeling my stock of sympathy and patience being frittered away in the first few minutes, "You shouldn't say things like that, Ernest." I had a little chart on my desk which told me who everyone was, provided they stayed in the same place.

"In any case," I went on, "it was not a very sensible thing to say, because you don't know that it is true."

"But I do know, Mr Curtis," said Ernest, "and I'm David That's Ernest under your desk."

I realised I was sticking my neck out but, being in the middle of a period when the experts maintained that complete freedom of speech was vital to the learning process, thought that I had better see this through to the end.

"Right, David. How can you possibly know that was you said was true?"

"She told me," said David solemnly. He was evidently a boy who didn't like his word to be questioned. "She was going to show me on the bus but we didn't have time."

I decided to cut my losses and start again.

"What I mean," I explained slowly, "is, do you notice anything to do with their size?"

One girl looked puzzled.

"Are we still on about the spots on her bottom?" she asked.

"No, Freda, we are not. It is Freda, isn't it? Good. Forget all about spots and Jane's bo.... well, forget that. Let's look at Simon and Jane and then tell me something about their sizes."

"Jane's fat," volunteered Freda.

"No. Well, maybe, but that isn't what I meant. Think about their height."

With exaggerated mime I jiggled about with my hands to give the impression that Simon was about eight feet tall and Jane some species of dwarf. "I know, Mr Curtis," said Adele, "Simon is high."

"Is he? I mean, yes, he is. But we usually use another word instead of 'high'

when we are talking about people. Do you know what it is?"

Eventually, by every means other than actually engraving it on their heads with a chisel, I drew from them, as the text books say, the word 'tall'. Another half hour of solid flogging by me and cheerfully puzzled endeavour from the children and we arrived at our first destination – "Simon is taller than Jane."

Still going by the book, I realised that this was the time for consolidation. I sent Simon and Jane back to their places, smirking at a difficult job well done, and brought out Charlie and Adele. I looked around in anticipation.

"Now, who is taller?" I asked.

"Simon," they all called with the self-satisfied air of those who, having won through to the truth, will not be shaken by cunning ruses.

Only Charlie, shuffling sheepishly around at the front of the class, remained unmoved by this mass demonstration. He put up his hand.

"Yes, Charlie," I said hopefully, "What do you think?"

"I think I've peed my britches," said Charlie. Amidst the general concern which followed this remark, Adele came up and took hold of my hand to comfort me.

"Don't worry about Charlie," she said quietly, "he's daft, but he can't help it." I wondered how long there was to go to dinner time. When the long morning was eventually over and dinner time did arrive, I found I was in for further revelations. We started by washing our hands and combing our hair, and that was a bit of a shock after the sort of thing I had been used to. Then we all went into the hall, where the tables were laid for a meal, and sat, talking quietly, at previously allocated places.

I was again most impressed, being accustomed to something that looked like a Cecil B de Mille crowd scene with accompaniment from the 1812 overture played loud. There was still more to come. Mr Charles stood up from his place at the head of one of the tables.

"I'm sorry, boys and girls," he announced, "but one of the ovens went funny this morning, so we shall have to wait about ten minutes. I'll let you into a secret, though. Mrs Worth chose the pudding today – see if you can guess what it is."

There were shouts from all over the room.

"That's it, Malcolm – you've got it! Jam rolly-polly. I have an idea that most of you knew. Now, until dinner is ready, who's going to give us a song?"

In my experience this should have been the signal for a blank silence, but not a bit of it. A dozen hands shot up and there were calls of "Me, Mr Charles!"

Eventually, after an eeny-meeny-miny-mo routine, one boy was selected. He walked out to the end of the room, grinning with delight and, without wasting time on preliminary announcements, launched himself wholeheartedly into one of the popular ditties of the day. He not only did the words and music, but put in all the actions and accompanied himself on an imaginary guitar as well. It would be exaggerating to call the result musical as, although he went up and down in the right places, it was not necessarily by the right amounts, but it certainly could not be faulted for enthusiasm. As he reached a breathless conclusion, the audience erupted into rapturous applause.

I leaned over to Mrs Worth who was officiating at the table next to mine. "Is the cabaret a regular feature?" I murmured. "Pretty well," she said, "you'll find there's little time for being miserable. It gets a bit like Butlin's at times, but the children love it."

By this time the meal was ready, Mrs Patterdale and Elsie serving as the children took up their plates. After asking for my likes and dislikes, one of the older girls brought my meal and, feeling as though I had been up most of the night without food, I attacked it gratefully. The Head had been right. Without anything but the usual basic ingredients, Mrs Patterdale had added a spice of genius and the result was superb. Just as we were savouring the last few crumbs of the rolly-polly, Mr Charles again stood to address the assembly.

"It's really Norman Coates' turn to pick the pudding for tomorrow, he said, but you all know he's away with a broken wrist. I hope some of you are going to write to him, by the way. I'll see he gets any letters you would like to send. Now, I'll tell you what I'm going to do. As he's just joined our family, I'm going to ask Mr Curtis if he'll choose for tomorrow. Now then, Mr Curtis, what would you like?"

I wasn't used to being pushed into the public eye in this way and for a moment the only two things I could think of were crepes suzette or prunes and custard.

"Apple pie," hissed Penny.

"Do you think I could ask for apple pie?" I said.

The suggestion was greeted with beams from Mrs Patterdale, applause from the children and a serious, "It's right smashing is t'apple pie," from a red headed boy at my table. It seemed that, with the help of my technical adviser, I had chosen well.

I was helped through the afternoon's activities by Mr Charles and, at a quarter past three, we were packing up in preparation for the busses coming. After the children had gone, I was walking around tidying up the room when Mrs Worth came in. She sat on the edge of the desk and smiled.

"How's it gone?" she asked.

"I can truthfully say there hasn't been a dull moment. I feel I've learned more today than all the time I was in college. I also feel as though I'm going to be a stretcher case before the end of the week."

"It gets everyone that way at first. You'll get used to it."

"The way I'm feeling at the moment, I'm not sure that I'm going to live long enough. My, my! You wouldn't believe that eight or nine small children could be so shattering, would you?"

"As I say, you'll get used to it. In a day or two you will find you are thinking of them as children instead of oddities. It gets easier then. Well – must go. I've some shopping to do on my way home. Remember me to Peter."

"I won't guarantee that. He has enough girls to occupy his mind without adding you to the list. In any case I would probably become insanely jealous."

"I bet you say that to all the sub-normal teachers you meet. Bye, bye, then – see you in the morning."

"Cheerio, and thanks for all the help."

I realised that, in spite of the rigours of the day, I was looking forward to the rest of the week.

Having had a much larger lunch than usual, I decided on something light for the evening meal. With some artistic prowess I made an arrangement on each plate of a couple of lettuce leaves, some slices of tomato and a pink, transparent substance which the man at the shop called boiled ham. I was just putting the finishing touches to this with a few tastefully hacked radishes when Peter burst in.

"Hello, Ken, how's it gone with those potty kids, then? What the hell's that muck. Have you bought a bloody rabbit?"

"You uncouth swine'" I said amiably, "men have died for less. In reply to question number one, I have had a most enjoyable but tiring day with those kids who are not, as you put it potty. Well, not proper potty, just a bit. As for the second query, have you no soul, no aesthetic sense, no thoughts beyond the crudity of bangers and mash? This is a melange of delicately contrasting flavours, colours and aromas, but I wouldn't expect you to know about that."

"Yes, I can see its' been a good day. I can always tell when you start talking like a literate half-wit. I'm bloody hungry. I went to York to see this customer and I've found out they don't eat over there. They live on beer and ancient bloody monuments. Fabulous feller, mind you, but seemed to think all I wanted to do was drink. By the time we had everything settled it was too late for a meal, so all I've had is half a bag of cheese and onion crisps I found under the car seat. I wonder how they got there? Anyway, I want something more filling than that rubbish."

"Like I said, no soul. I'll tell you what, though. Listening to your drivel has made me feel a bit peckish, myself. I'll open a tin of new spuds and I think we've got some bully beef somewhere. That should pack it out a bit."

We exchanged our usual stories of the days events. I went on at some length about how tired I was.

"Tiring! What do you mean, tiring? Start at ten and finish at three with a couple of hours for lunch. You don't know you're born."

"I know it doesn't seem much compared with you having to sit all day forcing strong drink down at someone else's expense. All I say is, if you feel you need a day's rest, don't spend it at an E.S.N. school."

"Come on! You're all the same, you bloody teachers. You put on a good act. How's Penny, by the way? Now, there's a nice girl."

"She's fine and, as far as I can make out, she's forgotten all about you. In any case you know enough girls already without getting interested in her. Off hand I must admit I can't think of any nice ones, but then, nice ones wouldn't want to know you, would they? She's married anyway, as you well know."

"So that's the way the wind blows, is it? Our disinterested friend has evil designs, has he?!

"Nothing of the sort. Some of us can admire people for their minds, but you wouldn't understand that. I just happen to think that Mrs Worth is a very nice person. Certainly far too nice for a nasty, lascivious, ex-member of the licentious soldiery like you. Seriously, Pete, life is so much more pleasant when you are working with pleasant people and that's the way it is. No more, no less."

"We shall see, we shall see. Meanwhile, your fairy flaming godmother will look after your best interests."

"If you mean you – don't bother. Let's get washed up and I'll buy you a drink before I start preparing for tomorrow. That is unless your harrowing experience in York has turned you against the stuff."

"For your sake I will try to overcome my loathing," said Peter at the same time as he was putting on his coat, "leave the washing up. It'll still be there tomorrow."

Next day I learned yet another lesson – that a good thing is worth doing again – and again – and again.

When I went into the room I saw that Ernest, one of the Mongols, was sitting in my chair at my desk. On his chubby face was an expression of pure ecstasy. The others were grinning broadly and waiting to see what I would do. Pretending not to notice anything unusual, I went and sat on my chair, and, of course, on Ernest. I opened the register and started calling the names to the accompaniment of squeals of delight from all and frenzied wriggling from Ernest.

"Now then," I said sternly "where is Ernest? He should be here by now. There will be trouble for him when he comes. I'm not having people coming late. Does anyone know where he is?"

Eventually I reacted to the cries of "you're sitting on him, Mr Curtis!" and stood up.

Ernest shot out like a rabbit, smiling with pleasure.

"As a teacher," I thought, "I may not have mastered this lot, but as a knockabout comic I'm going down big."

What I failed to realise was that I had created a precedent. Every morning and afternoon Ernest was on my chair until the day I left. It was probably the longest running comedy act in the business and playing to the same audience every time at that.

The lesson organisation of the school was simple in the extreme. Having spent the morning through the fog that surrounded the understanding of words and numbers, the children indulged in activities of various kinds in the afternoons. Each class had its own supply of equipment for painting, music, games and so on, and the fields were there for everyone to use when the weather was suitable.

One morning a new consignment of games and play apparatus arrived and was distributed around the classes as usual. Amongst the more orthodox things like bats and balls and ropes there were some strange machines in various sizes described on the invoice as 'pogo sticks'. I decided that at the first available opportunity I would put these into use. It so happened that that morning was warm and fine so I took my class out on the field to instruct them in the art of pogo-ing or whatever the correct term might be.

"Now then," I said "has anyone had a go on these before?" No one had.

"Right, I'll show you how it's done. You hold your stick in front of you like this, grasp the rubber handle at the top, put your feet on these two step things and bounce up and down."

They were quite amused the first time I picked myself up from the floor but the spectacle palled after the fourth and fifth attempt and they started to show signs of restlessness.

With a pitying smile I agreed to their requests to have a go and felt a bit humiliated when, with the exception of two girls who had found following the progress of a worm though the undergrowth to be more to their liking, they all mastered the things inside five minutes. I made up my mind that I wasn't going to be beaten by a bunch of youngsters of supposedly inferior intellect. With a bit of secret practice I would master this thing or die in the attempt.

After school dinner, therefore, instead of retiring to the staff room for a go at the crossword puzzle and a coffee, I sought a secluded spot between two huts and prepared for action. Thinking about it scientifically after picking myself up for the sixth time, I came to the conclusion that a hard tarmac surface, though more likely to cause serious injury, would be better from the stick's point of view so I moved from the grass on to the pathway. To my gratification I actually managed to stay aloft even though, rather than making forward progress, I seemed to be drilling a hole in the path. Flushed with success, a few more attempts brought movement, albeit backwards. As a careful search failed to reveal a reverse gear, I assumed I was at fault and started again. A little more concentrated effort and I was actually going the way I was facing, somewhat shakily it is true, but at a very fair speed.

Thinking more of the control and effort needed to maintain progress, I paid no heed to the possibility of traffic at the approaching crossroads so it was, I suppose, my fault that I failed to notice another pogoist coming round the corner. The predictable result was the surprised noise made when two pogoists clobber each other amidships, and a heap of bodies on the floor which upon investigation showed to be Mrs Worth and myself.

Penny was the first to recover. "Fancy bumping into you!" she said.

"Are you badly damaged?" I asked, "I don't know whether these things are taxed and insured."

"I think I shall recover, but I have a feeling that I've had about as much as I want of this particular form of transport. The magic seems to have gone."

"May I give you a lift, them? I think I'm going your way."

How long this insane conversation could have been kept up will never be known because at that moment we both stopped to listen. From behind the next building we could hear the now familiar thump, thump, thump.

Into view came the Head, pogo mounted. He was concentrating grimly, looking neither to right nor left so he was unaware of our presence. There was about his steady, unhurried progress and his upright stance a sort of dignity befitting his status. We looked at each other as he bumped sedately along the outside of the hall, round the corner and out of sight.

"This is a solemn moment," I said.

"What makes it seem all right is that he's so much better at it than we are. That's just as it should be, isn't it?"

"You know, on my first day here, he told me to keep a sense of humour. I can see what he meant. Having said which, in my case, this is all done with strictly educational aims, even though I'm not sure what they are. Anyway, I've a feeling that we are about to start the afternoon's business. Do you mind if I say, against all the odds, I'm enjoying myself here?"

"I don't mind at all. Do you mind if I say it's nice having you here?" "I most certainly do not. Thanks very much. And now back to the old

grindstone!"

We parted with slightly conspiratorial smiles.

When I reached home that evening Peter, who had spent the day badgering people locally, was beating out a minor conflagration with a towel.

"Chips again, I see," I remarked.

"Of course it's bloody chips, you don't think this lot started by making strawberries and bloody cream, do you? Don't stand there like a china dog; get something to put this out before the flaming house burns down."

By the time I had found something that might be useful, the fire was more or less under control. I peered into the pan with some interest.

"I take it these blackened sticks are the chips," I said.

"Of course they're chips, and done to a turn. Why this pan sets fire to the bloody building every time we use it I shall never know. You'd think that in this day and age it wouldn't be beyond the wit of man to design a chip pan without this inbuilt tendency to spontaneous combustion.

I reckon the makers are in league with the insurance people."

Just how this would benefit either party wasn't too clear, but I didn't press the point.

"What are we having with these chips?" I asked. "Tomato soup".

"Well, it's different, I'll give you that".

The meal was served in what he claimed to be the continental manner, chips on one plate and soup in another. Removal of the outer black coating revealed raw potato.

"These things are as hard as rocks," I complained.

"Then dunk 'em in the soup. On second thoughts tip 'em into a bag and give 'em to the deserving poor and we'll go out for a sandwich."

In case it should be considered that undue prominence is being given to our culinary experiments, it should be pointed out that this is not in the expectation of improving British eating standards, but simply because meal preparation loomed fairly large in our lives. Apart from work, Peter's girlfriends and the odd visit to the local, we spent our time either cooking, a bit of walking, and either playing or listening to music. When playing the saxophone I pretended to be Johnny Hodges, and Peter either browbeat our old piano or plucked the double bass. I preferred the bass. He could only play one wrong note at a time on that.

There were evenings when we invited similarly minded friends along for a sort of orgy. Some would bring musical instruments and 'have a blow' as the saying is. Peter would sometimes prevail on some young ladies of his acquaintance to join us and there were occasions when men, driven wild by drink and desire, were seen to put their arms round a girl's waist. This was late on in the evening, of course, when things were getting a bit out of hand.

Sometimes the man with the off-licence round the corner would be inundated by a request for as many as three bottles of his genuine French/Spanish plonk. It was said that, after thus depleting his stock, he spent the rest of the night after removing his shoes and sometimes his socks, trampling around on sticks of rhubarb to make a new vintage.

These, though, were high days and holidays. In general ours was a sober and even an industrious household. Meals were made, washing up was done when there was no more clean crockery, and a minimal amount of dusting and tidying was undertaken. Parents paid periodic visits to see it didn't become too squalid and we returned the compliment, hoping to be properly fed for once and bearing gifts in the form of bundles of dirty washing.

On this particular evening we settled down as usual to hear some records and to talk over the events of the day. I played down the pogo stick episode as Peter was going through a period where he imagined myself to be the sole guardian of the ratepayers' money, and I felt sure he would regard our little amusement as a misuse of same. Anything thus regarded led to highly emotive monologues which sent me to sleep.

I told him instead about the visit by Ernest's mother. She had swept in that morning trailing Ernest behind her like a full rigged man-o'-war towing a dinghy. It transpired that she had cadged a lift on the school bus, a highly illegal procedure because of insurance complications, and then ignored the rule about always calling at the office first when visiting the school.

Apart from sitting on him first thing every morning and afternoon, I could think of nothing I had done wrong to Ernest. I had to admit to myself that it was not easy to think of a suitable ending to a sentence beginning, "Mrs Halford, I sit on your son, Ernest, twice daily because...." I was already seeing myself in the headlines in the Sunday papers as the instigator of some new sexual perversion when my mind was set at rest.

"Now then, Mr Curtis," said Mrs Halford, "Ourern we never right fond of school 'til he come 'ere. Now he seems to have right taken to you and he's that disappointed when t'school's closed. Well now, there's Ourive, isn't there, y'see?"

"Ourive?" I'm not quite sure...."

"Yes, Ourive, she's Ourern's sister; Ive – Ivy, y'know. Well, now, I want her to get in here too. So I want you to have a word with Mr Charles because I've been to t'education in town and I can't make 'em understand."

"I'm afraid it's not as easy as that, Mrs Halford. You see, this is a special school and...."

"That's what I'm getting at. If Ourern could get in, I don't see why Ourive can't. Sh's always been quicker than him, though she is a year younger. He never stops talking about it doesn't Ourern and he's come on a treat since 'e's been here, so it's only fair that Ourive should come too, isn't it?"

"I'll tell you what, Mrs Halford. It's nearly time for assembly, so you leave Ernest here and I'll take you over to see Mr Charles. He'll explain it much better than I can."

Peter said he thought it was a silly story but that he suspected that it was costing the ratepayer and that this was no way in which to etc., etc. I went to sleep.

The term was drawing to a close and, as Mrs Charles had been given the go ahead by her doctor to return to school I knew that the time was approaching for me to be moving on once more. I felt sad about it because I thought that,

139

in a small way, I had managed to 'get through' to some of the children. I would be sorry to leave them, even though they left me feeling like a limp lettuce at the end of the day. I would be sorry to leave the staff and, in particular, Penny Worth who, without doing anything in particular, had by her cheerful presence, made each day a bit brighter. I would miss those meals, too, and the unfailingly jolly Mrs Patterdale.

To my relief, Mr Charles had decided that it would be better for the children if my departure went unannounced so, once again, there was no fanfare of trumpets to mark my exit. After saying my goodbyes to the head and the rest of the staff, I walked down the drive with Penny.

"It doesn't feel as though a term has passed since I called at your flat," she said. "A couple of weeks at the most," I agreed, "though, in another way, I seem to have been wrestling with Charlie and Co. since time immoral as my aunt used to say."

"What does it feel like to be always moving on? I don't think I would like it. I always get so nervous at the thought of anything new, and yet you seem to take it all in your stride."

"Little do you know. Actually I do quite like seeing new places and meeting new people. I've particularly like that part since I came here, said he expressing himself very badly as usual."

"If you mean what I think you mean, thanks, Ken. I've liked it, too."

A bus appeared round the corner. It was Penny's. She held out her hand. "Well, bye, bye, then. I'll probably see you again sometime."

"Yes, of course. I hope so. Bye bye and thanks for everything."

"And so endeth another chapter," I said to myself, and wondered what Peter would have thought up for the evening meal.

CHAPTER SIX

The next few terms were comparatively uneventful as far as schools were concerned. This is not to say that this period was completely devoid of incident but, by and large, the schools to which I was sent were well established and competently run secondary moderns so that all I had to do was to fit into the accepted pattern. Mostly they steered a middle path, refusing to become hysterically pro or anti those who, having discovered some supposedly new method or philosophy, could not believe that anybody (including, presumably, themselves) had ever been educated before. Neither were they supporters of the sit-em-in-a-line-and-beat-em-if-they-don't-understand persuasion. Like most schools and most teachers they used common sense and understanding and imagination in varying combinations and, as most teachers are sensible people with an interest in their job, they did pretty well with the human material at their disposal.

My salary had received a couple of boosts so that I was now officially a "Head, Group 2", although no one in authority had yet seen fit to entrust me with the responsibility of actually being one. I was in danger of sliding down into that comfortable rut again, particularly as I had eased the transport problem by buying a car. This was not an unmixed blessing.

The vehicle in question was a small Wolseley of nine horsepower, born in nineteen thirty something and bought from an elderly neighbour who, because of her artistocratic demeanour and supposed connections with some famous family, was known as the Duchess. Deciding she had no further use for motoring, she took to riding round the village on an incredibly ancient sit-up-and-beg bicycle with a basket on the handlebars containing a tiny Yorkshire terrier which chewed anyone foolish enough to get too close. From this lofty position the Duchess would address the villagery on a variety of topics in tones of calm and unruffled superiority.

"Good morning, Mr Curtis", she called out to me one day, stopping in the middle of the village street so that traffic could move in neither direction, "I've just told Mr Bird what he can do with his toilet rolls at the exhorbitant price he's charging. I shall go home and spend the morning tearing up the Times to put in the lavatory instead."

I should have known it was foolish to buy anything from someone like that. She could, and did, ask a price considerably over the odds with the air of one doing a great favour, and the idea of complaining afterwards never entered my head. So there I was with this car and feeling rather honoured because, "I really couldn't let her go to just anybody, Mr Curtis. It had to be someone who would understand her and look after her. You will let me have cash, won't you? I find those cheques tiresome."

It had its good points. The upholstery was genuine leather and the paintwork where it had not been polished away, was still a deep, rich, rustless black. The little overhead camshaft engine was not at all bad, buzzing away smoothly until the big end bearings gave in one day after a madly rousing blind from Whitby, touching 50 m.p.h. on the down hill bits.

On the other hand, being one of the first small cars to have the engine perched over the front axle, but without the advantage of appropriate independent front suspension, the handling was unpredictable. This was not improved when, doing a crossed-arms Nuvolari thing with the steering wheel on one occasion, I found that I was wiggling the rim only, it having become detached from the spokes for some reason. Not unnaturally the car trundled on in a forward direction towards a stone wall which happened to be there at the time, the scrabble for the brake pedal being less frenzied than it might have been had we been proceeding at more than ten or so miles per hour.

In its youth, the car had possessed a sunshine roof but some previous owner had decided that the British climate did not warrant such a luxury and had sealed up the joints with a permanently sticky substance bearing a strong resemblance to tar. The question of whether this stuff did or did not make a waterproof joint was put beyond doubt one evening when returning from Filey. Two of Peter's more artificial and glamourous girl friends were in the back seat and discovered in the course of a rainy journey that the bucket in the back was not for making sand castles. After spending a couple of cold and wet hours catching the water coming through the roof and then trying to chuck it out of the window, they didn't react too favourably when we suggested they should look on it as part of life's great adventure. After what they said, Peter thought he might as well cross their names out of his little book.

In spite of its failings, this was a car of character and I loved it dearly, particularly as it was the first four wheeled vehicle I had actually owned, not counting a thing made of planks and pram wheels with which I terrorised the neighbourhood when a child. It is true that I no longer had the pleasure of being alone in an early morning world. I could, of course, have got out of bed at the same time as I used to and gone for a walk, but somehow I never did. There were considerable compensations, though. I would often use a 'country' route through the little used side lanes instead of the busy main roads, and there were mornings when it was a real effort of will not to head for the Dales or the Lake District. I did, indeed, spend a lot of time at weekends exploring Wharfedale and Wensleydale and Swaledale, parking the car in some remote spot and pottering about on foot. The rugged heights of Swaledeale and the pastoral calm of Wensleydale appealed to me particularly in their contrasting ways, and I had many happy hours discovering new places and new friendships and a great peace.

Mostly these outings were taken alone, as Peter had other things on his mind. He had come in one evening with a strange light in his eye.

"You'll never guess who I saw today," he said. "You're right, I won't," I replied.

"Joan Bramall!"

"Good heavens, no! Not Joan Bramall of all people! Who's Joan Bramall? "You know very well, you silly devil. She was in the fourth form when we were in fifth."

"It's a funny thing, I don't know if you've ever noticed, but girls in the form below you at school look like bits of kids. Then when you've been left for a couple of years or so they seem quite different and you wonder why you never noticed them before."

"What the hell are you drivelling about? I thought we were talking about Joan Bramall, but if you can't remember her, which I don't bloody believe, then there's no point."

"As a matter of fact I do remember her. She was, I recall, blonde and very shapely for her age and she had brains, too, because you tried to make a pass at her one night on

145

the way home from school and she dotted you one with a copy of 'Travels with a Donkey through the Cevennes' by R.L. Stevenson."

"A little misunderstanding. We had a good laugh about it this afternoon." "You mean she let you get close enough to talk to her without aid of amplification?"

"Well, actually, I asked her if she would have lunch with me, and she did." "You didn't give her beans and chips at Wooley's cafeteria, did you?"

Of course I bloody didn't. She's not that sort of girl. She's working at her mother's place – hairdresser's, you know, and she's a smasher."

I looked at him with interest, but said nothing. There were signs here which were new and, as time went on, it became pretty obvious that a new phase was indeed starting in Peter's romantic life.

For one thing he was lavishing money on this girl without the immediate prospect of bundling her in the back of his car and spending the next few hours in some quiet cul-de-sac. Then again, after quite a short time, he had actually been to her house and had converse with her parents, a procedure against which he had always counselled strongly in the past.

There came a time when, no doubt against her better judgement, Joan was to be brought to the flat. It was, Peter stressed, strictly so she could see where he lived and maybe imbibe a small dry Martini. She was, he told me, very interested – talented would be a better word – in music, so there might be the odd record played, but definitely no smoochy stuff with the lights turned down.

"You know, I've remembered something about this Joan of yours," I said. "Do you recall that tine we were watching a netball match at school and Miss Burbage went on something alarming at one girl for wearing white knickers instead of brown? That was Joan Bramall. I remember all the details with great clarity. There was Harry Pullan and Reg King and Jack Webster and a few more and every time this girl jumped up to whang the ball into the bag thing, you made some remarks which had us all rolling about on the floor. It will occur to me soon what it was you were saying."

"Look here, Ken," said Peter in a most uncharacteristic wheedling voice, "you won't mention anything of this to Joan when she comes, will you? After all, there are things which we grow out of, aren't there? And what's more, I don't want to hear any of your disgusting filthy bloody jokes or any of your usual bloody bad language either."

"That's more like the Peter we all know and love. In any case there's no need to worry. I've arranged to go out."

So the affair bloomed and highly satisfactory it was, too, for Joan turned out to be not only pleasant to look upon, but a vivacious and pleasing personality as well. Peter, it seemed, was being tamed without even noticing that anything was happening.

Then, one morning, I received a card from the office telling me that I was to be employed at Crickley Main Road Boys Secondary Modern School in my usual capacity of assistant teacher from the start of the next term. This was another of those small towns, only half an hours run from the centre of Frontown, where I had never been because it was in the opposite direction from my usual touring haunts. Peter, in his capacity of roving salesman, knew most places round about, so I asked him about it.

"Crickley?" he said, "Bloody hole."

"Oh, come off it, Peter. According to you, everywhere is a bloody hole. It can't always be true. What's it really like? What do the people do for a living?"

147

"Queue up at the labour exchange, mostly. It used to be the big place for shoddy and mungo and all that stuff, but there's not a great call for that nowadays so most of the places are shut down."

"What the blazes are shoddy and mungo?"

"Didn't they teach you anything at that blasted school we went to? It's a mystery to me how you are so bloody ignorant and I know so much. Shoddy and mungo are sorts of cloth made out of riving up old rags and such. People have made fortunes out of it."

"But they're not any more?"

"No. I think there may still be a bit of it, but it's a dead alive hole, anyway. I never go there now – it's not worth my time."

So, on the first day of the next term I drove into Crickley, unperturbed by now at starting a new place, and located the Main Road Boys Secondary Modern School. Peter had not, for once, exaggerated in describing this as a dead alive hole, and the school appeared to be the deadest place in it. It was a typical Victorian affair of blackened bricks, just the width of the pavement away from the Main Road after which it was named. If there wasn't much going on in Crickley, there was plenty going through it. Cars, motorcycles, vans, buses, but mainly lorries, thundered past incessantly.

I looked at the school with an expert eye but, even then, failed to see the significance of the larger than usual number of broken windows and the peeling paintwork. As I stood there, a man of about my own age, bespectacled and dark suited, with the air of a bishop or a butler visiting an aged aunt, approached and asked if he could be of any assistance.

"Thank you, I wonder if you can tell me where to find Mr Castleford, the Head?" "You're not an inspector by any chance, are you? You don't really look like one, but one likes to be sure."

"No, nothing so distinguished. My name is Curtis and I'm starting teaching here. I'm from the County Supply Staff."

"Ah, that's all right, then. Pleased to meet you, old boy. My name's Mackinnon and so am I."

"Are you really? That's a surprise. I was beginning to think that this Supply Staff was a myth and that I was the only wandering teacher in the Riding. I've never met another all the time I've been on Supply."

"You're about to meet several more, old boy, if they remember to come back after the holidays. There are only three permanent members of staff here, you know, and five supplies. That's not counting Castleford who doesn't."

"Doesn't what?"

"Count. His contribution to the educational life of Crickley is negligible." "I'm sorry, but you've left me behind a bit. Why this peculiar set up?"

"I gather that you haven't been fully informed about the state of the roll at this establishment. We are, in fact, presiding over the last rites. Did you happen to notice a large box made of glass on the top of a hill as you came along?"

"Yes, I did see something of the sort. I thought at first it might be the school I was looking for."

"Come next term it will be. The authorities in their wisdom are joining together the two existing boys secondary moderns and putting them in that new monstrosity in the sky. No girls, you notice. They go away and play in their own place at the far end of town. So, you see, this place is on its last legs."

"Hence the broken windows and absence of paint. I suppose the regular staff have taken other posts?"

"That's right. Jim Booker – he's the Deputy Head and a decent bloke apart from a tendency to snappishness because he's carrying the place on his own – anyway, Jim and the other two are going to the new school when it opens. The only one not fixed up is old Cass."

"Which must be a worry to him, I would think. How is it he's left on the shelf?" "You'll realise when you meet him. He's got all the paper qualifications – good degree and all that – but precious little else. He spends Fridays locked in his office with the Times Ed., going through the small ads., and filling in application forms. He gets loads of interviews, too, but that's as far as it goes. Sad, really."

We had been walking along corridors and up a flight of stairs as we talked and were now on the first floor. Tucked away under the roof, it looked like an afterthought. There was just one short landing on which were three doors labelled 'Stockroom', 'Secretary', and 'Headmaster' respectively. Each of these rooms, I was told, had a second door leading to an identical landing and flight of stairs on the other side. Although at the time this seemed merely eccentric, I was to find out quite soon that the peculiar layout played a part in Certain Happenings, but more of that anon, as they say.

I knocked on the Head's door and was answered by muffled yelp which I took to be an invitation to enter. Having done so, I had the feeling that I wasn't quite as welcome as the flowers in May.

Sitting near the desk, their chairs in very close proximity, were a small, bespectacled man with dark hair slicked backwards from a face which I could only think of as shifty, and a large, excessively blonde lady. I assumed the man to be the Head and suspected that the beacon like red of his countenance was not its usual shade. The blonde, presumably the secretary as she had pretended to pick up a notebook and pencil when I went I, had an assured half smile on her face. She also had, I couldn't help noticing, slim and shapely legs and a pleasant face, but the rest of her was definitely over- developed. In particular, her top half, which was inadequately contained in some sort of floral garment, was constructed on more than generous lines and coming, as it did, about on a level with the Head's face, could have something to do with his unusual colouring. I decided that, as there were no holes into which I could crawl, I had better put a brave face on it and pretend that I had noticed nothing.

"Good morning. My name is Curtis – County Supply Staff. Reporting for duty. Mr Castleford, I presume?" I said, trying to appear casually at ease, but sounding more like a cross between H.M. Stanley and a policeman giving evidence.

"Yes, right. Good morning. Rather busy just now. First day of term, you know. Staffroom's downstairs. Have a word with my deputy, Mr Booker. He'll tell you what to do. See you later. Close the door as you go out."

I said, "Er.... right, thank you." and shuffled out feeling very foolish. The look which the secretary gave me wouldn't have fooled a boy scout and did nothing to ease my embarrassment.

Downstairs in the staff room I located the Deputy Head, perched on the edge of an aged and springless sofa, drinking tea.

"Yes, I've got a timetable for you," he said, "you'll be taking 1B for registration and then I've given you some P.E. with the fourth year and some English and Maths with the lower forms. Sorry I can't ask you what your likes and dislikes are. It's a matter of having to fit in with whatever there is to do at this stage."

That's all right. I'll get by at most things, though I can't pretend to know much about P.E. It's usually a specialist subject, isn't it?"

"So it is. Here and now we are specialists in everything. Personally I don't give a damn if you do Swedish drill provided they are reasonably occupied. I believe Mac has told you that this place is closing down. Well, the lads know it, too. What with that and the irregular staff – no criticism, but it's not the same as a well-established lot – things get lively at times. Don't stand any old buck from any of 'em. It's no good trying to paint a rosy picture for you, because you'd find out soon enough it wasn't true. We've reached the stage where the main object is survival and then teaching if you have any time left. There's a cane on my desk and you can have it to wave at them any time you like. We don't use it indiscriminately, but you have my full permission to cane anyone you feel really deserves it. Right. Let's get 'em in."

There was a great deal of shouting and pushing and general chivvying about before the boys finally lined up to Mr Booker's satisfaction and then started to file in to school. It was undoubtedly true that there was a feeling, stronger than I had ever experienced elsewhere, of 'them' and 'us', and the two sides showed little evidence of liking each other very much. Mr Booker stood on the stage as the boys came into the assembly hall, and he had in his hand a cane which he swished from time to time to make sure that everyone could see it. The rest of the staff were strategically placed to thwart any attempts at mutiny. Accepting the fact that it put me in mind of films I had seen of the exercise yard at Sing Sing, all appeared to be going well, when my nerves were suddenly shattered by a fiendish screech from my left. The urbane Mr Mackinnon had on his face an expression of diabolical hatred and he was bellowing in an unseemly manner.

"Johnson!" he yelled, his features contoured with anger, "Get you hands out of your pockets and stop treading on the heels of the lad in front of you or I'll come over there and knock your stupid head off and come and see me at playtime and it had better be without that look on your face."

He turned to me, closed one eye momentarily and murmured, "Speak roughly to your little boy, and beat him when he sneezes. He only does it to annoy, because he knows it teases. I quote."

"That was a very good performance," I whispered back, "you had me fooled for a minute."

"Thank you, old boy. See – Comrade Castleford approacheth and doth take the stand. That's a rare treat. I should prepare to contemplate the infinite for a while if I were you."

Rare it may have been for our Leader to come amongst us, but it was no treat. He grumbled and harangued for a full twenty minutes in a petulant sort of way that had boys and staff alike glassy eyed. He swept off the stage, leaving it to his deputy to close the proceedings, and we went off to our class rooms.

My first year maths group no great problems, either disciplinary or academic, and it came as no great surprise to find that schoolchildren in small quantities are much the same anywhere. I casually mentioned something of the sort later on when we were in the staff room having our coffee break. Connor, another of the Supply Staff and a foreigner from down south by the sound of him had no illusions.

"You wait 'til they've weighed you up," he said, "Bloody hooligans, the lot of 'em. You may think you're getting on all right and that they're a lot of angels, but I'll tell you one thing – don't turn your back on 'em. That's right isn't it, Mac?"

"In your rough London way, you have revealed an element of truth," replied Mac, "though there is a tendency to overstatement. Nevertheless, Mr Curtis – what's your other name – Ken? – well then, Ken, I believe you are taking 4B for P.E. after break. I merely suggest that you are likely to find them less amenable than the last lot you had. As friend Connor says, it might be advisable to keep facing them."

There was something in what Connor and Mac had said. If ever I saw a bunch of people looking for trouble it was 4B. it seemed as though some sabre rattling might be called for. Only half of them had any sort of kit to change into, so I pointed out that they must all have the correct gear or a note from home explaining why not.

"Why do we 'ave to do it?" asked a pimply, dark haired youth.

"There are many good reasons," I said, "but the only one you need to worry about at the moment is that I say so. So we shan't waste anyone's time you can come and see me at dinner time and I'll explain things more fully to you then. What is your name, by the way?"

"Battersby. You needn't bother to explain. I'm not going to do it anyway."

He turned to the others "I reckon nobody can make me do it if I don't want to. I reckon none of us should do it, don't you?"

There were murmurs of assent from some of the boys and a sense of expectancy as they waited to see what I was going to do.

"Nevertheless, Battersby, you and your comrades will

do P.E. and you will do it in the proper kit, unless there is some medical reason why you shouldn't."

"Nay, I reckon I don't need no medial reasons. You can't make me if I don't want to. And you can't 'it me because it's against the law."

"Is that so? Well, as you have so much respect for the law, I'll remind you that the law of this school says that you will do as you are told. I am telling you now that in five minutes from now we are going to start P.E. wearing the proper kit or as near to it as we can manage. I see you have shorts with you. You now have four minutes in which to change."

"I don't see why I should."

"Right. You, boy – what's your name?" I selected one of the quieter and more reliable looking ones. "Right, Frankland, go to Mr Booker, give him my compliments and ask if he will be good enough to let me have his cane for a few minutes."

We sat looking at each other in silence until the cane arrived and I called Battersby out, hoping against hope that he would not add fuel to the fire by doing anything else to make the situation worse at this stage. He came out.

"I am not going to ask you again if you will go and change, Battersby," I said, "you have already said far too much. Put your hand out."

He took a couple of fairly heft swipes with no further sign than to tuck his hand under his arm for a moment then, without a word, he picked up his shorts and went towards the changing room. The rest, after a glance at me, followed.

From their behaviour during the rest of the lesson, it seemed that I had won the first round, but it gave me no satisfaction. If we went on like this, I thought, I would be able to control them, I might even teach them, but there would be none of the camaraderie of 4L at Pitdale. It seemed a hollow victory, but, I reflected, better than being trampled underfoot and letting anarchy reign. I hated violence in any form and I recognised that I was trying to convince myself that I had done the right thing. One thing was sure; if any of the theorists had been in my position they would have found it a very different matter from writing a book in the security of their own study.

I knew it was a weakness, but I couldn't help telling Battersby to stay behind at the end of the lesson. I knew I wasn't really doing it to give him a final warning as I pretended but, in a peculiar sort of way, to offer the olive branch. This, I realised, was behaviour that no strong person would countenance for a moment.

"Now, Battersby," I said, being very strong, "you know what happens to people who cross me. I'm sorry it had to happen in my first lesson with you," (getting weaker), "but that's the way it is. Now I'm sure you're not the sort of boy who is difficult as a regular thing," (positively crawling and lying, too, for he looked every inch a candidate for the Mafia), "so let's not see it happen again. You can go."

"Yes, sir," said Battersby, respectfully.

I turned away and, as I did so, had an unpleasant tingling sensation in the small of my back. I recalled Connor's words – "Don't turn your back on 'em." I looked round quickly. Battersby was walking peacefully through the door.

"Kenneth, my lad," I said to myself, "you must be sickening for something. You've never behaved like this before."

The next lesson was with one of the younger groups and they were decidedly noisier than the first lot had been. After a few minutes I managed to quell them into complete silence and reasonable attentiveness. Speaking in a quietly purposeful voice I outlined to them the sort of behaviour I expected.

"Every time you come into this classroom," I said, "I expect you to be sitting up quietly as you are now. I do not expect to hear a sound."

I paused dramatically and, from immediately above my head came, loud and clear, the sound of running footsteps. There were two pairs as far as I could make out, the first to pass being lighter and quicker than the following ones. Punctuating this performance at regular intervals was the sound of doors being banged. As I listened to the noises growing alternately softer and louder, I felt like Father Brown on that occasion when he deduced all sorts of things through hearing the footsteps of the arch-criminal tearing up and down a corridor. The big difference was that I could make neither head nor tail of it. For perhaps a couple of minutes we all listened intently as the chase went on overhead until the sounds stopped as suddenly as they had begun.

Some of the boys looked as puzzled as I did, others exchanged knowing leers and, of course, there were the few who would have evinced neither surprise nor interest had the Archangel Gabriel appeared chasing Donald Duck upside down on the ceiling.

Later on, when I saw Mac for a few moments of freedom with a cigarette in the toilets, I described this performance to him and asked whether he knew of any explanation.

"Oh, yes," he said, casually, "that's old Cass playing in and out of the windows with Mrs Reynolds upstairs."

"Why would he want to do that?" He looked at me in surprise.

"Did nobody ever tell you about the birds and the bees, old man?" he asked.

"You mean this is just a simple case of the old Adam? Our leader has what you might call evil designs on Mrs Reynolds?"

"In a word, yes. He fancies her something rotten, which only goes to show that my old dad knew what he was talking about when he said it takes all sorts to make a world. He had a neat turn of phrase, my old dad."

"The said Mrs R is certainly not my idea of the perfect little woman."

"Nor mine, old man, I do assure you. It's only fair to add that old Cass fancies anything he suspects of being female. He leaps about in an uncontrolled way when he sees that picture in the geography book of an Eskimo lady in her winter outfit."

"I wouldn't have thought that Mrs Reynolds was the type to run away, judging by the look she gave me this morning."

"Worse, old boy. She sets her sights on anything male and then proceeds to work her way towards it in that relentless way that women have. So watch out – you could be the next. Curiously enough, the only one she doesn't care for is old Cass, ironic really. That's why she starts this chase routine. By the time they've done three laps of the course, he's so flaked out he hasn't the energy for anything else when she lets him catch her."

"I take it this is a fairly regular performance, then?"

"Except when he's in Bristol or Banff on interview at the ratepayers' expense, it's a daily thing with a matinee on Tuesdays. Come to think of it Fridays are usually out, too, because that's his Times Ed. Day and even he finds little that could be called erotic in that."

I told Peter about this during my recital of events that evening. Being the sort of thing he might well have done himself, I thought it would arouse some fellow feeling.

"Bloody disgusting!" he exclaimed, "Guardian of public morality like that. He ought to be birched. There's no wonder this country's going to the bloody dogs. Lowering moral standards wherever you look."

"I only mention it because chasing girls has been one of the things for which you have been awarded medals."

"Mere innocent youthful high spirits. Different thing altogether." "Peter, you are the biggest hypocrite in the West Riding. You wouldn't recognise a youthful high spirit if you fell over one, and the last time you were innocent its beyond living memory."

"One matures, Ken. One realises ones responsibilities. Ones mind is not always on lust and such, like one's is – I mean like yours is. Your trouble is that you ought to find yourself a nice girl like Joan. It would cure this disgusting bloody carnal outlook which people find so objectional."

"I don't know why I bother to talk to you at all. I suppose there is a tiny kernel of common sense in the middle of all that verbiage. But you're wrong in one way. Joan is a great girl and she's just right for you – but not for me. She likes getting tarted up every night and heading for the bright lights and all that, and so do you. Now, as you well know, I'm all for a bit of that myself now and again, but as a way of life it would drive me potty."

"I didn't mean we should both go out with her, you clot. I meant someone as nice as she is but with your comic ideas."

"There you have it. There aren't any girls with my comic ideas. Now with you it's different. Unless the scales fall from her eyes in the near future or I go and reveal all to her Mum and Dad, Joan will probably marry you, and she will make a very good wife. There is even a chance that you will be a good husband."

"Yes, I expect I shall," said Peter with his customary endearing modesty.

Back at the school the battle continued. It was rather like being part of a small rearguard unit keeping the enemy at bay whilst the main body regrouped at a safe distance. Our commanding officer was more of a hindrance than a help, but the rest of us put up a pretty good containing action without, however, any hopes of ultimate victory.

The head appeared in public on a few occasions and, in between times, carried on filling in forms, travelling the country for interviews, and chasing Mrs Reynolds round the landings.

It was, on one occasion, instilling a little culture into the lives of 2B by reading at them Mr de la Mare's poem about "The Listeners." Having sorted out the more difficult words and established that the man was not trying to sell brushes, both the brighter boys had some idea of what it was all about. I went through it again, without interruptions or explanations and, though I say it myself, I was giving a rousing dramatic performance. I had just reached the bit where this chap knocks on the door a second time and "Is there anybody there?" he says, with a great crescendo, followed by a long, pregnant silence. Well, actually it was followed by a long, pregnant mooing sound from the direction of the ceiling and then the customary sounds of the chase. I decided that, as far as I was concerned, Mr de la Mare would have to get along without pregnant pauses.

One day, when the Head was not engaged in any of his usual activities, he attended a staff meeting at the urgent request of Mr Booker. Mrs Reynolds also came along to take the minutes of the meeting and to rub her leg against mine under that table. This was, apparently regarded as normal committee procedure by the others as they had all gone through it at some time or other. After some discussion on administrative points connected with the closure of the school, we proceeded to more interesting topics.

"It's about the fourth year day out, Mr Castleford," said Mr Booker, "everything is fixed up except deciding which members of staff are going."

"Yes, yes, I know all about that" said the Head tetchily, "what do you want me to do about it?"

"Well, as you know, we need four staff to go with them and so far we only have Mr MacKinnon and Mr Curtis. Everybody else will be going with their own year groups and I'm already down to go with both the first and second years so I think I've earned a rest."

"What you mean is, you want me to go?"

"That's right. I've kept you out of everything else, but we must have someone senior with the fourth years – you know what they're like."

"Goodness knows how I'm supposed to get all my work done, but all right. If there's no alternative I suppose I'll have to go. Where is it going to be this year – Blackpool? Bridlington?"

"Pen-y-Ghent." "Penny what?"

"Pen-y-Ghent. It's a mountain. One of the three peaks. You're going to climb it. Mac will tell you more about it. It's his idea and he's the route leader."

"Come on then, Mr MacKinnon. What is all this nonsense. I'm not going to get dressed up in shorts and boots and ropes for anyone."

"I don't see that being really necessary, Mr Castleford," said Mac., "it's only a hill really – just over two thousand feet – and there's no rock climbing or anything of that sort. Just a gentle amble in an upwards direction. The coach will take us to the bottom, we walk over the top and the coach picks us up at the other side. That's all there is to it. Then we relax as our magic carpet whisks us off through the soft sunset for tea in a chippy in Ingleton."

"All right, them. You'd better be right. But that still leaves one short."

"If Mr Castleford is away, I shan't have a great deal to do," said Mrs Reynolds sweetly, giving my knee a squeeze that brought tears to my eyes. "I would enjoy making up the fourth."

"Right, then, that's settled," said Mr Booker hastily, "coach leaves here at 9 o'clock on Thursday the fourteenth. You'll need sandwiches for one meal, of course."

"And some decent walking shoes and a good waterproof," added Mac., "Pen-y- Ghent tends to get a bit boggy in places and there's nowhere to shelter if it rains."

"I do let myself in for some things," groaned the Head, "I hope you know what you are doing, Mr MacKinnon."

"Oh, yes, sir. I know what I'm doing all right," said Mac cheerfully, and the meeting dispersed.

On her way out Mrs Reynolds cornered me. "I knew our chance would come," she hissed between pursed lips, looking like Sophie Tucker doing a ventriloquial act, "I've seen the way you've been looking at me. Don't worry – we'll find somewhere on our own."

I was, I must admit, torn between smugness that a whole lot of woman had selected me for her attentions, and panic at the idea of being seduced by a fourteen stone sex-symbol in some remote bog hole half way up a mountain. Being a hypocrite, I gave in to the gay cavalier image for a while, though resolving at the same time never to be caught alone with la belle Reynolds. It was easier said than done.

For the next few weeks I kept having notes handed to me by small boys and purporting to come from the Head who, they said, urgently required my presence upstairs. Having a fair idea of when the Head was in residence I contrived by skilful lying, to evade these traps until one day when I was horrified to read, "Dear K. Guess what? I have your car keys. You can collect them from my office at any time. Joyce."

I knew when I was beaten and, having the nearest thing I ever got to a free period when Connor and another chap took the whole of the top half of the school for what they called singing, I scaled the heights to the office.

"Mrs Reynolds, you are a perisher," I said as I went in, "come on – let me have those keys please."

"You'll need to ask much nicer than that," she said, leaning up against me like one of the larger members of the cat family, "I don't know why you keep avoiding me. I don't suppose it's every day a girl offers herself to you, is it?

This sort of conversation was way outside my experience and I was finding the room unpleasantly warm and far too small for the sort of manoeuvres I was beginning to see as desirable. I had visions of the classes below being thrown out of their stride by hearing the running of footsteps taking the usual route but in the reverse order. As I edged round the desk I saw, lying on it, a magazine. It was open at a page on which were depicted, in revolting detail, a naked man and woman in such bizarre juxtaposition that I shied like a startled horse.

"Do you like it?" asked Mrs Reynolds.

"Like it!" I said, "I've not exactly let a sheltered life, but that makes me sick." "There! I knew you were different. That makes it more exciting."

"You're probably right, but at the moment all I want are those keys. Come on, Joyce, don't mess around, please."

"All right. You can have them if you come and get them," she said, and dropped them down the front of her dress. I was, as they say, nonplussed.

"Now you're embarrassing me," I said, sure of only one things; that I would walk home rather than go fishing around in the dark recesses of Mrs Reynolds' anatomy.

We stood looking at each other for a few minutes. "You're not going to get them, are you?" she asked. "No, I'm not."

She undid a couple of buttons and produced the keys.

"You do a lot for a girl's ego, don't you?" she said as she threw them over. "Thanks. I'm sorry if I've been churlish, but I don't like being pushed into situations. It happened once before and I don't intend it to happen again."

"I see. But don't think you are going to escape. There's a long time to go yet."

I left with the uncomfortable feeling that I was fighting a war on two fronts, and one of them too big and too determined for my liking. Peter's advice, when I rather tentatively mentioned such parts of this episode as I thought were fit for him to hear, was a return to his cruder pre-Joan philosophy.

"There's no problem, Ken. Take her out in the country and roll her about in the hay for half an hour. That'll cure her."

"What a disgusting suggestion. I've not the slightest intention of rolling anywhere with Mrs Reynolds. Apart from the sordidness of it, I would probably be crushed to death. No, I'll take every precaution against her feminine wiles, and hope for the best. I suppose I can always yell for the police."

"Then you're bloody doomed," said Peter cheerfully.

The day of the outing dawned, not bright and clear, but wet and windy. An inspection revealed that the boys of Crickly Main Road Boys Secondary Modern School had as much idea of what constituted sensible clothing for a fell climbing expedition as an Australian aborigine. Winkle picker shoes, tight trousers and long jackets were de rigueur at the time for the well dressed layabout and were much in evidence. The 'rain proof outer garments' which he had stipulated, ranged from a large ex-army gas cape worn by a very small boy, giving him the appearance when in motion, of a partially deflated barrage balloon on castors, through a miscellany of cheap plastic macs, to one Humphry Bogart type belted raincoat and trilby hat.

Mr Castleford was there, looking even more tetchy than usual and proving that the boys were not alone in their sartorial inexperience by wearing a dark blue suit, grey overcoat, shiny black shoes and an umbrella. Mrs Reynolds had a transparent plastic mac and hood, a pair of high heeled Russian boots and an innocent smile.

Mac called the roll and, even after a ten minute allowance for the late comers, one boy had still not turned up. Each boy, having once answered his own name, considered the proceedings at an end and started conversing in the piercing scream, which was the norm for social intercourse.

"Harrison!" yelled Mac, "Is Harrison here?"

I blew several loud blasts on the whistle, which I had thought it wise to bring along to warn struggling mountaineers or in case I found myself cornered by Mrs Reynolds. Little by little the noise subsided and Mac was able to make himself heard.

"Cor luvaduck," he said, wiping his brow with the spotless white handkerchief which he invariably carried tucked in his sleeve, "trying to make myself heard above you lot makes me feel like the late King Canute of whom you will not have heard. Is Harrison here yet?"

There was no reply.

"Well, that's it then. We shall have to start without him."

"'E won't be coming on t'bus, sir," said a voice from underneath a yellow sou-wester which contrasted tastefully with the wide shoulders and velvet collar and cuffs of the coat beneath.

"What do you mean, he won't be coming, Collins?" asked Mac. "'E told me. 'E's going on 'is bike."

"Going on his bike!" What on earth are you on about, boy? Does anyone else know anything about this?"

Everyone, it appeared, knew all about it. They hadn't seen fit to mention it because Mr MacKinnon had not asked where Harrison was. Harrison, who was an undistinguished sort of boy with the average tendency for getting into trouble was, it seemed, a keen cyclist. He had set off at some early hour in order to make sure that he arrived at Halton Gill before the coach party.

"If this is true," I said to Mac, "that lad deserves a medal. Apart from the fact that he seems to be capable of finding out where Halton Gill is and how to get there, it's forty five miles if it's an inch, and most of it hilly."

"You're right. I'll believe it when I see him, though. It's ten to one he's still in bed."

We boarded the coach without too much disorder I caused more confusion than anyone by bobbing up and down the aisle in an effort to ensure that I was not sitting next to Mrs Reynolds. I was wasting my time. She so arranged matters that, without once moving from her seat or appearing to speak to anyone in anything other than a normal chatty way, the only place left for me was next to her. I consoled myself by thinking there wasn't much she could do on a coach full of boys, but it would be exaggerating to say that I convinced myself.

In fact, the journey turned out to be surprisingly pleasant. Once we had cleared the outskirts of Frontown and started up Wharfedale, even some of the boys were sufficiently affected by the scenery to want to look out of the window and point out items of interest. The road is a never ending delight and, to my relief, Mrs Reynolds was unexpectedly knowledgeable having, she told me, camped around the area in her younger and, I presumed, slimmer days. Even the rain could not detract from the dignity of the fells, the ruined charm of Bolton Abbey and Barden Tower, the rugged, stony beauty of the villages and the sinuous, swift flowing river linking them all together. And all the time Mrs Reynolds and I were reminiscing or recounting some folk tale or snippet of history we had heard and generally behaving like cultured, civilised adults. She had, I decided, sensibly given up any ideas of hanky-panky and become instead a charming platonic companion.

I really was incredibly simple.

We eventually arrived, having consumed vast quantities of sweets, and greatly relieved that only two boys had needed to make use of the sick bags provided.

We climbed down from the coach and there was tiny, grey Halton Gill, built out of the material of the fells and looking as though it had grown from them, rather than being made by human hands. And there, too, sitting on a wall, looking snug in sou- wester, cape and leggings, and munching a sandwich, was Harrison. We more or less mobbed him as we tried to find out about his epic journey. When I asked him what sort of a trip he had had, he was very casual about it.

"All right, sir. There were nowt on t'road so I were able to get on all right." "Well, I reckon you're a hero," I said, "it's at least forty five miles, you know." "Forty eight, sir. It's nowt really. I've done a lot more nor that, sir, wi t'club." "I still say you've done remarkably well, and so does Mr MacKinnon."

I turned to Mac who had left the shepherding of the flock into a manageable unit to our lord and master.

"A very good show indeed, Harrison," agreed Mac, "now, hurry up and put your bike on the coach and then you can come with us on the climb."

"Nay, sir, I'll take my bike with me," said Harrison.

"Good lord, lad, we're going straight across there," said Mac, pointing to the waste of ground tilted up into the sky on the other side of the wall, "you can't ride across that."

"I know that, sir," said Harrison doggedly, "but I can push it, and If I can't push it, then I'll carry it. I've done this sort of thing before, sir. I'm not leaving my bike.

"So be it. I only hope you know what you're doing. At any rate we can get some of the others to give you a hand if it gets too much."

We moved over to the main group where the Head appeared to be getting steamed up over something.

"Where in God's name have you brought us, MacKinnon?" he hissed as we drew near. "There's damm all in the place – not even a pub. It's the end of the bloody world."

"It is a trifle remote, old sir," said Mac, "but over yonder hill" – he gestured vaguely – "lies Horton-in-Ribblesdale which has several more houses and a pub. There is also a church which is, I believe, of some historical interest to those in our present party. However, as my old dad used to say, the sooner we start, the sooner we shall get there."

"I'll tell you one thing. I'd never have come if I'd known, but seeing you've got us here we'd better get the thing over."

"Personally, I'm looking forward to it," said Mrs Reynolds, "come on Mr Castleford, we'll help each other along."

The rain had almost stopped and the wind was driving the tattered clouds over the fell tops as we started climbing. As usual, it took about ten minutes for our once compact party to spread itself out forwards, backwards and sideways over the landscape until we resembled the hosts of the Israelites searching for the promised land.

In a sense, Mr Castleford's description had been right. There were no outstanding features, no footpaths, nothing but the tough grass underneath and the ridge of the hill above. What Mac and I knew, and kept to ourselves, was that, having attained the brow of the hill we could see in front of us, another one would appear, and then another and another until you began to think that this mountain had no top, but just as succession of ridges going on for ever. My private preference would have been to start at Dale Head and tackle the sharp end first where you could see where you were aiming for, but this was Mac's party and I was happy to let him take charge.

Not so Mr Castleford. He moaned and grumbled and fell into holes and tripped over tussocks and puffed and panted. He sat down in a small rivulet and tried to light a wet cigarette and nearly cried.

"Are we nearly there?" he asked in a tremulous voice, spraying bits of wet tobacco around the hillside, "because I've about had enough."

"Not much further," lied Mac, "at any rate you could say in all fairness that we have made a good start. How goes it with the fair Joyce?"

The fair Joyce had fallen as much as the Head and with greater effect. Nevertheless, she remained unshakeably cheerful and grinned through a coating of mud.

"If only I could knock the heels off these dam' boots, I'd be fine."

So we continued to the first brow Mac going ahead with the more energetic ones, Mrs Reynolds and myself at the rear whipping in the stragglers, prominent amongst whom was the Head. He wasn't actually gibbering, but you felt he would have liked to gibber if only he had the strength. As expected, when we could see over the crest, there was merely a slight undulation and the hill continued as before. We paused to admire the view, which in spite of the greyness of the day, was superb. The Head, it seemed, was not mad about views. He sank into the wet grass, wheezing like a defective harmonium.

"God in Heaven," he muttered piously between gasps, "Oh God – Oh, my God." "Where's the top, Curtis?" he managed to gasp, "Is that it?"

"Well, no," I had to admit, "there's a good deal further yet." "Then I'm going back!"

"But there's nothing to go back to," I protested.

"I don't care. People live there. God only knows why, but they do. There's a road, too and that must go somewhere away from here. I'm going back."

"I really think it's better to keep together," said Mrs Reynolds, "apart from the fact that I'm enjoying it in a peculiar sort of way. I think it's fun."

"Fun!" snarled the Head, "You must be barmy. You please yourself what you do, but I'm going back and I'm going now."

He painfully picked himself up from the grass, took a deep breath and started purposefully down hill. His mistake was in looking over his shoulder to see where Mac was disappearing over the skyline so that he could shake his fist and curse at him. This prevented him from seeing the boulder which tripped him up and sent him tobogganing down the slope on his behind. He was reaching a very fair turn of speed when some obstacle barred his further progress and he executed a graceful loop, coming to rest in a boggy patch with his mouth full of sphagnum moss. We deemed it our duty to hurry the boys away out of earshot of the quite inexcusable language which was causing the pewits and curlews to scream in the gusting wind like something by Wagner.

As we climbed on, we occasionally looked back and saw the little black figure bounding, crawling, falling its way downwards until at last it disappeared. The fells returned to their immense, timeless dignity. The air was clean with the tang of the hills in it and we were getting our second wind and beginning to enjoy the challenge of it all when, quite suddenly, we were on top. As mountains go, two thousand feet isn't much to shout about, but everything is relative, and battling with the wind along this high plateau with valley after valley and hill after hill as far as the eye could see was dramatic enough for us.

The slog was over as we tramped cheerfully along, Harrison wheeling his bike, Mrs Reynolds limping and singing quietly selections from her repertoire of marching songs which could only have originated in one of the more disreputable units of the army. With the satisfaction of difficulties overcome and objectives achieved, we eventually came up with the advance party at the point where the ground suddenly drops away in a series of vertical crags. We sat down and looked beneath our feet into Ribblesdale.

"Pardon me for mentioning it," said Mac, "but I don't seem to see our revered leader, the worthy Dr Castleford, scholar of Oxenford. You haven't mislaid him, have you?"

"He'd had enough after the first bit and turned back. The last we saw of him, he was rolling in the general direction of Halton Gill, bouncing in spectacular fashion over the contour lines. He didn't seem to mind too much which way he was going so long as it was downwards."

"Foolish man. There's no sort of transport from Halton Gill unless he waits for the mail van tomorrow morning. With a bit of luck we may not see him for days."

"We should be so lucky," said Mrs Reynolds feelingly.

A few of the boys had recovered sufficient energy to walk around and savour the novelty of their situation or to peer over the edge with the respect for high places which both Mac and I had instilled into them. My old friend Battersby, however, seemed to be completely devoid of either fear or imagination and was standing too close to the edge for our peace of mind. Mac called out to him.

"Hoi! Battersby...." he managed to say, and then we were both leaping at him, grabbing his legs and dragging him along the ground away from danger. Apparently under the impression that he was a bird, he had stuck his hand in the pockets of his voluminous plastic mac and then raised it over his head just the moment when there was an unusually strong gust of wind. The mac had filled and belled out like the spinnaker of a racing yacht and there is no doubt that we had prevented him from joining his ancestors then and there. He had the decency to look white and shaken. There was no need for us to say anything and, anyway, I had the feeling that my voice would have trembled a bit if I had tried.

"Right," said Mac, "it seems as though the time has come for us to move on. Gather your belongings together, follow me and stick to the path. There's to be no hurrying, no running and no passing."

The rest of the journey was beautiful, exhilarating and without surprises. When we reached the coach, Harrison announced his intention of carrying on in the way he had started and pedalled off up the road accompanied by the combined cheers of the rest of us. I wondered how many others there were who had interests or hobbies or just the strength of character and initiative to do what he was doing: boys we would never know about because the atmosphere of the school prevented us from getting close enough to them. In my own mind I knew that we were only doing half a job, but I also recognised that it was all we could do under the circumstances. Feeling closer to these boys than I had ever done, we went together into Mac's 'chippy' which turned out to be a highly respectable café, and consumed large quantities of fish and chips and bread and butter, our appetites whetted by the keen air and the exercise.

On the coach, Mrs Reynolds collared me before I had time to claim the seat left vacant by the Head's departure. She put her raincoat over her knee, grabbed my hand and put that there too. To everyone's surprise I leapt to my feet and, swaying in the aisle, started to lead some community singing in a sepulchral and tuneless bass. After their initial astonishment the boys joined in and, being happily indifferent to subtleties of key or pitch, at a level which was more in keeping with their own voices and the mood of the songs. So, in good order, we returned to Crickley where we were met by a troubled Mrs Castleford who said she had been pestered by a lunatic ringing her up and claiming to be her husband. She said he babbled quite a bit, kept laughing wildly and, although, being on the telephone she could not, of course, see him, she had the distinct impression that he was foaming at the mouth. We told her not to worry, that her husband had decided to come back on his own and would, no doubt, arrive in due course.

Next morning we heard his story. Suitably edited and making allowances for his distraught state of mind, it seems that he had roamed in a wild sort of way around Halton Gill where the few people had slammed the doors and fastened the shutters on catching sight of him. He had then tottered away with some sort of notion of walking the four or five miles to Litton or Arncliffe (he didn't know they were called that) and after half an hour or so, was overjoyed to hear the sound of a tractor. This eventually appeared coming towards him, driven by a man about a hundred years old who, he thought, had probably made the tractor himself in his youth.

He made this person understand that he wished to go down the valley towards a bus or train service and offered him untold wealth if he would turn round and help him on his way.

"Tha wants to go through Arncliffe," said the ancient, "I'll tak thee to a mile t'other side if tha can stand on t'back wi'out tumbling off. Tha can put thi brass away; I doan't want it."

Mr Castleford clambered gratefully aboard, found an insecure perch somewhere near the back axle and they lumbered off but, he was horrified to notice, without first turning round. Sensing a dark plot to steal his money and dump his body in a bog, he beat the driver around the shoulders with what was left of his umbrella, this relinquishing his hold on the mudguard. The driver regarded him solemnly as he lay in the road. "Now what's up?" he demanded.

The Head pulled himself off the floor. "You said you were taking me to Arncliffe," he croaked, "why are you going this way?"

"'cos it's t'way to get theer. Tha were walking away from Arncliffe. Next place on t'way tha were going is Foxup and I reckon tha wouldn't care for Foxup. There isn't no road at all after Foxup. No, it's a right quiet place in Foxup – not like Halton Gill."

Misunderstandings thus sorted out, they continued gaily until he was lifted off the machine and propped up against a wall a mile the other side of Arncliffe as promised. Here he prayed and, he said, it was as well he had led a good life because providence sent him succour in the shape of the local vet returning to comparative civilisation after an emergency call. He remembered little of the rest of the journey, the details of which had jumbled into a nightmare of lifts and buses and trains. He was convinced that at some stage he was transported in a balloon, but we pointed out to him the unlikelihood of this. What was certain was his eventual arrival at his door at two o'clock in the morning, accompanied by a large policeman who had to wait some time before Mrs Castleford was able to identify her spouse with any clarity.

"You know, there's a moral in this somewhere" said Mac to the rest of us in the staffroom later that day. "Here's a lad, namely Harrison, with no background to speak of, hardly any academic attainments and frequently in bother with authority. He turns out, against all the odds, to have character and, if I may use the expression, guts. Then there is our leader, brilliant product of an ancient university and highly respected by all those leading citizens who don't know him very well. What does he turn out to be, one asks oneself? All right – don't bother to answer. But I know which of the two I would trust my life to if it ever came to that, which heaven forbid."

We agreed that it was odd and that you never could tell.

The final day in the life of the school would have saddened those who had built it with high hopes of hundred years before. We all, by previous arrangement, left our cars at some distance from the school and made sure that none of the boys knew where they were. Somehow we struggled through the day without violence on either side and, at four o'clock, were lying exhausted and relieved in the staffroom when Jim Booker came in.

"Come and have a look at this," he said, and his tones was so serious that we followed him without a word.

He led us to the outside toilets.

"What do you think of that?" he asked.

The doors to the cubicles were made of good solid wood, which had stood up to the misuse of generations of hefty boys. One of them was split from top to bottom and embedded in the crack was a garden spade.

"I've tried to get it out and I can't even move it," said Jim. "I'll tell you something. Whoever did that has more strength than any of us and next term he's going to be at the new school."

"God, it's nasty," whispered Connor, "Real nasty. I'll tell you something too, Jim. When you get up there, don't turn your back on 'em."

We moved away quietly, collected our belongings and went home. The school was really dead now – and there were no mourners.

CHAPTER SEVEN

Just when I was beginning to think that it would never happen, a card arrived instructing me to report to the Junior and Infants School at Washford, a village near the County Town, as Head. My first reaction was panic, but a moment's thought convinced me that a mistake had been made so I rang up the office to tell them.

"No, there's no mistake, Mr Curtis," said the quiet voice of Mr Elsworth, "I think it's time you had a chance at a Headship and you'll like this one. Nice little place. Yes, you've worked for this, and I'm sure you'll get on very well. You can always get in touch with me if you need to, of course, but I'm sure you'll manage."

As even Peter knew nothing about Washford, I went to see the Divisional Education Officer in the County Town as soon as the opportunity occurred so that I could learn more about my first command. I think that, beneath the excitement, I was still panicking in an unobtrusive sort of way. The improvement in my status was immediately noticeable when I arrived at the office. The clerk to whom I put my request to see the DEO did not, it is true, fall to his knees when I told him who I was, but he passed my message on and within two minutes I was being ushered into the presence, which was very gratifying. Not only that, but once inside the holy of holies, I was greeted more as a colleague than a hired servant and invited to sit down in a comfortable chair instead of the hard backed buffet which officialdom seemed to reserve for common teachers.

"Pleased to see you, Mr Curtis," said the DEO, "good of you to call and see me before taking over at Washford. Cigarette?"

I was struggling hard to break the smoking habit but thought the old pals act might prosper with the aid of a little tobacco and accepted. Not having any matches to offer, the hospitality was a bit one sided, but I sat back, crossed my legs and blew quantities of smoke towards the ceiling to show how much at ease I was with this sort of carry on. The subsequent choking fit was cured by sticking my head out of the open window for a few minutes.

"Now then," said the DEO patiently, "if you're quite sure you are feeling all right, perhaps you can tell me just what it is you would like to know."

"Yes, of course," I gasped, wiping my eyes, "sorry about that."

I cast around for a reasonable explanation for my behaviour but, on the spur of the moment, could think of nothing better than blaming it on an old war wound which seemed to lack conviction. I decided to move on to the next item.

"I'd like to know anything you can tell me about the school." I said, "How many children there are, names of the staff, what kind of area it is in – that sort of thing."

The DEO pressed a button which produced a female secretary, like a genie out of a bottle only more attractive.

"Get me that file on Washford Junior will you Jane?" he asked, and then turned to me again. "There are one or two things I think you ought to know that I can tell you without the records. You will be taking over until the permanent Head is appointed, which should be at the beginning of the spring term. There is a rather unusual feature in that we had to put a certain amount of pressure on Mr Brackthorne, the old Head to retire this year. He wanted to go on until he was sixty-five, but we thought it better to have a change. I really shouldn't say any more than that. There is one thing, though. He was reluctant to hand over his keys and there is just a possibility that he might turn up at the school. I wouldn't presume to tell anyone like you what to do if this should happen. I leave it to your discretion, of course."

My casual assurance, already suffered from a surfeit of tobacco fumes, was even further eroded. Reading between the lines it seemed that, not only was I expected to run the school for the first time in my life, but that there was a distinct likelihood of it becoming a double act. I felt this was going a bit far; that I was being victimised; that I should, in my own interests, express my profound dissatisfaction at being thus made to carry the can; that I should do it immediately and in the strongest possible terms.

"Of course, naturally," I said, "such an occurrence will not be allowed to interfere with the running of the school."

I was on the verge of adding that this was just the sort of thing we Heads regarded as a legitimate challenge to our authority, but thought better of it.

By this time the statistics were available and I was told that I would have under my control about 150 children, aged from five to eleven, four female and one male members of staff plus the usual caretaker, dining room people and so on. Washford, it seemed, was a pleasant village, part agricultural, part depending on the nearby pit. After some further discussion on details I rose to go.

"Pleased to meet you," said the DEO holding out his hand, "give me a ring if you have any problems. I'll try to get along to see you in a week or two when you've had a chance to settle in."

Peter had surprisingly little to offer in the way of advice on my new appointment except, predictably, that I should "make 'em know who's boss," which was precisely the thing that, at that moment, I didn't feel like doing. The more I thought about it, the more convinced I became that I was not cut out to be a leader and that the whole thing was going to be a ghastly failure. I had no desire at all to boss anyone about, and the prospect of imposing my will on what I envisaged as a group of hard bitten and vastly experienced teachers filled me with alarm. I also came to the conclusion that, despite my own experience of the past few years, I had been wasting my time and knew no more than when I was at college.

It was actually true that I was ignorant to a remarkable degree on such administrative details as what you did with dinner money after collecting it from the children, what returns were required by whom, how stock was requisitioned and so forth. These matters had always been dealt with behind closed doors and, with my usual lack of initiative, I had never thought to ask. It seemed a good idea to go to the school before the opening day and see what I could find out. Peter was giving himself a day off so we decided to go together in the Wolseley.

"One thing I will say," Peter remarked as he settled into the passenger compartment, "these are damned comfy seats. The only trouble is that the agony starts the moment the bloody thing gets mobile. Are you sure the wheels have got any flaming tyres on?"

The comments were not new and I ignored them, concentrating on the task of navigating through unknown territory. After traversing the County Town we went through one of the posher suburbs before turning down a country lane which, in about three miles, brought us to

Washford. It was, I was pleased to see, a real village with a Victorian church, a pub that could have been eighteenth century, three of four shops, and an incongruous mixture of country cottages and a few rows of nineteen twenty's type terraced houses. The top of the pit winding gear could just be seen above a belt of trees in the distance but everywhere else there were fields, looking a little soiled as everything near a coal pit always does, but fields nevertheless.

The school was a tidy, one story building, typical of its size and time with, as we discovered when we went in, classrooms opening from a central hall and toilets across the yard. Tucked away in one corner was a stock room and the Head's room – my room – balanced by the staff room on the other side. In between were the pegs and sinks of the cloakrooms and the caretaker's store. It looked well cared for and smelt of floor polish. "There's nothing much wrong with this place, Pete," I said.

"Bloody smashing," he agreed, "My – it takes you back a bit, doesn't it?"

"Does it? Yes, I suppose it does if you haven't been in a school for years. We professionals regard it in rather a different light, so don't expect me to go all nostalgic and sentimental like you."

"Sentimental! Me! Rubbish. You know I look forwards, not back. It makes you bloody think, though, all the same."

"You'd be doing something more useful if you gave some thought to this little lot," I said.

I had found, in rooting through the Head's desk, a varied collection of papers, forms, books and files. As none of them looked particularly secret we went through them together and in a surprisingly short time our efforts were beginning to make some sort of sense of the system. We were just beginning to sort out a pile for me to take home for further study when a middle aged lady wearing a long coat and carrying a shopping bag, appeared in the doorway.

"I saw the car outside," she said, "and thought I'd better come and have a look. I'm Mrs Ross, the caretaker, and I suppose one of you gentlemen will be the new Headmaster."

I admitted to being the one, feeling the strangeness of talking to one of my staff for the first time.

"We did call at your house, Mrs Ross," I said, "but there was no reply, so we came straight up to the school."

"Aye, I've just been doing a bit of shopping. Well, Mr Curtis, I hope as you'll find everything to your satisfaction."

I told Mrs Ross how impressed both Mr Lee and myself were at the standard of the cleanliness of the school, that we had only just finished remarking on how tidy everything was, and how we had said that one could, if so inclined, eat one's meals from the floor. In fact, I bossed her about something awful in the way advocated by Peter who was, I noticed, nodding his head and grimacing in approval. Mrs Ross was clearly pleased at this performance and eager to supply any information I required and, indeed, volunteered some gossip which was not only unprofessional but probably libellous as well. By the time we were ready to go I had a very fair idea of the background of most of the children and had been given a potted biography of the staff as well. With the exception of one Miss Lane, of whom she disapproved, Mrs Ross was of the opinion that all were paragons of hard work and virtue. I gathered that Miss Lane was a hard worker too.

"But Mr Brackthorne," she concluded "he were a funny 'un. I shouldn't talk of the Headmaster like this, I know, but everybody knows and I'm saying nothing that I haven't said to his face. 'Mr Brackthorne,' I've said, 'You're a funny 'un,' I've said."

"Well, I don't expect you will have to deal with him again, will you?" I said, crossing my fingers tightly under the desk.

"No, I don't suppose I shall, and let me say, I wish you well, Mr Curtis. We could do with some new blood round here. Well, if you don't mind, I'll get off and get a bit of dinner ready. I'm a widow, you know, so I've only myself to do for. Well, like I say, I hope you enjoy it here, Mr Curtis, and I'll say goodbye for the time being."

"Well," I said to Peter when she had gone, "there goes the most important member of the staff. Unusual to have a woman caretaker, but she seems to know what she's doing."

"She's a bloody treasure is that one, and no mistake. If you'll take my advice Ken, you won't go throwing your weight around with her like you have a tendency to do."

"Right-Oh, Pete," I said.

In spite of my natural disinclination to wake up in the mornings, I did like to give myself plenty of time to travel in an unhurried fashion and then to sit and ponder for a while before starting the serious work of the day. On my first morning at Washford I rather carried this to excess, partly because I miscalculated the travelling time required and partly because I had been awake most of the night remembering all the things I had forgotten. When I arrived, Mrs Ross was still clattering about with buckets and things and expressed surprise at seeing me.

"My, my! You wouldn't catch Mr Brackthorne here before the stroke of nine – and not always then. He were a funny 'un, though, was Mr Brackthorne. And you've such a long way to come, too, and in that old car. I'll tell you what, Mr Curtis; you go into your room and get on with whatever you have to do, and I'll make you a nice pot of tea. You'll need something after coming all that way – and in that old car, too."

And so was born the procedure which was to become a matter of daily routine, and my first perk. After a preliminary walk round I settled behind my desk in my room with my pot of tea which my caretaker had made for me, and took out of the drawer the school log book. Things would doubtless go wrong, problems would accumulate and multiply, and there may be a fire, pestilence and flood, but nothing was going to detract from the magic of this moment – not even the possible arrival of the late lamented Brackthorne, breathing fire and thunder. I opened the thick, leather bound volume and ruled a line under the last entry. Then I put the date in the margin and, after a suitable pause in which to savour the solemnity of the occasion, wrote in my most flourishing style, "Today, I, Kenneth John Curtis, commenced my duties as Head of this school."

I'd waited a long time to be able to do that.

After a while I heard the sounds of others arriving and although, as usual, I had it all planned out, couldn't for the life of me decide what to do next. Here, shut in my room, I was safe; outside was the great wide world and it was strange and alien and I didn't really want to have much to do with it. I wondered what Peter would do, being accustomed to meeting new people every day with an eye to flogging them things they didn't really want. Actually I knew very well what Peter would do. He would invite them all into the office, clap them all on the back, press strong drink upon them and there would be a surfeit of bonhomie. I knew that wasn't my style.

I stood up, took a deep breath, strode into the staff room and announced in clear ringing tones, "Good morning! My name is Curtis. I'm the new Head." It was precise, authoritative and nobody heard it because the room was empty. Wherever the teachers were, it wasn't in the staff room. Feeling a bit deflated I peeped cautiously into the first classroom. A stocky, middle aged female who looked as though she spent the formative years of her life playing hockey or breaking horses, turned from her desk and called out to me.

"Hello there!" she bellowed, "You'll be Mr Curtis, I suppose. Come in, come in. Glad to meet you."

It wasn't at all as I had planned it, but the ice was broken and within a few minutes word had got around, the others came in and we were all sitting on the desks, chatting away ten to the dozen.

There was Mrs Eldon, my robust friend who was, surprisingly, in charge of the five year old reception class. The immoral Miss Lane turned out to be mousy and fifty-ish, most disappointing when I was expecting Mata Hari, and there was Mrs Kennedy, kindly, bespectacled and white haired. Supplying the glamour was Miss Bullinger, not long out of college, dark haired and pretty and then there was the only male member of the staff, Mr Lewisham, who looked four or five years younger than myself and capable and athletic. I had the feeling I was going to get along fine with all of them.

"You'll be wanting me to take the assembly so you can get on with your work, I suppose," said Mr Lewisham, "We've usually shared it around between us, so it's no problem."

"I'd rather planned to do it myself," I said, "As far as I know, there's no office work needing immediate attention. In fact, I can't see there being anything until the diner money has been collected and, anyway, I want to introduce myself to the school. They'd better see what I look like, even if they don't reckon much to it."

"But Mr Brackthorne always had such a lot of work to do in the office," said Mrs Kennedy with concern, "Are you quite sure you will be able to manage?"

"Of course he'll manage, Ethel dear," said Mrs Eldon, "I always said that Brackthorne was coming the old soldier."

"I really don't think that's quite fair, Poppy," interjected Miss Lane, "Mr Brackthorne had many problems to contend with. Maybe because we had known each other for so long he used to confide in me. I think he was a very brave man and very much misunderstood in some quarters."

I thought it up to me to do something about the silence which had broken out following this announcement, pondering as I did so that if Mrs Eldon's parents had wanted a Poppy, they must have been very disappointed. I suggested that, with the exception of the new five year olds, the children should be bought into the hall immediately after registration so that I could have a word with them. After this, I said, I proposed to help Mrs Eldon with what I feared would be a crowd of wet and worried newcomers. As the hour approached nine o'clock I kept a wary eye on the door just in case the errant Mr Brackthorne should appear but, fortunately, nothing of the sort happened and, at about quarter past, a child came to inform me that everyone was duly seated and waiting in the hall.

I strolled out looking wise, friendly, purposeful, learned and stern which was, I suppose, asking a lot of one face. The first hint that my expression may not have been to everyone's liking came when two small children on the front row clung together like the babes in the wood and started to whimper quietly. I did a quick adjustment to a cheerful smile which made them burst into tears and proclaim loudly that they wished to go home.

Mrs Kennedy moved in swiftly and pushed something into their mouths which effectively stopped any further speech and even made them look fairly happy.

As I prepared for action, I realised that I was feeling, in front of these children and teachers, just as I had felt in front of a class on my first teaching practice. I also realised that I had been standing there alternately frowning and leering for some considerable time without saying a word and, furthermore, without a word in my head of the speech full of high moral sentiments which I had composed the evening before. Fighting down and insane desire to break into a top-hat-and-cane type of dance routine, I grabbed a chair which was fortunately to hand and sat on it with my legs astride and my arms on the back.

"Good morning children," I said.

There was some giggling and a halfhearted response.

"You know, I think you can do better than that. I'll help you by telling you that my name is Mr Curtis. Now then – Good morning, children."

"Good morning, Mr Curtis," they all chanted back.

"That's better. Now – who can tell me what Mrs Eldon is doing just now in her room?"

A few hands crept up, but mostly there were the usual blank looks.

"We seem to be having to make two starts at everything this morning, don't we? Perhaps we still think we are on holiday. Now, just think hard for a minute. Mrs Eldon is very busy this morning. If we are very quiet indeed and listen very carefully, I think we shall be able to hear what she is doing."

Everyone obligingly stopped shuffling around; even the heavenly twins in the front row forgot they had started to snivel again and, sure enough, we heard in the distance the wailing of young children being introduced into the educational system.

"Now – what is Mrs Eldon doing? I asked.

Hands shot up and there was general agreement that Mrs Eldon was 'looking after the new kids."

"That's right," I said, "and there's a new kid in the hall now who needs looking after. Can you tell me who it is?"

There was a great deal of looking around until one bright spark, grinning all over his face, but up his hand and said, "Please sir, it's you sir!"

The rest got the point and joined in the merriment

"Yes, it's me. I'm a new boy this morning, too. The only difference seems to be that no one has offered to look after me so far. Would anyone like to volunteer to do that?"

There was more hilarity and a few braver souls put up their hands.

"Right, I'll tell you what I would like you do to for me. I want you all to help me. During the next few days I shall be getting to know you and to know my way round the school, and I shall need all the help I can get from every one of you.

Then, later on, I shall be able to help you instead, because that's really what I'm here for."

Then, in accordance with both legal requirements and my own wishes, we said a short prayer and departed to our rooms. I sat on my chair after they had all departed and pondered. Not a solitary thing had gone as I had planned and yet, apart from a regrettable tendency to fall into the trap of saying 'we' instead of 'you' like a Victorian nanny, I had a feeling that it hadn't gone too badly.

"Anyway," I thought, "for better or worse, that's it. The first impression has now been finished. And so to battle with the teeny-weenies and, worse still, their mums."

What with this and the dinner money that had been haunting my dreams, and one or two minor queries to settle, the time passed so quickly that twelve o'clock arrived without giving me chance to sit back and wonder whether I was doing all right.

"I suppose you'll be having lunch brought into your room like Mr Brackthorne always did," said Miss Lane, "there are one or two of the older girls who know just what to do, so you don't need to worry about it."

"Well, actually I had planned to have it in the hall with the children but, if you are sure nobody will mind, it would save time to have it in my room. It will give me a chance to have another go at balancing the books. Maths was never my favourite subject and I seem to have lost some money somewhere."

There was general concern at this and Mr Lewisham said, "I've never had anything to do with the dinner books, apart from my own, but I enjoy playing around with figures," – he glanced at Miss Bullinger who tossed her wavy hair like the heroines do in books, but without any convincing sign of displeasure – "I'd be pleased to give a hand if you think it would do any good. Two heads better than one and all that."

I told him I would be delighted to have his assistance and, as he was dining on sandwiches, we retired to my room with a pot of tea and prepared for a session of high finance. With an air of long experience, I pointed out to him the accounting procedures which Peter and I had discovered the day before.

"I see," said Mr Lewisham, far too quickly to put at rest my feeling of mathematical inadequacy, "that's straight forward enough. All it amounts to is that there are the class registers and then the summary register which you keep and which has to balance with both the class books and the bank paying in book."

"Only it doesn't," I said.

"I see. If you like then, I'll check today's figures while you have your lunch and then we'll see what that proves."

Ten minutes or so passed in silence broken only by the chewing and slurping noises associated with the mastication of some sort of roast animal followed by prunes and custard.

"There's nothing wrong with your figures," said Mr Lewisham, "and yet there's this discrepancy of £1.12s at the end. Therefore it must be elsewhere. We'd better look at the figures for last term, hadn't we? If this 'brought forward' figure is wrong then we've found it. Do we have last term's registers?"

"Funny you should ask. There's a letter somewhere from the office asking why they haven't been sent in, so I had a hunt round for them. I unearthed them from the bottom of that cupboard, eventually, which seems a rum place for them to be."

Together we plodded through the old books and, the more we checked, the more obvious did one thing become. Someone had been fiddling. It was only small amounts, but almost weekly and covered up in what even I saw was an amateurish way. We looked at each other without speaking for a while.

"Look, John," I said eventually, "this may or may not be what it seems but, in any case, nothing must be said to anyone else at this stage. If anyone wants to know how we've managed, we simply say we've sorted it out. Agreed?"

"Agreed. What I can't understand is why anyone wanting to pocked a quid or two didn't do just that. Why bother to make any entry at all? Nobody bothers to count heads at dinnertime. Maybe we should, but we don't, so nobody would have been any wiser."

"Yes, you could have done that – or any of the other teachers – but not the person we're both thinking about. The entries have already been made in the class registers by the time they come into the office, so some book cooking becomes necessary."

"It all points to one person, doesn't it? It's not very nice, you know."

"It is not. But don't forget we may be wrong. There may be some perfectly rational explanation for everything, so we must keep it quiet. I shall have to think about telling the DEO, of course, but nobody else need know."

That afternoon I did two things. First I wrote a statement in the log book and in the summary register stating that I accepted no responsibility for any errors prior to my arrival and then I rang up the DEO and told him to expect me on my way home that afternoon.

When I was shown into his office I apologised for disturbing him again so soon.

"It is rather sooner than I expected, Mr Curtis, but no doubt it is important," he said.

"If I didn't think so, I wouldn't be taking up your time."

I put the books in front of him and explained what I had found. He sat silently for a moment, fingertips together.

"Mr Curtis," he said eventually, "it is quite obviously that we must both draw the same conclusion from this evidence. I shall have to tell you a little more than I did yesterday. I now see that I should have done so at the time, but I think you will understand why I was perhaps over-reticent when you have heard what I have to say. Mr Brackthorne, when he was first appointed, before my time, was, I am told, a good and conscientious Head. His wife, however, became a permanent and very demanding invalid shortly afterwards and he lacked whatever it is that is needed to cope with this new situation. One result was that he started to drink more than was good for him; another was that he came to think that the world owed him a better living than he was getting. We had reason to think he was connected with one or two commercial enterprises which were only just on the right side of the law. I knew nothing about what you have just shown me, but it fits into the general pattern."

He paused for a while, weighing his words carefully before continuing. "You may be wondering why we didn't do something about the situation, particularly as his effectiveness as a Head was decreasing steadily. Well, we felt sorry for him in a way and possibly even more sorry for his wife. As long as he was not having a bad effect on the children we felt that he should be allowed to carry on until he retired. By the time we found out what was happening he didn't have long to go. That was why we wouldn't let him go on beyond sixty, of course, as I told you. If we had known about this business sooner it would no doubt have forced our hands."

There was another pause. Anything I could have said would have been superfluous so I waited for him to go on.

"Are you prepared to leave this with me?" he asked. "May I ask what you are proposing to do about it?"

"Certainly you may. I shall see that the account is straightened out and that will end the matter."

"And Mr Brackthorne will not be involved?" "As far as I am concerned, no."

"Then I agree."

"I'm pleased to hear you say so, and I thank you for

bringing this to my notice. You were perfectly right to do so, of course."

I left wondering how it was that I never seemed to have a straightforward carry on when I started a new school.

By the following day all feelings of trepidation or even of strangeness disappeared and I was relishing the thought of another session in charge. It was not, I decided, because I took delight in being a position to say to one man come and he cometh or to another, go and he goeth, because the necessity to do this had not arisen. I thought it was probably the satisfaction of being the chap people came to for a final decision, but had to admit that, lurking deep down somewhere, was another and less worth reason. I felt a childish pleasure in thinking that I could, if I so wished take time off to visit a neighbouring Head, call hi Fred or Joe as the case might be, and discuss with him matters of importance while other people got on with the work.

"Come and look round my place Joe (or Fred)," I could say, "Let me know what you think about the art work (or the school dinner or the state of the drains)."

In fact I never did anything of the sort and, because I failed to see the truth for far too long, there was something else I failed to do which was far more important.

I took the attitude, at this early stage of being in charge, that I was simply a bird of passage and that, until the permanent Head arrived, it was my job to see that the place kept ticking over satisfactorily and nothing more. In consequence, although I could see room for improvement here and there, and although I knew I could order plenty of new reading and reference books to replace the museum pieces being used, I failed to do so. These things, I thought, should be left to the new Head who may have different ideas from myself. It was some time before I realised how wrong I was, and that the only way to run a school was to forget that I was there for only a term or two, pretend it was forever, and act accordingly. That way the school is alive and any new Head would rather take over a place with a life of its own that somewhere giving the impression that rigor mortis had started to set in.

None of these thoughts worried me, of course, on that second day. I walked with a light step, spoke cheerily to all and even sang a gay snatch.

"A fish is an animal with dirt on its face; a tum tum it tumty tum disgrace," I intoned, and small children looked at me in wonder and went to tell their friends.

It was in such a mood that I went into my office and sat behind the desk, hands in my pockets and a silly, self-satisfied smirk on my face. As I sat thus, thinking of nothing except how good it was to be alive and powerful, I noticed that the door was slowly and silently opening. I watched, fascinated, as a male head appeared and one eye closed in a ridiculously conspiratorial wink. It was not, I decided, a very nice head, reminding me in some ways of my one time leader, Mr Castleford, but with more pronounced tendency to rattishness. The hair was black and shiny, and under the thin nose was a dark horizontal mark, presumably masquerading as a moustache. The colour scheme was carried through to the black bordered finger which proceeded to tap one side of the nose, accompanied by another leering wink, which seemed to be intending to convey the message that this thing and I were, in some way, companions in some nefarious enterprise. I felt that, had its owner thought more about it, the face would have said "Psssst ...."

I was not flattered, but I was interested. "Yes? What can I do for you?" I asked.

By now the body to which the head was attached had slithered into the room and closed the door quietly behind it. I was quite taken aback to realise that here, in front of my very eyes was the archetypal spiv of the wartime black market. The attitude, the expression, the clothes, even the East London accent when it started to speak, were so true to type as to seem a parody.

"Nah then, Guv," said the person.

"Good morning," I said, "is there anything you are wanting?"

"Well, nah, there may be something you're wanting, eh? You'll be the noo boss, eh? Old Bracky what was 'ere before, well, him and me did a lotter business togever, di'n't we? 'Ad some good fings going, we did. So, yer see, I fought I'd give yer the charnce o' carrying on, like, see? Good business we done since during the war, me and old Bracky." He sighed sentimentally, "Cor good times them was, in the war. Seen this room full of 'ams and sideserbacon, I 'ave. still, we 'aven't done so bad since, either. Cor, we ain't 'alf taken some mugs."

It may be that he realised his approach was not being particularly subtle, or it may be that he caught sight of my expression, but a sudden anxious note crept in as he continued, "All in a good cause, o'course, all in a good cause. School funds and all that yer know. Give quids away, we did."

"Look, Mr..... I don't think I caught your name.... Mr Smith, of course; well Mr Smith, I'm here as Headmaster and not as a trader and I certainly have no wish to carry on in the way you suggest Mr Brackthorne did. On the other hand, if you have some honest scheme for raising money for the school, I'm prepared to listen, without making any promises."

"That's the ticket, cock," said Mr Smith amidst a paroxsym of winks, "money for the school, ain't it? I knew you was a bright one, soon as I see yer. Well, nah then, I can get anyfing, see, from nylons to dirty books. It's distribution what's the problem, see, so the kiddies push 'em rahnd and abaht and what we make goes to school funds, see? Then o' course, we keep a little bit for commission fer you and me, eh?"

"How much commission?"

"Cor, you're a quick one, mate. I fought you'd catch on quick, soon as I seen yer. "Ere's another sharp one like old Bracky,' I fought. Well, now, take them barth salts what we did larst year. Good line they was. Luverly box wiv flahrs all over it and a scent that knocked yer dahn. 'Alf a crahn they was, and that's cheaper than in the shops. Well – cost to me, sixpence; school fund, tuppence; Bracky and me shares one and tenpence, twentyfive – seventyfive."

"You what!" I exclaimed, astounded at these revelations.

"Oright, oright – forty – sixty then. I see you're a sharp 'un. But that's as far as I go. Forty-sixty and I'm doing you a favour."

"Tell me, Mr Smith, these bath salts. Where do you get them from and what are they made of?"

"I can't tell you all me secrets, y'know, but these come from a mate o' mine whats an industrial chemist. Well, 'e's only in a small way, yet. Makes 'em in a shed at the end of 'is yard, but we all 'ave to begin somewhere, don't we? And don't fink there's anyfing in 'em to do anyone any 'arm, cos there ain't. Washing soda, mostly, and there's noffing wrong with that."

"I see. And you say that Mr Brackthorne was a party to all these activities, was he? Made himself a tidy sum, I've no doubt?"

"Cor, I'll say 'e did. O'course it were better in the war." The memories of the golden age overcame him again and he all but wiped a tear from his eye. "Full of 'ams, this room 'as bin. And sideserbacon. And that there cupboard cram full o' coupons. Cor, we 'ad some good fings going, Bracky and me. Yes, 'e's made a bob or two, I can tell yer. Mind you, there's still good fings if yer look arahnd. There's always mugs, ain't there?"

"Yes, I suppose there are, Mr Smith. I must admit that you have surprised me this morning, and I'm not quite sure what I ought to do. One thing I am quite sure about is that I am going to ask you to leave and don't bother to come back."

"Whatdyermean? You ain't mug enough to frow these charnces away, are you?"

"That's about the size of it. I'm on the side of the mugs. No will you please leave."

"Not so quick, made, not so quick. Bracky and me 'ad good fings going and I don't see why I should give 'em up so easy. Look, I'll tell you what I'll do – I'll go fifty- fifty, and that's more than I ever did with Bracky."

"Mr Smith, I don't seem to have made my meaning clear. I am not a violent man so I will not make threats, which I wouldn't carry out, but if you don't leave this room

and this building immediately I shall call the police. I have a feeling they are not your best friends."

"Oright, oright. I'm going. Cor, yer not like old Bracky. You're a bloody mug, you are. I don't know what education's coming to."

He departed, leaving me wondering what further revelations there would be before the term was over.

I was surprised to find how easily I assumed the mantle of authority as the weeks passed. I became on familiar terms with various officials at what was always referred to as 'the office', parents called to see me on a variety of matters concerning their offspring, and some of the members of the local committee visited now and again. I enjoyed all this immensely and had to keep reminding myself that my main job was not socialising, but so to organise, encourage and cajole my small unit that the education process was as successful as we could make it.

Major changes were neither necessary nor desirable, but I made smaller ones here and there within the rather strict limits which I had imposed on myself, and I was vain enough to believe that the school improved greatly in both spirit and achievement. Sober reflections made me admit to myself that this was mainly because there was now a Headmaster who was actually visible around the place, but that didn't stop the odd twinge of possessive pride now and then.

I made a point of teaching each class for one or two periods each week – with the exception of the reception class which frightened me to death – and so grew to know the children individually. What a change it was to have no disciplinary problems at all! Whether the children were cowed by me exalted position or whether I had gained in confidence and expertise, or wether they were just extraordinarily amenable, I don't know, but teaching or chatting with them was a natural affair with no sharp edges.

One afternoon at about two o'clock, when I had almost forgotten about him, I had a visit from the notorious Mr Brackthorne. There was a discreet tap on the office door, I invited whoever it was to enter, and this rather seedy looking person, middle sized with a straggly moustache, grey hair in need of cutting, and an ill-pressed suit, appeared almost apologetically in front of me. He smelt like a brewery and reeled ever so slightly with a circular motion like the mast of a yacht in a calm harbour. When we spoke it was with the careful enunciation of one who suspects that an excess of alcohol may have made his speech a little more blurred than he would wish.

"My name," he announced, "is Brackthorne. You will be Mr Curtis."

We shook hands and I told him how pleased I was to see him, which was not strictly true. Interested would have been a better word.

"Good place you got here," he said, "nice people. Ver' nice people. More than you can shay for that blurry shower at the offish." He hiccupped solemnly. "Whoops. Shorry about that. I've just been, or there again, I've just had...... yes, tha's better... ... I've just had a little picklerup."

"Picklerup?" I queried. He guffawed loudly and sank into a chair, where he sat deep in thought for some moments.

"Whadyeronabout?" he demanded aggressively, "Picklerup, picklerup – there's no such blurry word as pipip..... whatever it was I just said. I know that because I'm blurry Headmaster. Hey! Whadyer doing in my chair?"

"Now, Mr Brackthorne, I have a lot of work to do. You will understand that; so I really must ask you to leave and let me get on with it."

He looked at me in wonderment for some time and then it seemed that the mists began to clear and he made a brave effort to return to his formal manner.

"Pick – me – up," he said slowly and distinctly, "that's what I've had – a picklerup. Been ill, you see. Been ver' poorly indeed. Got to do what th'blurry doctor says, eh? You can understan' why I need a pick... pickm'up, can't you?"

"I see. I'm sorry you haven't been well," I said, wondering how on earth I was going to get rid of him, short of calling for reinforcements and putting him out on his ear.

"I will now, with your permish, proceed to the objec' of my visit thish aft'noon," he said, with yet another change of mood, "With your kind of permishishish, I shall proceed to the objec' of my visit this aft..... no, I've said that. With your blurry permishshshsh," he went on, sounding like a soda syphon, "I shall go an' have a brief word with Mish Lane. Old frien's y'know. No need to show me the way. I used to work here y'know. Did I tell you I used to work here? Now you seem a nice young chap, but there's one thing I can't unnerstan'. Whadyer doing in my blurry chair?"

"Mr Brackthorne," I said with a hint of desperation, "you just stay sitting down in that chair, seeing you have been ill, and I shall go and get Miss Lane to come here and have a word with you. Now, don't move. Please don't move – I shall be back in a moment or, rather, Miss Lane will be here in a moment. You just stay there in that chair."

There was a resounding snore. My visitor's hands were clasped across his tummy, his eyes were tightly shut and on his face was the blissful expression of a small child who has gone to sleep after opening his presents in the early hours of Christmas morning. I tiptoed out.

On the way across the hall I met John Lewisham.

"I have comrade Blackthorne in my office and he's kettled," I told him.

"He would be at this time, wouldn't he? It was one of the aims of his life ne'er to spend an afternoon sober if he could help it.

"In that case, he's well on target for today. For some reason he wants to see Miss Lane, so I'm going to take over her class. I can't have him wandering around the school in the state he's in.

I really don't see why not. He did it for years. The kids just thought he was eccentric. As for Miss Lane.... well, I can only assume that nobody has told you."

"Told me what?"

"Well, it's a bit difficult to put delicately and I don't like saying things..... but dammit, it's common knowledge and you're bound to find out sooner or later. Well, you know that she – Miss Lane, that is – is in receipt of a special allowance, ostensibly for being in charge of the infants department?"

"Yes, of course. What about it?"

"Not for that at all. She used to go with him to his caravan in Primrose Valley every weekend – hence the special allowance, for a post of special responsibility.

"You're joking!"

"No, really, I'm not. Well, you wouldn't, would you – not about that. It's one of those well kept secrets that everyone knows. I have friends in schools miles away from here who can give you chapter and verse."

"Good Lord. I must have had a very sheltered life. Infamy piled on infamy! Anyway, I'd better get a move on before the party in question comes to and starts wandering around. The condition he's in, he's likely to start thinking he's in Primrose Valley now, and heaven knows what might happen then."

What the meeting was about I made no attempt to find out, but Miss Lane came back to her room after about a quarter of an hour, twittering about how poor Mr Brackthorne was so misunderstood and looking rather red around the eyes. When I got back to the office he had gone. I saw him only once after that, and under rather peculiar circumstances.

Mrs Ross came to me one morning with my usual pot of tea and an unusually worried look on her face.

"Now then, Mrs Ross," I said, "you're looking a bit under the weather this morning. Nothing wrong I hope?"

"As a matter of fact, Mr Curtis, there is," she said "you know my little store room near the boys' cloak room? Well, I keep most of my stuff in there as you know, and you'll bear me out that only last week I got a new crate of soap and half a dozen mop heads and some floor polish and a few more odds and ends."

"That's right. We checked the requisition together. What about it?" "They've gone!"

"What do you mean, Mrs Ross? What's gone?"

"The soap and the mops and the polish. They've all gone, Mr Curtis, and it's my responsibility. I lock the door, as you can bear me out, so the kiddies can't get in there in case they get their hands on the ammonia or such like and hurt themselves. But they've all gone."

"Well, I can see why you're worried, Mrs Ross, but let's have a quiet think about it for a minute. First of all, you're quite sure you put the things in that room and nowhere else?"

"Certain sure, Mr Curtis. I can show you the empty spaces on the shelves where they was. But I've looked everywhere else, just in case. There's no sign of them anywhere. I know where I put them and they're not there now."

"And you're sure the door was locked?"

"The only time that door isn't locked is when I'm inside the room. I do it automatic like. You know that, Mr Curtis. Whenever I come out, I lock that door, just in case the kiddies, you see, might get their hands on..."

"Yes, yes, I understand. And very right and proper too.

Now, let's think. Is there anyone else, apart from you and me, who has a key to that door?"

Mrs Ross pursed her lips and looked at me with an unwinking stare.

"Yes, Mr Curtis," she said, "there probably is. But it wouldn't be right to say. What I do say is this – it's done at deader night."

"What makes you think that?"

"I've got me reasons, but it wouldn't be right to say. You mark my words, though – at deader night it's done. From where I live you can see the front door of the school and all I say is, if anyone watched at deader night, which I can't do seeing I have to be up early to get the school ready, they'd see things."

"You could be right, I suppose, but there's one big snag. We've no reason to think that whoever it is will be coming back, have we?"

"They'll be back, all right. Tuesday the crate of soap went, but I didn't tell you 'cause I wasn't certain sure that I might have left it somewhere else. Last night the mop heads and the floor polish went. There's only one thing left that anyone would want, and that's a big box full of new stuff like scouring powder and bleach and pan-scrubs and such like. You mark my words, they'll go – at deader night, tonight.

"Right, Mrs Ross. I've an idea I'm making a fool of myself and, really I should phone the police and the office, but if you don't mind, I think I might come round to your house tonight and have a go at watching. I suppose there are no signs of anyone breaking into the school are there?"

"They've no need to do any breaking in, Mr Curtis. You come round to my house tonight and I'll give you a bit of supper and you'll be able to see a treat from my side window. If I was you I'd get someone to come with you and then you can take turns.

I had already decided that I would ask John Lewisham if he fancied the idea of playing detectives and it was no great surprise that he greeted the idea with enthusiasm. He invited me round to his digs for tea and then, after a leisurely drink at the local, we reported to the house of Mrs Ross to await deader night. We were invited into a comfortable room festooned with photographs of several generations of the Ross clan, a large currant cake was placed on the table along with some bottles of beer which we had brought with us, and we were ready for business.

We were fortunate in that our observation window, whilst giving an excellent if rather distant view of the main gate and entrance to the school, was itself in a dark corner of the village street and, unless we actually pressed our noses against the glass, we would remain virtually invisible. A street lamp near the school gate was a mixed blessing, illuminating parts of the path and wall, but casting pools of dark shadow as well.

At first Mrs Ross stayed with us, recounting enthralling stories of life as seen through this particular window, but she eventually departed to listen to a favourite radio programme and then retire to bed.

"You'll see him, make no mistake," she said, "at deader night you'll see him. I'd stay up and help you watch but I've got to be up early in the morning and I'm not as young as I used to be. The door's on the latch – just pull it to when you want to go. Goodnight."

John and I sat there, speaking in whispers for some unaccountable reason, peering into the patchwork of light and shade until our eyes ached and we felt more than a little foolish. After gazing at nothing for a couple of hours we had the excitement of the five or six revellers from the Fitzmaurice Arms discussing the prospects of the football season as they made their way home. not even a cat disturbed the stillness for another half hour and then it happened.

A vast but tatty looking American Ford, like a cross between an early flying machine and a raspberry blancmange, drove slowly past our window, stopped outside the school and then reversed up a cul-de-sac which adjoined the side wall. The engine was switched off and the lights extinguished, but there was no immediate sign of movement from within.

"Do you think this qualifies for deadernight?" I asked John, who had gone to renew his enthusiasm for one of the bottles.

"No doubt about it," he said.

"Then I think the play has begun. The classic set up for the big job is being enacted before our very eyes. I shouldn't be surprised if, at this very moment, the arch criminal is telling his moll that, after this one, it's the south of France and a life of luxury. Do arch criminals have molls these days, by the way?"

"Slightly démodé I would have thought. You're right, though – I don't mean about the moll. Someone's getting out, look. Loitering with intent if ever I saw it."

Two dark figures had, indeed, emerged from the car and, after a stealthy look round, the taller and slimmer of the two remained leaning on the open driver's door. The other weaved an unsteady looking course towards the corner, which he negotiated with some difficulty, fell up the step into the playground and then tacked his way towards the main door in the manner of a sailing boat in inexpert hands. After some delay scuffling around on hands and

207

knees, presumably in search of dropped keys, the figure disappeared into the building.

"Now, I think?" I said. "Now it is," said John.

We left the house and, keeping to the shadows as much as possible, worked our way carefully up the road towards the waiting car. We were almost level with him before the reclining figure saw us and shot a good three feet into the air.

"Ohmygord!" he said.

"Good gracious, it's Mr Smith, isn't it?" I asked, "this is a surprise, seeing you here at this time of night."

"Cor, blimey. Give me a shock, you did, creepin' up sudden like that. Cor.... you've no right to go creepin' up sudden. Might 'ave given me a bleedin' 'eart attack."

"You sound almost as though you had a guilty conscience, Mr Smith. You know Mr Lewisham, don't you? We were just taking a little stroll together before going home."

"Yes, o'course. Me too. Come out for a breff of air, I did. Noffin' wrong with that, is there?"

"Nah, nah, I'm not..... what the bleedin' 'ell was that?"

The sounds which had interrupted Mr Smith's little chat came from the school and comprised, in order of appearance, a metallic crash, the sort of splashing noise which a hippopotamus might make going in off the top diving board, and a sustained, high pitched human noise which I judged to be a cursing of an exceptional high quality.

"What was that?" I asked. "I don't hear anything. Do you, Mr Lewisham?" "The plaintive notes of an owl, maybe; nothing more," agreed John.

"I'm bloody off," said Mr Smith and, jumping into his car and slamming the door, he made an exit, smoking tyres and all, that would have pleased Al Capone himself.

It was a pity that, in his anxiety to depart, he should have done so backwards. Being a cul-de-sac, the shape of his car was altered considerably against the wall before, by now thoroughly demoralised, he finally departed at zero revs in a series of slow jumps, like an elderly kangaroo, having apparently elected to start in top gear. This exit from the scene of Mr Smith coincided with the arrival on it of his fellow conspirator who was, as expected, none other than the late Head.

He was dripping water from head to toe and seemed a trifle put out. His language, which was almost visible, did not improve when it dawned on him that he was on his own. Leaving a trail of moisture behind him, he lurched off down the road like a corporation water cart.

"I have a feeling," said John, "that we may have witnessed the end of a beautiful friendship."

"Let's hope so. Come on – we'd better lock the place up. I have the feeling he might have forgotten."

We went into the school and to the caretaker's store where we removed the trip wire and the large zinc bath, by now only partially filled with water.

"It worked better than I expected," I said, "Congratulations."

"Not bad, not bad," said John with quiet pride, "the old skill has not entirely gone. There are some advantages to a boarding school education, you see. On the whole I think we may call it a good evening's work."

"Yes. Well worthwhile. What on earth the powers that be would say if they knew, I shudder to think. I'll get in touch with the office tomorrow and get them to change all the locks, but I don't think there'll be any more trouble. Come on, let's get the place shut up and I'll give you a lift home."

At breakfast next morning Peter was anxious to find out why I had not turned up until the early hours, his mind only capable of envisaging one reason. However, I was feeling the effects of the night's excitements and promised further information in the evening.

"All right then, you miserable devil", he said, "but if, as I suppose, there's anything dirty about it, you'd better censor it. Joan's coming over to make the meal tonight."

Since Peter's association with this Joan, we had become marginally more civilised in our eating habits, scarcely ever having to retrieve bits of stew from the floor or call in the fire brigade. This was largely through example as, every so often, usually on her Wednesday half-day or on a Sunday, Joan would prepare a meal for us all and very good it would be too. Her ideas of cleanliness bordered on the fanatical, but she had the happy ability to produce something interesting out of very little and without all the cursing and general shambles which were an integral part of our system.

On this occasion she had made a goulash, using up the last of the paprika, which I had bought for a memorable creation of my own a long time before.

"You know, Joan," said Peter as we were relaxing at the end of the meal, "this fellow didn't turn up until the milk arrived this morning, and he's being very cagey about it. I reckon he's found some disreputable female company out Washford way."

"I don't believe it," said Joan, "Female company maybe, but not disreputable. I do hope so, anyway. He's far too nice to be on his own all the time."

She was, as I have said, a sensible, intelligent girl.

"You make me blush," I said, "but if you gather around as soon as Pete's done the washing up I will tell you a story that will make your flesh creep. It concerns two villains of deepest dye, nefarious deeds at deadernight and the unmasking of all this lot by the gallant and handsome young hero. That's me."

And so I told them the tale, mentioning no names, and perhaps, embroidering a little here and there. There was silence for a while when I came to the end.

"What a bloody turn up," said Peter, eventually, "I know you haven't said so but I reckon the chap you're talking about used to be the Head at that school. And what's more, we've been paying him a bloody good salary for being a crook.

You ought to turn him over the police. He's a flaming menace."

Peter's original notion that Joan's ears must not be sullied by anything in the nature of impolite language had died a fairly quick death.

"I'm not so sure, you know," said Joan, "He seems to be a lonely sort of man to me. In a funny sort of way I feel sorry for him. I think he needs sympathy and understanding."

"There you are," said Peter without batting an eyelid, "what did I tell you? Sympathy and understanding. What are you going to do about it, Ken?"

"I've had a quiet word with the DEO, that's all. Officially I know nothing. I'm not all that happy about letting him get away with things, but the main thing is to have stopped him."

Joan curled up her legs on the settee. "You're right, Ken," she said, "there's no point in punishing the poor chap just for the sake of it."

"Too bloody right, there isn't," said Peter. "I'm inclined to agree with you," I said.

At school, the next event of any significance was the Harvest Festival. This followed traditional practice in being a multi-purpose exercise. With the help of carefully worded begging letters from me, the children talked their parents into donating quantities of any merchandise which could, by the use of a fertile imagination, conceivably come under the general heading of harvest. The keen ones, who wanted their children to get on, went to immense trouble to buy exotic fruits and flowers and then create from them displays of great ingenuity and beauty. Those of lesser imagination or interest bunged a cabbage, a few carrots and a tomato in a box, whilst the ones whose interests lay elsewhere rummaged in the back of the cupboard to see if there were any tins without labels they wanted to get rid of.

On the morning of the combined show-service-sale, one end of the hall was hidden under a scented, coloured mountain which, as the day wore on, gradually became an orderly display. Mrs Kennedy and Mr Lewisham worked wonders with old desks, blackboards and corrugated paper so that children, passing on their lawful occasions, could not help but pause, admire and ejaculate "Ooh!" or "Aah!"

In mid-afternoon the parents arrived and sat facing the children and the display. There was much nudging, pointing, grimacing and waving. Suitable hymns and songs were sung, some accompanied by the shrilling of massed recorders – a sound calculated to make the more musically inclined adults wince visibly. Being by now rather addicted to the sound of my own voice, I gave a short but pleasantly witty address at the end of which, to nobody's surprise, I invited the audience to step forward and buy back the stuff they had already given good money for in the shops.

After a quarter of an hour of utter chaos the children started to drift off home with their parents, leaving us with a few nondescript items to dump surreptitiously in the rubbish bins. Teachers, who had been frenziedly taking money, thrust notes and coins into my hands and departed to the staff room for refreshment. When I had said goodbye to the last mother, an anxious person who wished to analyse her son's failure to master the intricacies of long division at the age of six, I put my head round the staff room door.

"Hey," I said, "who's going to help me count this lot?"

"But Mr Brackthorne always insisted on counting it himself," said Mrs Kennedy, He used to say we had earned a sit down and a cup of tea after all the hard work we had put in."

"Good for Mr Brackthorne. I think I've worked hard, too, so come on, somebody. Come into the counting house and bring your tea with you. I don't mind a cup myself if there's one to spare."

John Lewisham and Mrs Eldon came with me and before long we had agreed that the grand total was £36.18.7.

"I reckon that's pretty good. Don't you, Mrs Eldon?" I asked. "Considering its more than four times what we've ever made before, I should jolly well think so," she replied.

"Really? I wonder why that is. Were there more parents this time or were we over-charging, or what?"

"No," said John, "no more people, no bigger prices. Just one difference." "Meaning?"

"I know what he's getting at," said Mrs Eldon, "Think who counted the takings for the past goodness knows how many years."

"Oh, Lord," I said, "not that, too. Is nothing sacred?"

"I suppose not, where making a profit is concerned," said Mrs Eldon, "you may not know it, Mr Curtis, but Mr Brackthorne was always one for making a quick buck, as I believe the Americans say. The funny thing is that, in retrospect, he doesn't seem what you would call a bad man. Not really bad, if you know what I mean. And yet he was up to all sorts of tricks, you know. One year I remember he had covers for his car seats made as a needlework project yet, somehow, one never boiled over with indignation. I suppose we were wrong, really."

"It's difficult to sit in judgement, isn't it?" I said, "I did have some idea that he had perhaps been not quite as punctilious as he might have been but who's to say I wouldn't have done the same as you if I'd been here then? As for today's takings, I suggest we get them into the bank as soon as possible and leave it at that."

"An admirable idea," said Mr Lewisham, "and then it's next stop Christmas." We agreed that there was one thing to be said for this term – nobody had time to be bored.

As things turned out life became even busier than expected. Miss Lane took to having the vapours at unpredictable intervals, which left me learning how to cope with six-year-olds by the deep-end method of being left alone with them from nine until three-thirty every day. With the forthcoming Christmas festivities much in mind, and being unable to find any suitable published material in the time available, I decided to write, compose, produce and accompany (on the recorder) a pantomime appropriate to the situation.

The story had to be, of course, Cinderella, and I reduced it to the most basic version possible without losing all semblance of meaning. The songs were simple to the point of inanity, the tunes being such as could be tackled by principles who seemed to have a range, when stretched, of about three and a half notes. Running time was anything between ten minutes and half an hour depending on how long it took to locate the performers required for any given scene, prize them away from whatever it was they were doing and re-adjust them mentally to the new situation. This was followed by a period of immobility and silence from the rest of the cast in order to give the newcomer time to locate friends in the audience and wave to them as though they were about to embark on a lengthy sea journey.

What problems Francis Laidler had with Cinderella I know not, but I'm prepared to bet they were as nothing compared with mine. For a start I wished to allocate the main parts so, while they were in their customary state of ignorance of my presence, I cast a keen eye around the class. Without exception they were toothless, unkempt and snivelling. Reason and a closer inspection showed that I might have been a little harsh in my judgement, but a quick series of auditions revealed that those who could, at a pinch, appear on the stage in any role other than Quasimodo, were tone deaf and suffered from adenoids. Eventually a selection of sorts was made and a great deal of ingenuity and deception practiced so that those left out did not go home and complain to their parents, and those chosen were not given the chance of lording it over the others. Then the next problem appeared. Not one of the elect few could be prevailed upon to speak their lines in anything other than a sort of strangulated whimper. This was all the more exasperating as their normal day-to-day conversation was carried on in a strident, high-pitched screech that shattered windows and could be heard by their fathers working underground at the pit half a mile away.

Somehow these difficulties, if not overcome, were modified until a sort of semi- continuous performance evolved. The star performer was a doll-like blonde by the name of Caroline who played the title role and she was ably supported by the two ugly sisters whose parts ere taken by a couple of bosom friends – boys, of course, in true pantomime tradition – one of whom was short and fat, the other tall and thin. Indeed the only similarity between them was the hardly perceptible speed at which their minds worked but, once having got a routine it was there for life and the were so serious about it as to be genuinely funny.

For the public performance, at which my pantomime was but a small part, we had rigged up a stage complete with curtains and lighting contrived and operated with considerable panache and peril by John Lewisham, whose special subject was science and who thought he knew about these things. The parents turned up in force to see their progeny recite, sing, act and do all the other things which, quite rightly, make up a school Christmas.

We started off with a very passable mixture of seasonal songs by the choir, and then it was my turn. I wedged myself into a corner of the wings with my recorder and the complete score, words and music, on a postcard, and we tottered gaily through the opening chorus by the peasantry. It all went so well that I should have had a premonition of reefs ahead, instead of which I was busy congratulating myself as Caroline appeared on the stage for her big solo aria. At rehearsal this had always been delivered in a thin, piping little voice that went up and down in a fair approximation of what I was doing on the recorder and was not without a certain wistful charm. Not tonight though.

There were the expected noises from the mums on seeing Caroline togged up in her finery and I played the introduction to her tune. She smiled sweetly and her mouth opened and closed in perfect time but, I was perplexed to notice, without any sort of sound coming out. She seemed to have decided that, if she made no noise at all, she could make no mistakes so her song dragged on in a complete silence. Silent, that is except for an argument going on back stage between the ladies and gentlemen of the chorus as to which foot to use first in the thing we called a dance.

"It's your left foot first," came the disembodied voice of Peasant A. "'T isn't. It's your right foot first," riposted Peasant B.

"Left" "Right" "Left" "Right"

"It's your left 'cos Mr Curtis said so."

"It's not. It's your right. Look I'll show you."

There followed a brief respite and then, triumphantly, from Peasant A, "That isn't your right, it's your left you daft......."

In some respects these mining children had quite surprising vocabularies. Meanwhile Cinderella continued simpering and silently mouthing and everyone in the audience pretended that this was just what they had come for and applauded loudly when the entire cast, with the exception of the ugly sisters, shuffled on sheepishly at the end. No one seemed to know where the ugly sisters had got to but, as no harm could come to them, I didn't' worry too much and went out front as we theatricals say, to watch the nativity play by the older juniors.

It was very well done until they reached the scene where the shepherds were crouched cross-legged around their fire on the hill overlooking Bethlehem. There they sat looking serious in a carefully composed group with their striped dressing gowns on and towels wrapped round their heads, musing on the strange events of the day when from the East entered the Angel Gabriel and simultaneously from the West, the two ugly sisters, hand in hand. Cheering up at the sight of familiar faces they were about to join them around the fire when the Angel Gabriel, an intelligent lad from the top class, seized them and led them off, murmuring as he did so in a whisper which could be heard all over the room. "Hey up, two young 'uns, come wi' me. Tha's gett'n thisens in t' wrong 'oil."

When it was all over I said my usual few words but this time with a difference for, sitting in the front row next to the vicar and smiling condescendingly, was the man who was to take over from me as the new permanent Headmaster. After saying how happy I had been amongst them, I introduced my successor who, as befitted one who wore a beard, a velvet jacket and a green bow tie, started to tell parents how everything was going to be much better now that he had come.

I crept round the back into my – his – office and had a last look round. I couldn't help it; I resented this newcomer taking over the reins of MY school, talking to MY children, haranguing MY parents. There could be no doubt, I had enjoyed being a Head and I wanted to do it again but, for that moment, it was this place and these people uppermost in my mind. I took the log book out of the drawer.

"Today, I, Kenneth John Curtis, ceased my duties as Head of this school," I wrote and, as I signed it, I added aloud, "And a Merry Christmas to us all. God Bless Us Every One."

CHAPTER EIGHT

Towards the end of the Christmas holiday I had a phone call from Mr Elsworth. "Ah, Mr Curtis," he said in his usual polite yet leaving-no-room-for argument manner, "I thought I'd better ring you about your next assignment. First of all, though, I hope you are having a good holiday and I should tell you that the D.E.O. was very pleased with the way you handled things at Washford. Yes, very pleased indeed. Now, about next term, I'm sorry we can't find you another Headship straight away, but your turn will come again. I've found something different for you, though. You will be going to Kingstree House Special School. I know you will find it most interesting."

"Kingstree House," I repeated, "That's a bit better neighbourhood than you usually find for me. I know nothing about it, though. In what way is it special?"

"Well, it's a residential place, of course, but that won't affect you. You will work normal school hours. The children are E.S.N. and of course you've had experience of them at Carlton Royd. They are also deaf."

"Deaf!" I squeaked, "I can't teach deaf people! I've never met anyone who's properly deaf. You mean they really can't hear anything at all?"

"I'm afraid that is so, Mr Curtis. Very sad. They need someone like you, a person of sympathy and understanding. I may tell you there are not many of our colleagues I would be able to send to a school like this."

"But Mr Elsworth, be reasonable. I really know nothing at all about the teaching of the deaf. What use am I going to be?"

"You are one of our most reliable and adaptable people, Mr Curtis. You will find that Mr Green, the Head, is a most helpful person – a very likeable man indeed.

You will get along fine, I am quite confident of that. He will give you all the help you need. In the meantime the card with be coming along with all the usual details. If you have any queries, give me a ring, won't you? Cheerio, for now, then, Mr Curtis and a Happy New Year to you."

I had long passed the stage when I would work myself up into a frenzy of worry and indecision at the prospect of something new or unusual, but it would be right to call my mood thoughtful on hearing this news. I had instead ideas of getting books out of the library which would not only explain to me to go about teaching the deaf but would also teach me the deaf and dumb alphabet, or whatever it is called. It didn't take long to see that one week was hardly likely to be long enough for such an exercise. Then I realised that these children would presumably be unable to speak in an intelligible way and that really did worry me. Like many people, I found it acutely embarrassing to try and cope with those who had difficulty in communicating. I had, I admitted to myself, a strong desire to pass by on the other side whenever anything in the nature of abnormality touched the fringe of my life. There was going to be no chance of that from now on.

In spite of these thoughts, it was with more interest than doubt that I travelled the three miles through lovely lower Wharfedale to the village of Kingstree on the first day of term. There had been a heavy frost and in the low sunlight the landscape was like a stage backdrop in blue and silver.

The old Wolseley purred along in its best and quietest manner and I felt happy.

Kingstree House turned out to be an imposing Georgian Manor with extensive grounds and outbuildings situate, as the estate agents say, adjacent to the river. I had vaguely noticed it many times before but assumed it to be the home of some Frontown tycoon. Indeed, the only indication that this was not so, was a small, neat board on one of the gate pillars saying simply, 'Kingstree School, West Riding of Yorkshire County Council.' I drove through into a large courtyard, parked the Wolseley and wondered which entrance to try, or whether to simply walk in or ring for the butler. I was saved the trouble of making a decision because a large door into the main building opened and out came half a dozen boys followed by a young man in flannels and a sweater.

"Hello," he said, "Can I help?"

"If you don't mind," I said, "my name is Curtis and I'm on the County Supply Staff. I'm starting teaching here this morning and I'd like to see Mr Green."

"Sure; hang on a mo' and I'll take you there."

He turned to the waiting group of boys and broke into the gesticulations of deaf and dumb speech, at the same time enunciating clearly but quietly, I am going to see Mr Green. Wait here until I come back."

The boys, who seemed to be about fourteen or fifteen years of age, nodded and started their own silent conversations. Not really silent, though, for there were noises coming from them which I supposed to be their attempts at vocal communication. It put me in mind of the story everyone tells of going into a pub in remote Wales and all the locals immediately start talking in Welsh. I had the same feeling of not understanding a word but suspecting it was all about me.

My guide introduced himself as one Barry Elder, not a teacher but a general factotum who kept the children amused or occupied when the teaching staff was not doing so. We walked along a couple of nicely carpeted corridors, tapped on a heavy panelled door and I was in the presence of the Head. There was, I had to admit, a twinge of resentment that I was not the chap behind the big desk, but Mr Green's greeting was warm enough and obviously sincere. He was a man of about my own age, middle sized and with an air of neatness which stopped short of being dapper.

"Don't worry about the teaching this morning," he said after the usual preliminaries, "either Bill Dean, the Deputy Head, or myself will put you in the picture as far as possible and then, I'm afraid, it will be a matter of throwing you to the lions this afternoon."

So most of the morning was spent in walking around the place and listening to snippets about the background of the children and being given advice which I understood perfectly at the time and forgot ten minutes later. At about ten to twelve the Head announced, to my surprise, the he thought it was time to be getting ready for luncheon.

At most of my previous schools, getting ready for school dinner had meant a quick visit to the toilet, a rinse of the hands in water which was invariably stone cold and then into the dining room to belabour the children into some sort of order. Mr Green evidently guessed the trend of my thoughts and smiled.

"We are lucky in having a quite beautiful house to live in here," he said, "so we try to keep up a semblance of gracious living whenever we can. It helps to counter the tragedies we have to live with, you know."

After washing and cleaning my fingernails with much greater care than usual I was shown to the staff dining room and was duly impressed at the standard of gracious living which had been achieved. Although the room was dark with oak panelling, a huge refectory table, and heavy, leather seated dining chairs, it was by no means gloomy, for a tall French window faced a lawn sloping down to the river and, on this January day, a crystal chandelier burned brightly. At the head of the table sat Mr Green with, opposite him, his wife, who was also the matron. In between were the teachers – Arthur Roebuck, fiftyish and in charge of woodwork and crafts; Bill Dean, bald, round and cheerful like a scholastic Pickwick; Simon Wood, young and athletic; Linda Allen, young and shapely, and myself. We were waited on by two girls from the village, dressed neatly in black, who appeared to have a multitude of duties to perform, none of them particularly onerous.

I remarked that only a few bottles of wine were needed to complete the picture and was told that even that was supplied on birthdays and special occasions – after the customary whip round, of course. With the Head carving the joint and his wife quietly instructing her two young and somewhat giggly helpers, it was as unlike any school dinner I had ever had, as was one of Peter's concoctions from anything of the same name at a reputable restaurant.

Then, inevitably, came the reminder that life was real and life was earnest.

Mr Green took me along to one of the classrooms, which had been built into the stable block and introduced me to my charges. He used the method of communication, which was general throughout the school – quiet, carefully spoken speech, accompanied by sign language.

"This is Mr Curtis," he said, "he will be your teacher now. Come here, Tony."

A boy of about nine years of age, wearing headphones

and a large black box slung on his chest came to the front with a broad smile on his pointed features.

"Now, Tony," said Mr Green, "Mr Curtis is not as clever as you. He does not understand sign language, so you will help him to talk to the others. O.K?"

He turned to me and explained that Tony had partial hearing, which meant that, with the aid of his amplifier, he would be able to understand most of what I said and could also make himself understood. Anything I could not get over to the remaining five in the class he would do for me. It seemed a somewhat tenuous link to me but, being more than I expected, I was duly grateful. Then the Head left and I was on my own. In a situation like this there aren't really many alternatives. You can run away, you can sit down and cry, or you can try to do the job you are there for, however ill prepared you may be. Having a go at the latter I found within a fairly short time that I was making some sort of contact by means of primitive drawings on the blackboard and much gesticulation. It was painfully slow but most satisfying when a small point had been made and understood.

What made it more so was the fact that I was having to overcome difficulties as well as the children. The fact that I was capable of speech and hearing was a positive disadvantage to me in a situation where nobody else could do either. I was the odd one out and had to struggle and improvise to get through to them just as they would have to do when in the outside world. It was a sobering experience. There was so much I did not know, either, in the educational sense. I hadn't the faintest idea how much they could be expected to do, or whether there was any point in trying to get them to say words, or how you could tell whether they were reading properly or, indeed, at all, when they were not able to say things aloud.

The Head did his best to sort out some of the more immediate problems when afternoon school was over, but I had to accept that I would not be able to cope with the same expertise as the properly trained teacher. There was going to be, it seemed, a fair amount of groping about in the dark and hoping for the best. At least it took my mind off the business of not being a Head any more and I began to wonder whether Mr Elsworth was a cleverer man than I had given him credit for.

The next morning there was an assembly and I thought at the end of it that I had never had a more harrowing experience in my life. The most painful part, to me, came when the Head invited everyone to join him in saying the Lord's Prayer. Above his clear speaking of the words was the mumbo-jumbo wah-wahing, the mumblings and clicking's, and the distorted, mangled sounds which, to the children, represented speech. I must have looked a bit shaken, for on the way out Bill Dean came over to me.

It's a bit unpleasant the first time, isn't it?" he said, "but don't worry. You'll get used to it."

"I'm not at all sure I want to get used to it."

"If you stay here for any length of time you'll have to. It's like being a doctor, in a way. You have to concentrate on the job without getting too emotionally involved. You'll find it will come after a week or two. We've all been through it."

He was, of course, right. Although I never lost the feeling of, I suppose, pity, yet I found after a while that I could see them as individuals and, to a large extent ignore their physical and mental disabilities and concentrate on the personal characteristics, which a teacher looks for in any normal pupil. I found that there were certain aspects of teaching these children which I had to learn if any sort of contact with them was going to be made. There was no point, for example, in bellowing at them or clapping your hands to get attention. You just switched the lights on and off a few times instead. On those occasions when another member of staff wished to discuss some matter, which was not for general publication, it was possible to do so in an ordinary tone of voice instead of slinking off into a corner and whispering. It was as well to turn away, though, for some of them were pretty smart at lip reading.

Music was the subject that surprised me most. If anyone had asked me which of all the subjects it would be pointless attempting, this would have been the one; but not so. The Head was a competent and enthusiastic pianist and he pounded merrily away whilst Mrs Allen pointed with a stick at a large coloured chart suspended from the blackboard. In response to the signs written thereon, the children walloped or shook or otherwise produced noises from a selection of percussion instruments with considerable accuracy and evident enjoyment.

"Most of 'em can't hear a thing, of course," explained the Head, "but they can feel the vibrations and it gives them some sort of satisfaction. You were saying the other day that you play the saxophone, weren't you? Bring it along sometime and we'll try something together."

As a result of this invitation, the remaining music lessons that term were spent with the children painstakingly flogging their way through the percussion chart for 'Cherry Ripe' under Miss Allen's somewhat exasperated guidance at the same time as the Head and I were performing 'Sleepy Time Down South;. The resulting cacophony, which would probably have sent any forward-thinking music buff into ecstatic raptures, was completely lost on the percussion section.

On the whole, though, this was a sober term. We had our laughs; occasionally we were near to crying; at times there were moments of anger, invariably directed at parents. Most of these were desperately keen to help, although personal contact was necessarily limited when some of them lived anything up to two hundred miles away. There were some, however, like the Great Tycoon and the Eminent Surgeon and the Famous Explorer who seemed to prefer not to know. Curiously it was mostly the ones who had a fair bit in the bank who found caring for their odd offspring something they would prefer not to be seen doing. Maybe they had the idea that hefty contributions to the school fund were an adequate substitute for affection. They may have been big people to some folk, but we reckoned nothing to them at all.

Take the Famous Explorer, for example. he had a ten year old son by the name of Charlie with us. He was one of those of whom it was difficult to say whether he was backward because of his deafness or whether he was not really as deaf as his backwardness made him appear. Everything Charlie did was hard work but he was a cheerful, if somewhat solitary, character. He had a feeling for animals and was exceptionally gentle and skilful in dealing with the ones we kept at school. In woodwork he had made, with a great deal of unobtrusive help from Arthur Roebuck, a hutch for two young rabbits, which appeared on the scene one morning. To Charlie it was a palace amongst hutches and he sandpapered it for hours to make sure there were no sharp corners and rough edges. In his quiet way he was as pleased as punch when it was finished.

Shortly after the completion of this masterpiece there was to be a parents' weekend when those willing or able to do so would descend on us to spend a few days with their offspring and see what progress, if any, they were making towards being able to take some sort of useful part in life. The Famous Explorer had intimated that he would be coming and we lost no opportunity of telling Charlie how pleased his dad would be to see the piece of work he had created. Charlie could hardly wait. He hopped up and down each morning until someone told him how many more days there were to go and he cleaned out his hutch and polished it with loving care.

Late on the Saturday of the parents' weekend, the Head rang up London to find out why the Famous Explorer had not shown up. His face was white when he came out of his office. Everyone on the staff was waiting to hear what he had to say.

"His secretary tells me that he went to Switzerland this morning for a short ski- ing holiday," he announced quietly.

"She said that he did appear to have had an entry in his diary about some sort of appointment in Yorkshire, but that it had been crossed out".

He looked at us for a moment in an uncharacteristically bewildered sort of way. "What am I going to tell Charlie?" he said.

The mild, benign, quietly spoken Mr. Dean took off his glasses and polished them carefully.

"I don't know, George, he said, "I don't know what you're going to tell Charlie, but I have no doubt you will tell him something to set his mind at rest because you've had a good deal of experience at that sort of thing. There's just one thing I would like to say, though." He replaced is spectacles and looked round at us all, "I'd like to say that I hope that bastard breaks his bloody neck."

As far as I know he didn't because people like that rarely do, and the Head must have excelled himself at telling the tale to Charlie because he showed no outward signs of distress, either then or afterwards. Shortly afterwards a proper teacher arrived and I left. In spite of the shortness of my stay I had learned a lot. In particular I had learned how under-rated in the mind of ordinary folk like you and me, is the affliction of deafness. I hadn't realised until I lived amongst them, that there were children living in a world without music or birdsong or the humming of insects on a summer's day – children who would never know what these things were, however good they became at reading about them in books; children who had never in their lives heard a nursery rhyme or a fairy story or a simple joke or a riddle. And I think I learned how to help a little, without either condescension or embarrassment.

To say that I enjoyed my period at Kingstree would be wrong, but I did find it an experience both satisfying and humbling. Whether I did any real good there I doubt. This is a highly specialised field and all I could do was hold up one end and let the proper batsmen get on scoring runs at the other. I wasn't sorry when the familiar card popped through the letter box one morning to say that life was about to return to normal; I was to report on the Monday as an ordinary assistant teacher at a very ordinary Secondary Modern School in an ordinary sort of town. I reluctantly admitted to myself that I was, after all, a very ordinary sort of person when all was said and done.

CHAPTER NINE

For some time past, I had been sifting through the advertisements in the Times Ed. every Friday in the manner of my ex-leader and eminent down-ill mountaineer, Mr Castleford, and making application for those situations which appealed to me. All I wanted was the Headship of a Junior School in a pleasant country district, not too big to be a burden, but big enough to be interesting and adequately paid. There was only one snag; every teacher in Yorkshire, a few thousand in other parts of the country, and all those Heads with small schools in nasty areas were after the same thing. As a result, I might as well have fed my applications forms to the lions in the local zoo, but I persisted and was, on one occasion, actually called for interview. This was because the school was a local one and I was known to one or two of the parish councillors who, presumably working on the principle that the devil you know is preferable to any other, supported my application.

They must have been gravely disappointed because the interview was a total disaster. Without going into details, which I find too painful to contemplate, I did everything as badly as human ingenuity could imagine. I slept very little the night before and not at all the night after and it was several days before I smiled again, and the only in a wan sort of way.

I knew I wasn't doing so badly at the schools I was sent to and I had been assured by both the DEO and Mr Elsworth at County Hall that my spell as Head at Washford, though not likely to cause much of a flutter at the Headmasters' Conference, had been highly satisfactory. Yet I had this feeling that nobody who mattered knew anything about me. Since being on the supply staff I had seen not a single HMI, Inspector, Adviser or anyone else who could, as you might say press my suit in the corridors of power. I wasn't' exactly despondent, but I couldn't help thinking, particularly on those occasions when I was at the sort of run-down, down-town establishment to which Supplies were usually sent, that I was being left behind again and there didn't seem to be a great deal I could do about it.

One morning, however, towards the end of the Easter holidays, I was shaving in that leisurely way which indicates there is no need to go rushing after buses whilst eating a bacon sandwich. It was a pleasant feeling, particularly as Peter was chasing around frenziedly preparatory to going to Newcastle upon Tyne to placate some dissatisfied customer and squeeze another order out of him. I heard him go to collect the mail, which had just arrived. There was a moment's silence, and then he called into the bathroom.

"Hey, Ken. Guess where you are going next term!"

"It's not supposed to be a guessing matter," I yelled back, "and is nothing sacred to you? Those cards are private and personal".

"Then they should put them in a bloody envelope. I can't help it if I'm so quick at assimilating the written word. In any case you know you'd tell me, so I don't know what you're grizzling about".

"I suppose you're right. Tell me the worst, then".

"You're going to like this one. Friars Chapel Junior and you're going as the boss again".

I charged out of the bathroom to look at the card myself, not having the greatest faith in Peter's reliability as a purveyor of information, but for once he was right.

I didn't need to ask about Friars Chapel. I had been through it scores of times and knew that it was an ancient village with some stone cottages, a few shops, a couple of pubs and a Norman church. The reason I had been through, rather than to, Friars Chapel, was that it was slashed through the middle by the Great North Road. Night and day there was a ceaseless stream of traffic surging North and South, only the occasional motorist pulling up to slake his thirst at the Friars Inn.

Even the garage and filling station was hidden round a corner where only those with local knowledge stopped for a few gallons and a friendly chat.

Before calling at the Divisional Education Office in Sunby for further information, I went to look round the village and decided it would suit me fine. Apart from the bit bordering the A1, which was dusty, noisy and highly dangerous, the place had charm. It was still predominantly agricultural and quite unspoiled by modern development. The school I eventually found, separated from the highway only by a narrow pavement and about ten feet of playground, with plenty of paved space round at the back facing some fields. Having been built in the late nineteenth century when the shape of the village was already well established, it was on the edge of the housing, just where the road climbed a gentle hill and ran round a curve into open country again.

The DEO, when I ran him to earth in his office in the pleasant market town of Sunby, clearly regarded my visit as a non-event. I had already discovered, in the course of my dealings with them, that DEO's tended to be either penny plain or tuppence coloured. The penny plain had worked their way through the ranks from office boys and stamp lickers and were dour and knew 'the book' from A to Z.

234

The other lot had good degrees from ancient universities, oozed charm and were adept at delegation. This one, Mr Banks by name, was a penny pain and he was gruff, bluff and knowledgeable. He gave me the distinct impression that if he never saw a Supply Head again it would be too soon.

After imparting the usual statistics about the staff and the children, he said, "Go and see Henry Jones. He's the butcher in the village and he knows everyone and he's on the school management committee. You could see the Vicar, too, if you want. Being nominally a Church school, he's the chairman, but Jones will be able to tell you a lot more. Goodbye."

Suspecting he had seen as much of me as he thought necessary, I left and went back to Friars Chapel for another look round and a sandwich at the Friars Inn where I watched the traffic going past and thought how different it must have been in the days when this was a coaching inn. Afterwards I wandered through the narrow streets behind the main road and found the establishment of Mr Jones, Purveyor of Fresh Meat, Home Made Sausages and Meat Pies. I didn't bother to call, as there was a constant trickle of customers, each of who was engaged in lengthy and animated conversation. Instead I found the school caretaker, an elderly, garrulous man who welcomed the chance to open up the building and talk about it.

Like many village schools, it had started life as a one-roomed affair looking like a miniature church, and then had been gradually added to over the years. The back looked over fields, trees and grazing cattle; the front was a maelstrom of noise and vibration, particularly from the Scotland bound lorries which had to drop a gear to surmount the slight hill only a few feet away.

"Shaking the place to bits, they are," bellowed Mr Rispin, the caretaker, into my ear. "Gets worse every year with these 'ere articled lorries. I've told 'em, you know. 'This roof will come down one of these days,' I've said. Told Mr Banks to his face. 'You want to get up a ladder and have a look for yourself,' I said to him. Aye, getting worse every day, it is. It's not safe."

"If it's so bad, why isn't someone doing something about it?" I asked

"They won't spend any money, that's why. They're supposed to be building a new school, up Cray Pasture way. They've had the plans ready for years, but they won't spend any brass. It all goes to t'town, you know. I shall never see it, but this 'ere traffic gets worse and worse. These articled lorries it is. You can feel the place shaking."

He was right, too. There was undoubtedly a tingling sensation coming from the floor in this part of the building, but knowing that all caretakers are required to take a course in Pessimism before qualifying, I was not unduly concerned. On my way from the school I looked in at Mr Jones' butchering establishment, and, finding him alone, introduced myself.

"Well then," he said seriously and eyeing me up and down as though he were weighing be up for purchase as sausage meat, "Well. You're one of these Supplies, are you?" I agreed that such was the case.

"I see. Well, then, I've no doubt I shall be coming in to see how you are getting on. It's a good school and we're keen to keep it that way. You've got some good teachers, too. There's Mrs MacDonald with the little ones. She's been doing that job for thirty years so there's not much you can teach her. Aye, and then there's Mrs Carling; she went to college with Mrs MacDonald and they've been together ever since. That just leaves Miss Thomas; she's only been here about nine years, but she's doing all right".

I said I was pleased to hear it.

"Are you a church man, then?" asked Mr Jones.

"That rather depends on what you mean. I do go to church, but not every week and its not Church of England".

"That's a pity. It's a church school, you know. The vicar doesn't have a great deal to do with it, like in interfering with things, but he's very interested, and he's very high church. Some of us don't go all the way with him there. Near enough R.C. he is, but that's the way it's always been in this village. It's because of the De Faux family, you know, though they're abroad most of the time nowadays. Anyway, you'll need to get on with t'vicar."

"I really don't see any reason why I shouldn't. I've no intentions of trying to covert him."

"I hope not. Right, then. Jack Rispin is the caretaker and he looks after the church as well."

"Yes, I've met him, thanks. He was very helpful in showing me around. Right, Mr Jones. Thank you very much for your help. I shall do my best you know, and no doubt we shall meet again."

"Aye. I shall be calling round to see how you're getting on. It's a good school, mind, and we want to keep it that way. Good afternoon then."

It hadn't been an interview notable for warmth, I thought. In fact there had been a distinct frigidity about friend Jones that I was at a loss to account for when I thought of his attitude towards customers earlier on. On the whole I supposed it must have done some good calling, even though I had heard little that I didn't already know.

When the first day of term arrived, I contrived my first meeting with the staff much better than I had done at

Washford. There was only a tiny hutch of a Headmaster's office, so I persuaded Mr Raspin to make some coffee in the staff room and then issued libations of this brew to the ladies as they arrived. It was all most decorous and formal and rather old-world, but it gave us the opportunity to eye each other cautiously and to discuss such odd things as how children from five to eleven years old were sorted out into only four classes and so on.

I was teaching the top age group more or less full time as well as being in charge, so there's not going to be much time to spare. Fortunately, the county was becoming more open handed with its allocation of clerical time and I had the services of a secretary on Monday and Friday mornings. As she was a quietly competent person, this took away all the horror of having to balance books and such like, so that all I needed to do was a cursory and unnecessary check and then sign on the dotted line.

I had a pleasant surprise, too, during the very first assembly, as several of the boys were members of the church choir and instead of grunting resentfully during the hymns, they led the singing with a rare confidence and quality. As there were only about a hundred children altogether, there was a relaxed family feeling that may sound strange to parents who feel the house is overfull with just one precocious infant, but teachers will understand. I told them who I was and said what a pleasant place they lived in and then we had the Lord's Prayer and I was half way through pronouncing the benediction when I noticed that we had been joined at the back of the hall by a pale, earnest looking person wearing a long, black clerical garment. It rather unnerved me to be leading a religious service when there was a professional in the congregation, but the feeling turned to one of real embarrassment when

I saw him bobbing his head up and down in certain places and then crossing himself when I reached the end. The thought that my words could cause this sort of reaction really worried me.

In our family we had been bought up with the basic tenets of not touching anything that didn't belong to us, being polite to everyone, showing respect to those to whom respect was due, i.e., teachers, doctors and clergymen, and kow-towing to no-one. As a good non-conformist, my conversations with the Almighty were respectfully chatty, and I found that overmuch attention to ceremonial, however impressive and beautiful got in my way. I would not for a moment have claimed that this was either the right or the only approach, but it did for me, much better than the ornate vestments and gilded ornaments which I found so difficult to reconcile with the carpenter of Nazareth. So there I was, quite contented that everyone should worship in the way they found the best for them, or not at all if they felt so inclined, apparently sparking off genuflections in a serious minded priest. I was unhappy about it.

When we met after the children departed, there was the same guarded welcome that I had received from the D.E.O., Jones the Meat, and the staff. The vicar seemed to be quietly pleasant, if humourless, person and I could imagine him being dogmatic to the point of martyrdom – or fanaticism – if pushed too far. He told me he was most interested in the school, which was a good one and they wanted it kept that way. He added that he did not interfere with the actual teaching or running of the school but would be happy to help if asked to do so. I suggested that at some time I would be most grateful if he could show the older children round his church and tell us something of its history. He said he would be delighted to do so and we parted with marginally less ice than was evident when we met.

It seemed curious, I reflected, after an uneventful first day, that practically all my experience had been in badly housed schools in neglected districts where the teachers and others were almost universally helpful and cheerful, and here I was where every prospect pleased yet the people I had met were coldly cautious. As I said to Peter that evening, I was finding it hard going to penetrate this reserve. There was no animosity, but there was no friendliness either.

"Comes from living in the country all the time," he said, "you can't expect someone who has nothing to look at all day but grass and bloody mangold wurzels to be bursting with bloody laughter, can you?"

"I don't expect them to be laughing their heads off all the time," I said, "I'd just be happy if they made me feel a bit wanted. They all look at me as though I were planning to pinch the church silver or something. I feel like little orphan Annie."

"I didn't know she pinched the church silver. No, the trouble is you're pushing 'em too much. Slow and cautious, these country people. Stop trying to ram your city charm down their throats and they'll come round. Give them time. They're well known for being a bit slow are country folk."

"Come off it, Pete. You don't need a safari to get to Friars Chapel, you know. It's only three quarters of an hour from the middle of Frontown and there's about a million vehicles a day going through it. Anyway, it'll be alright".

It was, too. I decided I liked it so much that I rang Mr Elsworth at County Hall next day from the box in the village, as we didn't have such a modern innovation in the school.

"Hello, Mr Curtis " he said. "How are things going at Friars Chapel?"

"Fine, thanks. The reception hasn't been riotous, but I'm sure it's going to be all right.

"Yes, well, that's understandable. Now, what can I do for you?"

I told him as quickly as I could, before all my small change ran out, that I was so pleased with the place that I would like to apply for the post on a permanent basis.

"The only snag is that I've a feeling the final date is very near. Can you tell me whether it will be all right if I send in an application now?"

"Hang on a minute and I'll have a look at the list. Let's see..... ah, yes, here we are.... 'Friars Chapel J.M. & I. Applications to be in by the 23rd.... that's today, isn't it? Never mind, they always allow a bit of leeway. Have you got an application form?"

I assured him that I had a collection of them and he told me to complete one and get in the post without delay. If I addressed it to him personally he would see that it reached the appropriate department. This I said I would do and we just managed the odd word of farewell before the pips went.

I walked through the old cobbled streets back to the school. Birds were singing fit to bust, the sun was warm on my back, and through the gaps between the stone cottages I could see the fresh green of the fields and the trees. I liked this place and I was determined to pull out all the stops to further my application. On calm reflection I realised that, in fact, I didn't have any stops to pull out. I was known to nobody locally and I remained, as far as I could tell, a statistic where County Hall was concerned, only Mr Elsworth and the Washford D.E.O. being able to visualise me as a more or less live human being. Nevertheless, I was going to try hard to make somebody aware of me and the first objective was obviously to do my best here and now.

It was, therefore, with an entirely unjustified feeling of guilt that I went into school and found my office occupied by Mr Banks, the D.E.O. Although it was my lunch time, I felt I had to make an excuse for not being busy making timetables or scrubbing the floor or something.

"Sorry I wasn't in," I said, "I had to phone County Hall. It wastes an awful lot of time having to walk into the middle of the village every time to use the telephone. Is there no chance of having one put in here?"

"No," said Mr Banks, who was not one for beating about the bush, "there's no point spending money when there are plans for a new school."

"I suppose not," I agreed doubtfully, "but the new school won't be finished tomorrow, will it? It does seem to me to be an antiquated notion for any school to be without a telephone. I'm thinking of a fire or accidents – that sort of thing."

"I agree with you in the general way, but justifying expense to councillors is a different matter. Remember there are scores of rural schools in this area alone, most of them without the telephone. I can't very well support one without the others. Anyway, that's by the way. I was passing so I thought I'd call and make sure everything is all right. It's been a good school this, you know. Mr Thorpe built it up to a high standard and we don't want it to go backwards again."

It seemed to me that this concern about how the school was going to manage with me at the helm verged on the paranoiac, but thought better not to say so.

"As far as I know, everything is fine," I said "I met the vicar yesterday morning and we had a pleasant chat. I've seen Mr Jones, too, and I think I've seen enough to know that the staff are competent. It seems to me that I would have to try very hard to make a mess of things here, and I've no intentions of doing that."

"I'm pleased to hear it. Is there anything you want me to mention while I'm here – apart from the telephone, which you're not going to get?"

"No, we've had the buildings section people round and they have inspected it thoroughly. Naturally, there is a lot of vibration and that has some effect. All the buildings settle and move a certain amount, but there's nothing to worry about. It'll see your time out."

With these reassurances I had to be content, and it was a fact that over the next few weeks it seemed that I had rarely been in a school that gave less cause for concern. The children were a likeable lot made up of the usual mixture, but with no really bad ones amongst them. They all showed a readiness to learn and an absence of sophistication, which made the teachers' life a real pleasure. The vicar popped in once or twice weekly invariably during morning assembly, presumably to check up that I wasn't corrupting the young of his flock with some dreadful heresies. My attitude towards his bowing and crossing gradually changed and although I was never completely at ease with it, I did have a tendency to laugh rather than cry, which was, I suppose, irreverent, but I couldn't help it.

The teachers mellowed as we came to know each other better and it wasn't long before the staff room became as cheerful a place as any I could remember. The three ladies being who and what they were, did not indulge in anything approaching ribaldry, but they could see the funny side of things and were generous friendly souls.

One day I discovered the reason for the coldness which had characterised my early days. I happened to be climbing up to the top shelf of the stock room to get some books down for Mrs Carling who turned dithery at any height that was measurably above ground level.

"Mr Greer used to sleep in here," she said.

Dismissing the idea that she was about to recite a poem of some kind I asked for some elucidation.

"Who is Mr Greer?" I said.

"He was the Head before Mr Thorpe came," she said, "he was on the Supply Staff like you. I thought you would know him."

"No, we don't often meet each other, you know. Now you mention it, I remember seeing his name in the logbook, but I didn't know he was Supply. Was he such a hard worker that he had to come in her for a nap, then?"

"Oh no, he stayed in here all night. I know I shouldn't speak wrongly of a Headmaster, but he really was a very strange man. I suppose we were all a little bit worried when we heard that we were going to have another Supply Head."

"The mists being to clear," I said as I carted the pile of books into the classroom for her, "I thought everyone seemed a bit cool. I hope you don't think we're all odd."

"Now, you know we don't, Mr Curtis, or I wouldn't be speaking to you like this. We've all been saying how much we would like you to stay here. Do you mind if I ask whether you have applied?"

I admitted that I had done so, but that past experience did not make me optimistic over the outcome.

"I do hope you are wrong Mr Curtis," said Mrs Carling, "and if there's anything we can do to help, you may be sure we will all do it."

"Now you're making me embarrassed. I haven't done anything world shattering so far, but you have no idea how

pleased I am to hear what you have just said. Thank you very much."

I turned to leave when a though suddenly struck me. "Why on earth did this Greer person spend the night in the stock room?" I asked. "I understand that he lived rather a long way away. Somewhere near Clitheroe I think it was. Anyway, he brought his camp bed and put it in the stock room and just went home on weekends. Not always then, if all the stories are true.

He used to cook his breakfast on a primus stove when he got up in time, but he would sometimes be in bed when we started to arrive at school. I believe he used to get the dinner ladies to save him things for his evening meal."

"He must have had a constitution like iron if he could eat that stuff twice a day," I said, and this was no more than the truth.

The only regular black spot on the otherwise pleasant daily routine at Friars Chapel was the school dinner. I suppose I must have had worse in the Army, but it would have been difficult to say just where. They were prepared – cooked is altogether too complimentary a word – at the kitchen some miles away on a blasted heath at some time around midnight. The constituent parts were then put into large rectangular tin containers with lids on, and several of these fitted inside a much larger container with a handle at each end and a fastener like a safe door. The theory was that this device kept the food hot. Actually what happened was that the things either arrived at our school at about eleven o'clock and were left lying around for people to fall over until the serving ladies arrived, or the van broke down and we all sat getting more and more restless until the stuff eventually appeared.

Opening the tins was a task only performed by the initiated and then at a considerable risk. It involved either kicking the handle or belting it with a serving spoon, whereupon the lid fell downwards with a crash on to your foot, and a stench of stewed cabbage emerged. Everything, whatever its shape, name or texture, tasted of tinned stewed cabbage. They said that cooks who inadvertently made meat taste of, say, meat, were sent on courses to rid them of the habit. It was, of course, stone cold as well.

This did not prevent at least half the children staying for a school meal, even though none of them would need to travel further than about a quarter of a mile to get home. This was not quite the easy process it might seem, however, because for many of them the journey included a crossing of The Road, an exploit comparable in difficulty with most of the great voyages of exploration of the past. This was also put forward as a possible explanation for a curious phenomenon, which I discovered after I had been at the school for a couple of weeks or so.

I wanted to invite all the parents to an open evening later in the term and followed the usual procedure of writing a letter which Mrs Hardy, the secretary, typed out and then duplicated on our machine, which was of the kind used by Noah during the Flood. My introduction to the art of duplicating had been with a simple affair in which the melting of a gelatinous substance had been an integral part of the process. Crude it may have been but the only mechanical contrivance being a small hand roller, there was little to go wrong. This thing at Friars Chapel was one step beyond that. The paper still had to be fed in one at a time by hand, but there was a handle to turn, pressure to apply, a highly flammable liquid to squirt and other technical things. I had tried it once and finished up wading in a sea of screwed up paper, and in an alcoholic stupor through inhaling the heady fluid, which was oozing from every shaft and gear wheel. After that I left it to Mrs Hardy who was a gentle soul and appeared to have struck up some sort of understanding with the thing.

So there I was in the staff room one lunch time, stuffing these letters into envelopes and addressing them as Mrs MacDonald called out the names from the registers.

"Tony Smith," she said, "No.... don't put Mr & Mrs Smith – its Agnes Smith, you know, she never got married."

"Right O," I said "carry on."

"Susan Wright. That's Mr & Mrs Edmondson. It's her auntie really." "This is more difficult than you would imagine, isn't it?" "Press on."

"Alfred Stimson. He's not a Stimson at all really. You'd better address it to Mrs Capstick. He lives with her most of the time."

And so it went on. There were aunties, uncles, grannies and just good friends in surprising number. So much so, that I thought it worthy of mention to Peter that evening.

Joan had gone off visiting an aged relative in the metropolis, leaving him at something of a loose end and not over cheerful about it either.

"It's an odd village in some ways," I said, "there's this business of so many of them not seeming to know who their real parents are and not caring over much either, and then when they have got a normal family they do it to excess and have seven or eight offspring. There's one lot out there, the Springetts, who are so prolific that at dinner time all I need to do is call out "that boy next to Springett!" and the whole room comes to attention. I think someone ought to do a bit of research into the place. It makes a nonsense of all the national statistics."

"You don't need a bloody expert to do that. I can tell you why it is" said Peter. "Of course you can. Why didn't I just ask you first, I wonder?"

This thought brought the stark horror of the situation home to him and I had to take him to see Wilf at the "Dog and Goose" to get over it.

The next day, being a Saturday, we had planned to take the edge off Peter's loneliness by a visit to Frontown to select a record or two. We were just boarding his car – or rather his firm's car; still a Ford but less spartan than the original one – when he suggested that it would be a change to journey a little further and do our shopping in Bankford.

"Has the phonograph reached Bankford yet?" I asked.

"Somebody was telling me there's a bloody fabulous record shop there. They've got lots of obscure Ellingtons that you can't find anywhere else. It seems worth a try. Anyway, I'm driving, so you haven't much option, have you?"

I said I was perfectly happy to be driven to Bankford, that I would enjoy browsing round this shop if it existed and that my sole purpose for that day was to make him happy. He said he should think so, after all he had done for me and so, with these and other pleasantries, the journey through the streets lined with factories and terrace houses was accomplished and we parked the car without too much difficulty.

Finding this record shop of his entailed a fair amount of questioning of innocent citizens, most of whom appeared to find difficulty in understanding our pleasant cultured accents, and then slogging up and down the steep hills around which the town is built. It turned out to be a place with a modest frontage just off one of the main shopping streets and as we found out when we entered, was deceptively large inside. There were quite a few people looking through the racks and amongst them, with an unusually serious look on her face was my old colleague from Shipham, Mrs Worth.

I went over and murmured to the back of her head, "Cheer up. It can't be as bad as all that!"

I hadn't thought these words as having any particular sinister connotation so it was with some surprise that I watched Mrs. Worth shoot six inches vertically into the air and then come to land facing me. I was relieved to see her face take on the old familiar smile.

"Oh, Mr. Curtis," she said, "I am a fool, jumping like that. I was miles away and you gave me quite a shock."

"I should think he bloody well did," said Peter, who had joined the party, "no finesse, that's his trouble. How are you, anyway?"

She assured us that, in spite of leaping about like a startled rabbit, she was not a nervous wreck and had, in fact, rarely felt better. We assured her that we had rarely felt better either, the conversation being up to this stage remarkable for its unanimity, rather than originality. We went on to explain how we happened to be in Bankford and she said she was selecting some records for the school.

"That's why I was in the clouds when you spoke to me," she said, "I was trying to think of something both suitable and different but I must be very unimaginative. I keep coming back to the same old things like Eine Kleine Nachtmusik and The Trumpet Vountary."

"Did you ever hear the story about that chap who asked the trumpeter to play a number by request?" asked Peter.

"Yes," I said.

"Well," he went on, "this chap said to this trumpeter, 'do you play the trumpet voluntary?' and he said, 'No. I get union rates the same as everyone else.'"

"First told by Joshua in front of the walls at Jericho," I explained.

"I think it was funny," said Penny politely, "and I didn't realise that Jeremiah

Clarke lived so long ago."

"Oh yes," I said, "it's not generally known that he and the Jeremiah in the Bible are one and the same. You know, the one who did all the weeping and gnashing."

"If you two are going to talk nonsense, I'm going to see what I can find in the jazz section. I wonder why they always put it in the flaming cellar?"

"All right, if you find yourself out of your depth with this intellectual conversation," I said, and Penny and I went on to chat about the ESN school and how everyone was getting on, and I told her of some of my travels since leaving Shipham and the time passed pleasantly and quickly. Peter eventually emerged from the cellar having unearthed what he claimed to be a little knowing Count Basie of about 1929. Penny looked at her watch, exclaimed that she should have been meeting a friend in a quite different part of town ten minutes previously and left with hurried farewells.

"Nice girl, that," said Peter, "she'd just do for you if she weren't married." "There's no need for sarcasm. All you need to do is use your bloody brains for a minute."

"Go on then. Don't keep me in suspense."

"Right. It's all because of the Great North Road, isn't it?"

"How do you mean, the Great North Road? Do you think it's the petrol fumes that are doing it, or were you thinking of Dick Turpin?"

"Try not to be stupid. Think what happens. Fred goes to visit his girlfriend on the other side of the road. By the time he gets across, it's too late to come back so he stays where he is. Either that or some poor wench is wandering on the wrong side of the wringing her hands and crying out because she can't get back to mummy and daddy. Friendly cottager takes pity, gives her a bed for the night, Bob's your uncle."

"You have a coarse mind, but it's an interesting theory nevertheless."

"Of course it is. An even if they do survive all the temptations of the place and manage to get married like all decent people do, there's not much to do in the evening when you've only half a village to amuse yourself in. If you're on the wrong side you can't even get to the pub for a pint."

"You have a one track mind," I said, "though to be fair, the track is a bit straighter and narrower since you met Joan. Mrs. Worth and I are colleagues with educational interests in common, that's all."

Peter used a coarse military expression and we went to find the car and return home.

On the following Monday the sun shone and I took my class out on the back playground to teach them how to play what I called non-stop cricket. Friars Chapel was a delightful place to be on such a day. Running alongside the playground wall was a rough lane leading to a farm, on which we parked our cars. Beyond this an ancient hedge, all sizes, shapes and shades of green sheltered the profusion of wild flowers growing amongst the grass up to the woods. Even the roar from the road was reduced to distant rumbling.

I explained to my class the basic rules of this game. At each end of the pitch was a post about five feet high on the top of which was a vertical piece of wood a foot or so square. The batsman used a thing like a thick overgrown table tennis bat and I bowled with a tennis ball. In contrast to my performances at the real game, I had found that I possessed some skill in throwing at this board and could even catch the ball, as often as not when it was returned to me by a fielder. When I did miss it, I could always pretend to be looking at some child and shout unnecessary instructions to him.

It was a game calling for speedy reactions and, unlike ordinary cricket; there was little time for loafing around and admiring the scenery. In the first innings the teams, of mixed boys and girls, made very meager scores, but when we started again, some of them showed that they were well on the way to mastering this thing. Michelle Brown, the daughter, as far as anyone knew, of an ex-merchant navy seaman and a lady who looked as though she could have been the village blacksmith, led the recovery. She spotted the speed and direction of each ball as soon as it left my hand and used her considerable strength to belt it all over the playground. It travelled with such force that the small number of children capable and willing to stop it wore themselves out running all over whilst the others wisely cowered out of harm's way.

Matters were getting a bit desperate when I saw a car come along the lane and pull up at the school gate. What with my eagerness to put a bit of space into the attack and my inquisitiveness to find out who was in the car, things started to go awry. Not being careful enough in looking where I was going, I tripped over the base of the stand which then fell on top of me, enveloping my head in the jacket which I had hung over it. So there I was, thrashing about on the floor in pitch-blackness trying to disentangle myself and saying things under my breath. When I eventually broke free I lay there on the playground and looked up into the faces of the DEO and Obediah Smith.

"Good Morning," I said.

"Good Morning," said Obediah, "tha' can get up."

Having scrambled to my feet and dusted myself down I grinned somewhat nervously.

"Thank you," I said, "I do seem to be behaving in odd ways when you come round don't I, Mr. Smith?"

"I see you have met," said the DEO coldly, "do you think you could spare a little of your time to show us round?"

"Of course, I'll be delighted. Would you mind waiting in my room for a couple of minutes? I'll make arrangements for my class and then I'll be with you."

After my guests had departed I appointed Sheila Lacy, a sensible girl with lots of personality, to act as umpire-cum-deputy-teacher, a procedure which was fairly normal whenever I was called away from the class. I then appealed with every confidence to their pride, integrity, honour and any other qualities I could think of, to behave in a manner befitting the occasion and threatened to clump them all if they didn't. Then I went in to do the conducted tour.

There wasn't really all that much to see. The teachers were introduced as we came to them and the children exhibited interest and acute indifference in about equal proportions. One or two who were prepared to treat Obediah as a figure of fun were quickly quelled by the murderous scowl, which I gave them from behind his back.

We arrived finally in the room nearest the main road. This was possibly the oldest part of the school and, partly because it was so incredibly noisy, partly because it was too big for an ordinary classroom, its function was confined, in the main, to that of dining hall. Being surplus to normal requirements, this gave the service ladies plenty of time to set the tables beforehand and clear away afterwards, a boon indeed. It had in its way a certain dignity, the most obvious architectural features being the arched windows and the stone projections each carrying a carved head, which supported the curved roof beams where they met the wall.

I explained to Obediah, when he remarked on the vibration, that some concern had been expressed about the safety of the building, but that I had been reassured on this point. The DEO gave me a glance that said, "Why don't you keep your big mouth shut?" as Obediah turned to ask him whether this was so.

"Yes, Alderman Smith," he said – it had never occurred to me that I ought to be calling him anything other than plain 'Mister' – "the buildings section have had men down here and submitted a full report."

"When?"

"It will be about a year ago, now." "What did it say?"

"It said that there had been some movement over the years, but that this was now negligible. There is nothing to cause concern."

"Nowt's negligible where t'kiddies are concerned. I should have it checked again right away and then have it seen to regular. Let me know what happens."

"Right, Alderman Smith" said the DEO.

"We'd better be getting on, then. I've a lot of places to see today," said Obediah, and led the procession out to the car. As the DEO walked round to unlock the driver's door, Obediah turned to me and spoke very quietly.

"You're doing all right, lad," he said, "keep trying. I reckon it won't be too long before you'll be ready for a place of your own. Good morning to you."

I went back into the school feeling ten feet tall and with an almost irresistible desire to burst into song. Passing the game which was still in progress, I patted on the head, one Steve Wilkins, a curmudgeonly youth who had been made to stand on one side for cheating, and implored him not to be so naughty. I then rang the bell for playtime ten minutes early.

It was only about a week later and I was just settling my lot down for the first period in the afternoon when there was an almighty crash and two piercing screams from the dining room. I rushed in to find the two servers white faced and trembling, and looking at the smashed remains of a trestle table.

"What on earth has happened, Mrs. Barrett?" I asked.

"Ee, Mr. Curtis, it's a mercy, that's what it is. Just to think.... ee, it's a real mercy."

"It doesn't look much like a mercy to me," I said, "what's happened, Mrs. Osman – do you know?"

"Nay, Mr. Curtis, we was washing up and I heard a bit of a noise like and I looked up and there's this thing falling from the roof and, crash! It came down on this table and look what it's done. Mr. Rispin always said as this roof would come in and now it 'as."

As I could see nothing wrong with the roof, this seemed a bit far-fetched and yet when I looked again, there did seem to be something different. I pulled aside the remains of the table and saw what it was. Leering up at me from the wreckage was one of those stone heads that had finished off, I thought attractively, the beam supports at the top of the wall. I lifted it with some difficulty, for the weight was considerable, put it on another table and inspected it closely. "Good Lord," I said, "these things aren't carved out of the wall stones at all. They're just stuck on. Cement, I suppose."

"It's a mercy, Mr. Curtis," continued Mrs. Barrett, "just think what would have happened if that had fallen half an hour earlier."

I thought, and turned as pale as my companions. At that same table had been sitting eight small children. There was little doubt that had the stone fallen when they were there, at least one of them would now be either dead or seriously injured.

"Excuse me," I said, "I'm going to ring the office straight away about this. Unless they do something today we'll make arrangements to eat in the main hall."

The journey to the telephone box was done in record time and it was just unfortunate that it was not until I was starting to dial that I realised I had no change with which to feed the thing. I rang the operator and asked her to give me a reversed charge call to the DEO's office and to speak to Mr. Banks personally. After a short silence she came back with the news that Mr. Banks could not accept a reversed charge call from Mr. Curtis.

"Tell him the school roof's fallen in," I said.

In a remarkably short time the DEO's testy voice was barking into my ear. "Now then, Mr. Curtis, what's all this, what's all this?"

I explained to him what had happened and I spelled out what might have happened.

"It is in that room where we discussed the safety of the building with Alderman Smith, if you remember," I said; just to make the position clear.

"I know, I know. I'll be over as soon as I can get hold of Jackman from the Buildings Section. Don't' go home until I get there."

They arrived within an hour; the buildings expert borrowed the caretaker's ladders to make a personal inspection and then pronounced his verdict.

"I'll have some men up this evening to remove all the rest of these things. It's a miracle they haven't fallen off years ago."

"What about the rest of the roof?" asked the DEO.

"It won't fall down yet awhile, but I'd advise you to push the starting date of the new school into next year's estimates. Even if it means putting something else back a year or two, it will have to be done. This isn't going to last for ever, you know, and we shall probably get lumps of plaster falling before long, even if the structure itself doesn't collapse.

It's a mercy that no one was hurt today."

I agreed that the phrase had occurred to me too.

By the time I arrived at school next morning there were no stone heads to be seen and there was one brand new table. It seemed the office could move quickly when the need was there.

The weeks passed without hearing anything from County Hall about the Headship, until one morning a printed letter arrived thanking me for my application (I could see no reason for their gratitude) and informing me that an appointment had been made. Although it was what I had been expecting, I couldn't help a twinge of disappointment and, I suppose, resentment too, that no credit appeared to have been given for my work during the term.

The following day, Jones the Butcher paid his first visit to the school since I had first met him in the shop. In contrast to that earlier occasion, he seemed excessively fulsome.

"I thought I'd better look in and see you," he said, "or else you'll have gone before I get the chance, and I wouldn't want that to happen."

I said that I had been rather surprised that I had not seen him before this. "Well, it's a busy life, isn't it? People in public life like you with understand what I mean. What with running a business and then all these meetings we've been having lately...."

He shuffled around in his chair, lit an obnoxious pipe with more than necessary care and generally looked embarrassed and ill at ease. As I showed no signs of breaking the silence he got up and looked out of the window, which, as it faced directly on to the outside toilets, can't have been much of an inspiration to him.

"Now then, Mr. Curtis," he went on, "it's only right that I should tell you something. Don't think because the other managers and me haven't been round to see you that we don't' know what's going on. There's not much goes on in a village that folks don't know about."

As he paused to relight his pipe, my mind was doing a rapid survey of the last few weeks to see what misdemeanors I might have committed which would warrant this approach.

"So, you see," he went on, "all of us reckon you've done a right good job here. We've been very pleased indeed... yes, very pleased we've been. If you hadn't been doing well, there would have been somebody round to see you, and no mistake. So it's only right I should tell you, we think you've done very well."

I mumbled some sort of thanks and started to feel embarrassed myself.

"Nay, there's no need to thank me. You see, we would all be right suited if you were staying on here, but it's too late for that now. Aye, it's a pity, but there it is. I'll tell you the truth of the matter. When we looked through the applications we never even gave yours a second thought and I'll tell you for why. It's because you're on this Supply Staff. We've had some funny experiences with your people and we reckoned you were all tarred wi' t'same brush. We were wrong. There, I've got it off me chest and I feel better for it. Now, before I go I want to say two things to you. T'first is to tell you again I'm sorry you're not stopping and t'second is to say that if ever you need any help with

259

references or testimonials or owt like that, you've only got to ask. Now I'll say goodbye and get back to my business and let you get on with yours."

He departed leaving me pondering on many things, not least amongst which was the difference between the speech I had just heard and the oft-quoted concept of the Supply Staff being the elite of the profession. There was no doubt that since I had joined, the number of Supplies had increased enormously and the service had attracted too many people who wanted the extra pay and also welcomed the constant changes as an opportunity for avoiding responsibility.

"Never mind," I told myself, "who cares about fiddling little places like Friars Chapel? We now have the great Obediah on our side, and he's mustard. Look out for greater things, my boy."

CHAPTER TEN

ECUMENICAL INTERLUDE

Whether it was the work of Obadiah or whether the Authority began to realise my true worth at last I don't know, but I suddenly found myself in great demand as Supply Head in schools of various shapes and sizes. I was not overwhelmed with requests to take over distinguished Grammar Schools or thousand-pupil Secondary Moderns, for which I was profoundly grateful, as my ambitions did not lie in that direction. There seemed to be, however, a number of smaller schools awaiting new Heads because the last one had either retired to an asylum, disappeared under mysterious circumstances, or shot himself. It was at these where I was required to spend a term or so attempting to straighten things out as best I could in readiness for the arrival of the new permanent boss.

In fairness, there were others where no straightening was necessary and where it was possible to relax and enjoy the company of well meaning children and cheerfully competent staff. The others were not bad schools, but they were undeniably difficult, situated for the most part in unlovely areas with high unemployment, few amenities and no sense of community.

The private advise of one of the older and more experienced of my College lectures came often to mind.

"Start off by being a bastard," he told me, "you can always relax later, but it's impossible to do it the other way round. And remember the two most important words in the teacher's vocabulary – persistency and consistency."

Peter would have found the first part of this dictum easier to follow than I did, but I managed to approximate to it where I thought necessary and things usually turned out pretty well. In doing so and in coping with new situations and meeting new people I learned a lot about my job, about life in general and about myself.

For example, the question of Church schools, of whatever denomination, was one that had so far not taxed my brain to any noticeable extent. I had been called upon to serve at a few Anglican establishments and found them unremarkable in every way and, indeed, practically indistinguishable from the ordinary county schools. The religious education programme might, it is true, include visits by the vicar, regular or spasmodic according to his enthusiasm, sense of duty and courage. Judging by the sounds of hilarity and generally clatter emanating from the room being used for religious indoctrination on these occasions I deduced that he would have been more usefully occupied looking after the needs of the deserving poor.

The rector of one parish, renowned locally for the compelling power of his sermons, confessed to me on emerging in a dishevelled state from a melee with the top year juniors, that this was the hardest work he did all week and, he suspected, ineffective to boot.

What started me thinking more deeply about the subject and, eventually, to disagree with the whole concept of church schools, was being sent as Head first to the Roman Catholic school in the small industrial town of Corborn and then, with a swift change of allegiance, to the Church of England establishment just across the road. It was a small incident at the latter, insignificant and even mildly amusing in itself, that set me going.

I was standing in the hall one morning before school when, with the maximum amount of disruption and ill-concealed delight, a posse of older boys carried in for my inspection one of their number who was leaving a trail of blood across the floor from a gash in his leg. After dismissing the ghouls who were clearly disgruntled at being thus deprived of the pleasure of examining the damage at closer quarters, I turned to the sufferer who was standing patiently oozing blood over his boots.

"Now then, John," I said, "what's happened to you?"

"I was kicked sir," he replied and, after a dramatic pause, "by a Catholic, sir."

An unremarkable story, yet it disturbed me more than a little. I was in the unique position of knowing both lots of children and knowing that, in every way but one, they were practically impossible to tell apart. Yet, here they were, growing up practically within sight of one another and already believing they were different and accepting that difference must, in the end, mean violence. The thought challenged all my beliefs in what Christianity was about.

To tell small children that there was only one way and that non-acceptance of this would leave them without hope of salvation could not, I felt, be accepted under any circumstances whether it was propounded by Catholics, Methodists, Communists, Nazis or anyone else. It all started by dividing the world into 'them' and 'us' and I decided then and there that any system, which encouraged divisiveness, would get no support from me. Not that I expected this to start any ripples in the Vatican or the Methodist Conference mind you, but I felt grateful that I had been able to see two so-called 'rival' camps from the inside and wished that others might have the same opportunity.

To go back to the beginning of this particular posting, I had known there was something peculiar afoot when I had a phone call from the County Hall instead of the usual postcard.

"Ah, Mr Curtis," said the voice of Mr Elsworth at its most urbane, "I thought I'd better have a word with you about your next school. You'll be going as head again, for two terms I would think until the new man is appointed. It's a nice school, Junior and Infants, with about 200 on roll. Have a word with the D E O about staffing and so forth. It's in Corborn; the Roman Catholic school."

"I knew there' be a catch in it," I said, "I'm not a Catholic, you know".

"Oh, no", he interrupted, "You are the Head and this is your school. You won't take assembly and you won't take R E but in every other respect you have the final word. You will have County's full support on that."

"I'm delighted to hear it," I said, "but what's all this about Sister Somebody-or- other? Do I take it I have a nun on the staff?"

"That's right. She's only just out of probation but a nice girl and very efficient. You'll like her. Well, there we are then. Any problems, just give me a ring. Goodbye."

I put the phone down and turned to Peter.

"Hey! Guess what!" I said, "I'm going to be a Catholic."

"Bloody Hell!" he said, with what I thought was a singular lack of appropriateness, "you'll need a drink."

"I think I do" I said.

Apart from the usual gurgling noises we sat in silence for a while, both considering the implications of this sudden translation into unknown realms.

"I'll tell you one thing," said Peter at last. "I thought you would. What is it?"

"You'll need to be careful. Be on your guard or Father Flat Hat'll have you in the fold."

"Not likely. I suppose by upbringing I ought to be anti-Catholic but I'm not. I'm anti-me-being Catholic though."

"Don't be so sure. You'll be there all on your own with 'em all looking at you as a damned soul in need of saving. Come to think of it, not without bloody good reason either. No, you'll have to watch out mate."

"There's a nun on the staff," I said, with a touch of awe.

"There you are; Penguins as well. Your days of freedom are numbered.

They'll be lighting candles for you and whisking you off to mass before you can say 'Hallelujah'. There's just one thing you ought to do in all fairness, though."

"What's that?"

"When you meet Father Flat Hat you ought to tell him that if he ever gets around to hearing your confessions he'll need to bring his sandwiches and a drop of something to drink. Talking of which, let's pop down to the pub to see if Wilf has any Irish stories you can tell 'em to liven up the staff room."

It was alright for him. He could go off and spice up his sales patter with a few of Wilf's dubious stories about Irishmen, but I could see I would need to tread warily.

My doubts, as usual, turned out to be groundless. I did my customary visit to the D E O followed by a recce of the school before term started and found it much like anywhere else.

There were rather more religious pictures than usual on display and each room had a crucifix and a few little painted statuettes dotted around which seemed slightly alien to me, but pretty harmless. There was, if anything, less evidence of the presence of children than I would have liked, with somewhat austere cleanliness the dominant feature until I arrived at The Head's room, which gave clear indication of having been tidied by a mechanical shovel. I remarked on this to Mr O'Leary, the caretaker, who was acting as guide.

"No, he wasn't a great one for tidiness wasn't Mr Rafferty, sir. No indeed, that he was not. Never noticed any mess, but just put things down all over the place he did. I'd go round every night regular as clockwork, just picking up all the things he'd dropped and putting them in his room here. I hadn't to put them away in cupboards or drawers though. He wouldn't have that. That he would not. A good Catholic mind you, sir – not a better in the town."

This seemed an appropriate moment for the big confession. "I'm not a Catholic, you know, Mr O'Leary," I said.

"You are not? Well, just fancy that now. Not a Catholic. A fine Catholic was Mr Rafferty and a fine man, too."

There was a pause while he gave the matter thought.

"I doubt he wasn't all that good a schoolmaster, though. A bit too high in the sky he was for most of the time. I reckon maybe a bit less holiness and a bit more making the little devils get their noses in their books would be no bad thing."

And this, to my surprise, was the attitude of all the other members of staff but one when I met them on the first morning of term. They didn't put it in quite the same way and there was unstinted praise for Mr Rafferty's personal qualities, but mention of his teaching prowess elicited knowing smiles in which even Sister Mary Joseph joined. And there was another surprise; Sister Mary Joseph was young, petite and pretty and smiled a lot – characteristics, which, I thought only, occurred to nuns in Bing Crosby movies.

The one member of staff who had no part in this cosy pre-school session was a Mr Rathbone who came in a cloud of tobacco smoke just as the bell was going for the days work to commence.

He was middle-aged, large and flabby, and sloppily dressed in a scruffy pair of flannels, roll-necked pullover and a sports coat with bulging pockets and ragged cuffs. We just had time for a hurried greeting before he blundered off to his room. He turned out to be one of the very few really unworthy members of the teaching profession I came across during my years rambling around the Riding. Always in the act of catching up and never quite making it, he also gave distressing evidence of a lack of time spent in personal hygiene. I had the feeling that we would never become great friends.

A study of his records showed that he had used a circuitous back route to gain entry into the profession. Starting life as a tailor, he augmented his income by part-time teaching at an evening school and then, when his business showed signs of going down the drain, managed to get a full-time post telling other people how to be tailors. From there he had progressed to general teaching by the manipulation of friends in High Church places and so became the pain-in-the-neck of our little place.

Nobody – even the children, whose standards of etiquette were not of an exacting nature – liked sitting near him at lunch time. Without consideration for the needs of others he would grab the largest portion, which could be, accommodated on his plate and then shovel it indiscriminately into his mouth and over anyone within spraying distance to the accompaniment of sonorous belchings and internal squirtings. Fortunately this stoking process was completed in five minutes or so when, if there was nothing to finish off on the children's plates, he would leap up, trample over everyone's feet and stalk off to his classroom. There he would lock the door, read his newspaper for a few minutes and then sink into a noisy sleep until the bell went for the afternoon session."

He was also the only bigoted member of staff with the unwavering dogmatic faith which brooks no argument and which can start revolutions. Only once was I tempted to ignore my instructions about non-interference in matters of religion when, in the course of a staff room conversation he referred to Martin Luther as "the most evil man who ever lived".

"That's a bit strong, don't you think?" I suggested. "You may not agree with him, but there have been millions who do."

"Exactly. That's why I say he's the most evil man who ever lived. It's historical fact."

"And would you teach that to the children?"

"I never mention him. If any of them asked me, of course I'd tell them. Why shouldn't I?"

I mentioned something of this to the D E O when I saw him next.

"Let it be," he said, "that's firmly under the heading of R E and not your business or mine. If it worries you, I can tell you that Arthur Bryan who'll be taking over from you as permanent Head will sort it out. He's R C of course, but a liberal minded man. He'll be in a better position that you to deal with that sort of thing."

And there I had to leave it. Otherwise we all got on well together and it seemed that my way of doing things met with general approval. There were only two children who could be classed as problems but, as always, they took up an inordinate amount of my time.

The first was a boy of 8 whom, when the mood came upon him, was a menace to other children and adults alike. On these occasions he would let fly with fists, feet, teeth and any implements coming to hand, screaming and cursing the while. If the moon was in the right quarter or whatever it was, the slightest suggestion of criticism would send him off into one of his big spectaculars so that he sometimes got away with behaviour which wouldn't be accepted from anyone else. This was grossly unfair, of course, but in the perceptive way that children have, they recognised that Paul was different and had to be treated accordingly. Even so there is a limit and some remonstrance was considered necessary when, for example, he tried to carve his name with a penknife on the boy next to him or to see what the effect would be on the girl in front by pouring polycel paste into her knickers. Then the balloon would go up and an emergency call would go out for my assistance.

In spite of our efforts the situation grew worse and I wrote a letter to his parents suggesting that we should meet to discuss further action. There was no reply. Another couple of weeks went by with further uproars and our combined stocks of applied psychology, common sense, experience and patience rapidly dwindling to zero.

Two more letters went home without reply and it became increasingly clear that sooner or later some innocent bystander was going to get seriously hurt in the blast unless we acted quickly. Not only that but Sister Mary Joseph, in whose class Paul spent most of his time, was going to have a nervous breakdown and I was nearing the stage of provocation when I was likely to do him a permanent injury. Twice I called at the house and, although no one answered, I had the feeling that I was being watched. The D E O and the county psychologist were alerted, more as a gesture than in the hope of any real help, and it was left at that, with the rest of the school continuing its unruffled way.

I had arranged a day trip to the coast; route maps were duplicated, all the usual precautions taken to reduce the possibility of children casting themselves off piers or being abducted from amusement arcades, and letters were sent to parents asking for the money for the coach fare. Sister Mary Joseph came to me the morning after these had been distributed.

"Guess what!" she said, "Paul's brought in his money for the trip!"

"I don't believe it!" I said, "after all the times I've hammered on the door and thrown stones at the windows! If you weren't here I'd be tempted to say something very rude."

"When I've gone you can say it for both of us. There's no note – no message of any kind. He just banged it on the desk. I suppose we shall have to accept it?"

"I'm afraid we shall, but the prospect of Paul undiluted on a coach and on the top of dangerous cliffs is a bit daunting. The trouble is he's quite capable of ruining the day for everyone else. How did he behave on that walk you took them on last week?"

"He ran across the road without waiting, threw stones at a cat, and when we got in the wood he broke a branch off a tree and tried to remove Jeanette Morley's head with it. He came all the way back with me holding his hand tight while he trod on my feet. I wasn't happy."

"You should have told me. Look, Sister, I'll tell you what we can do. I'll write another letter to his mother asking to see her. She won't answer it, of course, but I'll also say that we have received his money and that he can go on the trip provided there is no further trouble between now and then. How long is it? A couple of weeks? He'll never hold out that long."

We didn't hear anything even when Father O'Rourke, bullied by Sister Mary Joseph, tried to make contact at the house. The first time Paul misbehaved I dumped him in the car and sped off home with him. I needn't have bothered. Even his sterling endeavours to kick the door down brought no response and I restrained him from attempting to smash the window with a milk bottle. The letter I had written containing a final warning about the trip was pushed through the letter box and I departed under the interested gave of the neighbours.

Two days before D-Day came the final episode. A solemn looking little girl with plaits came and told me that Sister Mary Joseph would be pleased to see me in her room. Pushing aside the unworthy thoughts that sprang unbidden to my susceptible mind, I realised this could mean only one thing and set forth in some haste. Sure enough the sound of combat reached my ear before I reached the room and on entering I found the class sitting in awed silence while Paul hacked away at where Sister's shins would presumably be. He was making up for the quietness of the rest by calling her names, which I hadn't heard since my army days.

Grabbing him by the collar and the sear of his pants I lifted him as one would a Swaledale sheep and carted him along to my room. After an unpleasant half hour, having apparently exhausted his vocabulary, he sat sullenly in an easy chair while I wrote my letter to his mother making it quite clear that Paul would not go on the trip and that I would be seeking advice of the Education Psychologist. As it was now home time, I put his money in the envelope along with the letter, pushed it though the familiar letter box and left Paul in the garden to find his own way in.

Paul didn't appear at school for the next two days. At 9 o'clock the following morning the children were assembled in the school yard in their best clothes and festooned with parcels holding sufficient food and drink to support a polar expedition. Groups of parents watched admiringly as their offspring stoked up on sweets before boarding the waiting coaches and then suddenly switched their attentions to the entrance gate where a loudly protesting Paul was being towed along by a belligerent looking female. Taking this to be his mother I went over to meet them.

"Good morning Mrs Dunn," I said, "I'm pleased you've managed to find time to come and see me at last, but it's rather inconvenient this morning. We shall be leaving on the school trip in a couple of minutes so perhaps you could call again tomorrow".

"I 'aven't come to see you," the lady replied, "I've brought 'im to go on this 'ere trip."

"There must be some mistake, Mrs Dunn. I wrote to you about that. Paul isn't going on the trip."

"Oh yes, he flaming well is. You're victimising 'im, that's what you're doing. I'll get 'is dad down to sort you out. Come on, Paul, stop that now and get on the bloody bus."

Paul fortunately did nothing of the sort but tore himself free from the parental grasp and streaked off in the general direction of home. Mother, however, was only just getting into her stride. My attempts to keep the discussion private didn't seem to appeal to her. In a strident voice she called on the assembled parents, the bus drivers and any passing pedestrians to witness what a bully I was and unfit to be in charge of harmless little children. Not only was she going to enrol her husband and his friends to tear me limb from limb, but she was going straight to the Town Hall to tell them what a viper they were nursing in their bosoms and from there to Father O'Rourke to bring down the wrath of God.

Seizing on a pause for breath I decided it was time to wind up the meeting and depart as quickly as possible for the seaside.

"Mrs Dunn," I said, "this is neither the time nor the place to discuss your affairs. If you wish to report me to the Education Office you have every right to do so. I shall certainly be making my report as soon as we get back. As for telling Father O'Rourke, you can tell Father Christmas for all I care. Good Morning."

There wasn't exactly applause as I climbed in a dignified manner up the steps of the coach and got my foot stuck in the door in my hurry to close it, but I saw some knowing nods and smiles as the mothers discussed this unexpected bonus to the morning's entertainment. As we swept out on to the road Mrs Dunn was belabouring Paul who had apparently been hiding somewhere and that was the last I ever saw of them. When I called to see the D E O next morning he already knew the whole story. "Yes, Mrs Dunn came to see me," he said. "She told me that Paul would not be happy at your school and insisted on a transfer. He's going to Tom Hardwick at Overcliff."

"That won't please Tom," I said, "and it won't please Father O'Rourke either, sending him to a State school."

"I don't suppose it will, but I've a feeling Father won't say too much about it. You might give Tom a ring and let him know what he's in for."

"It'll be a pleasure," I said.

That evening I told Peter something of the Paul Dunn affair.

"It's all right feeling relieved because someone else has the bother of trying to make him into a normal human being, but the top and bottom of it is that we've failed," I said.

"Of course you've bloody failed," he said sympathetically, and I can tell you why." It's because you're so stuffed up with daft theories that you don't' go about things in the right way."

"All right, then, we'll accept that we, the so-called experts – well, professionals anyway – have made a mess of it. How would you, the non-professional, the average man as you might say...."

"I'm not an average man," Peter interrupted, "and certainly not the average man."

"Of course not. Nobody is. But just for the sake of argument, pretend that you are. Now, what would you, the pretend average man, have done in this case?" "Plastered his head against the wall."

"Can't do it. I'd be clapped into clink." "Well, what can you bloody well do?"

"We can take what action would be expected from a reasonable parent."

"Well, there you are then. I don't see the problem. My parents were reasonable an they used to bang my head against the wall, so what's wrong with that?"

"Peter, they did no such thing. You forget that I spent many happy hours at your house during our formative years playing with trains and things and never once did your mother or your dad so much as raise their voices to you."

"Naturally they wouldn't do it when you were there would they? In any case my character was formed by then. I was perfect."

"Heaven protect us from the average man," I said. "Seriously, Peter, this isn't a one-off case. Every teacher has to deal with someone like Paul at some time, and even worse, they have to deal with the parents who, in nine cases out of ten, are the cause of all the bother in the first place. And it really isn't the answer to clobber the kids however tempting that might be. They get clobbered every day at home so it's lost any sort of meaning. Send 'em to the educational trick-cyclist and all you get after a couple of months of testing and case conferences is a report telling you what you already told them in the first place, wrapped up in a mystical jargon."

"Then clump his head, and to hell with the lot of 'em."

"I sometimes think you could be right," I said.

The second big problem at the school was something quite new in my experience and centred around a pathetic five-year-old. This thin, pale, silent, waif-like little girl was presented to us on the first day of my second term by her brother Matthew who, having completed his stint at our establishment, should by rights have been reporting for duty at the local Catholic secondary modern.

Mrs Watts, the reception class teacher, having enough problems of her own, sent them along to me to sort out.

"Now then, Matt," I said, "why aren't you at your new school?"

"Cos me mum said I 'ad to bring 'er 'ere," he replied. "Me mum says she's old enough."

During these exchanges the subject of our conversation was staring blankly at a point somewhere up above my head, one fist thrust inside her mouth and the other clutching a strand of tangled hair. She wore a dress of no describable colour, which appeared to have been shortened by a blunt knife bringing the waistline somewhere just above her ankles. The same implement had apparently been used to saw off the front of her canvas shoes so that the set of blackened toes thus revealed would have had to be bent double in order to be accommodated.

"What's your name, love?" I asked.

"She won't talk," explained Matthew, "her name's Treeser". "Theresa," I wrote. "I didn't know you had a sister, Matt." "No, sir," said Matthew, "Me mum says she were a mistake." I hurried on "When is her birthday?" I asked.

"Well, she doesn't really 'ave no birthdays but me mum says she's five."

"I need to know a lot more about her than that. Look, Matthew, you'd better get off to your new school. I'll give you a note explaining why you're late and I'll write another one telling your Mum I want to see her."

So started the formal education of the saddest little child I ever came across. Questions here and there revealed that few people even knew of her existence. She had never left the house since birth, never met any other children, had never seen the doctor or the priest or, indeed anyone outside the family who treated her as the would an unwanted pet animal. She lived in the basement of the old terrace house where, it seemed, she received adequate food, was kept reasonably warm and was not ill-treated in the usual sense of the phrase. It was just that in the first five years of her life she had been deprived of all normal human contact.

The staff went out of their way to be kind to her. Appropriate clothing appeared, she was washed, her hair was combed and the caretaker's wife gave her an old doll, which had belonged to her daughter.

We presume that this struck a chord somewhere for she took it with her everywhere she went, not carrying it as a normal child would carry a doll, but dragging it along by one leg or the remnants of its hair. Gradually she dismembered it until it became little more than a shapeless torso, but still it was the last thing she left when school closed in the afternoon and the first thing she went to in the morning. Apart from this she showed not the slightest interest in anything that was happening to her and she never made a single sound of any kind, either laughter, or crying or speech.

Then, suddenly, after several weeks there came the major break-through. Sister Mary Joseph, still looking far too attractive to be anything but a film-musical nun, burst into my office at playtime one morning in a state of excitement which I felt sure would not meet with the approval of Mother Superior.

"Mr Curtis, Mr Curtis!" she panted, "Theresa's spoken! It's a miracle, Mr Curtis!" She's spoken to me!"

"When I had put her in a chair and plied her with strong liquids in the form of instant coffee and plenty of sugar, she became coherent enough to tell me the story. Once every week she took the reception class for what we called Art while Mrs Watts was elsewhere instilling the rudiments of needlework. During this cultural feast Theresa had, for the first time, actually used the painting materials provided, not, it has to be admitted, in the manner suggested by Sister Mary Joseph, but in daubing the barely recognisable remnants of her doll and, incidentally, herself and the adjacent area, a brilliant red.

Sister, gratified at this performance, had made encouraging remarks to Theresa on how nice her doll looked.

"And then," said Sister triumphantly, "she spoke to me!" "What did she say?" I asked.

"She said, "It's bleeding like bloody hell!" said sister, and she was so pleased she never even blushed.

From that moment Theresa showed a gradually increasing awareness of the people around her. Originally this took the form of aggression. In the classroom she would aim a swipe at any child who came near her, and at playtime from her customary vantage point in the school doorway she would suddenly and silently leap out, hit some unsuspecting infant over the head and then retire smartly to listen with evident enjoyment to the resulting howling. Not surprisingly this development didn't improve her position in the popularity ratings and I could see that there would be problems ahead long after my departure.

In the meantime Theresa's parents became the unwitting cause of one of the brighter moments of my reign as a semi-Roman Catholic. Once again it was Sister Mary Joseph who was involved, appearing one day towards the end of the lunch hour requesting a private audience. Her expression was troubled and she was kneading her hands together in a distraught sort of way.

"Oh, Mr Curtis," she murmured tearfully, "I have a terrible confession to make!" "Then don't you think you are in the wrong department?" I asked, "Surely it's Father O'Rourke you want to see, not me."

"Oh yes, I shall see Father later, but I want you to know what has happened first," she said and told me this story.

Returning from an expedition to the shops during her lunch break, who should she see in front of her but Mr and Mrs Connor, parents of Theresa, proceeding homewards laden with produce from the local market. Well, Mrs Connor was laden, staggering along under the weight of two carrier bags in her left hand and a bulging string bag in her right. Judging from the way she was dragging her feet and wheezing, Sister judged that the parcels were heavy. Two paces in front slouched her helpmeet, cigarette protruding from the corner of his mouth, left hand in pocket and right hand clutching a pink newspaper, which he was studying with some interest. Being a young lady of spirit as well as spirituality, she couldn't help thinking that if she were Mrs Connor she would be tempted to bean her spouse with one of the bags prior to suggesting that he should help with the cartage.

It was at this precise moment, said Sister in awe-stricken tones, that Mrs Connor swung the string bag twice round her head in the highly approved manner adopted by the boy David when slinging stones at giants, and brought it down with a dull thud on the head of her nearest and dearest. The pavement was strewn over a considerable area with potatoes, carrots, a large cabbage and Mr Connor. Sister, horrified at what she considered she had done, fled from the scene and from the earthy conversation which as accompanying the carnage.

"Oh Mr Curtis it was horrible!" she said, "and yet the most terrible thing of all is that I don't honestly feel sorry. In fact I.... well, I even enjoyed it in a sort of way. What can I do, Mr Curtis? Can you forgive me?"

"My dear Sister Mary Joseph," I said, "Speaking strictly as a non RC, I'm not qualified to say what is a coincidence and what is divine intervention. I certainly have no power to forgive what I regard as a highly successful operation, because I reckon it needs commendation, not forgiveness. Those two deserve each other. Speaking as a human being I can think of a few more parents you could go to work on if you really think you can do it every time."

I heard afterwards that she did, indeed, confess to Father O'Rourke who indicated that some sort of penance was called for. I couldn't for the life of me see why.

This Father O'Rourke paid fairly frequent visits to the school, usually at a time when some sort of refreshment

might be expected to be on offer. He was rotund, elderly and scruffy and had a quirky sense of humour, which was often used to my discomfiture as a non-believer. I had the feeling that if I reciprocated in like manner it would not be too well received. He accepted unquestioningly his right to occupy the best chair in the staff room and to be waited on hand and foot. I was assured that he was, in spite of impressions to the contrary, a kindly man who did much good work in the parish. He was also the world's worst driver, his arrival being invariably accompanied by screeches of protest from his aged Morris. On my last day at the school, his approach was heralded by the usual racket augmented by a nasty metallic scraping noise.

"Now what have you hit, Father?" I asked as he came into the staff room.

"Oh, nothing much!" he grinned, "only that old car of yours. A drop of paint will see it all right I dare say."

I sniggered politely at this typical riposte and took little notice of the unusual silence from the rest of the staff. It was only when I had tidied everything up in my office and was preparing to depart for the last time that I saw that my car was lacking a yard or so of paint down the side and that the off-side wing was distinctly non-standard shape. I was a bit peeved. During the holiday I had it repainted and repaired and sent the bill to Father O'Rourke. I didn't expect a reply so I wasn't disappointed.

CHAPTER ELEVEN

Apart from the case of the bleeding boy recounted earlier, my defection to the Church-of-England-School-Across-The-Road passed without incident. Father O'Rourke I only caught a glimpse of on three occasions when he was more-or-less in charge of his car in the Corborn traffic and concentrating on the road ahead much more conscientiously than was his wont. The Anglican vicar came to see me twice at my new place, once to say hello, and once to say goodbye. On the first occasion he admitted that he wasn't all that enthusiastic about children individually, that en masse he loathed and feared them, and that he had every intention of leaving well alone. The situation was very different from the one a couple of terms later when I was sent to yet another C of E school.

This one was in the delightful little village of Sandwick Monkton on the edge of the Vale of York and quite a change from the sub-standard industrial conglomerations where I was usually called upon to earn an honest crust. There was a wide main street with a maypole fronting a dignified Georgian hotel and, along a side lane, the church, rectory and school. It would be fair to say that every prospect pleased and, as I subsequently discovered, the bit about man being vile wasn't too far off the mark either. The Victorians had had a go at improving the Norman church and, more recently and with more success, part of the rectory grounds had been annexed for a school extension. The rectory still retained enough garden to have made a fair sized public park and the house could have accommodated most of the county's poor along with their friends and relations.

The Divisional Education Officer, an uninformative and distant sort of person, had suggested that a visit to the rector, the Rev Uppingham, might prove useful so I duly sought him out in his study. He was a broad, red-faced man in his mid-fifties with a cheerful demeanour, unlike his wife who was tall, thin, sallow and unsmiling. She was obviously highly suspicious of my motives in making friendly overtures to her dog, a repellent, rat-like creature with an ultra-sonic yap and a strong desire to make a meal off my ankles. The rector seemed disappointed that I didn't feel in need of a drink and offered to conduct me round the school. It didn't please me particularly to realise after a while that he looked upon this as his personal property and, it seemed, on me as a hired hand who would, as a matter of course, agree with everything he said. Tiring a little of his "we do this here" and "of course I stopped all that" line of conversation, I asked him whether I was right in thinking that this was a 'controlled' and not an 'Aided' school and therefore much more under the authority of the Education Department than the church.

"Yes, yes; of course you've absolutely right old boy, but that's only an arbitrary bureaucratic distinction isn't it? It's still the school of the Church and that's the way we have to regard it, don't you agree? Now let's go and have a look at the church."

He was justifiably scathing about some of the Victorian alterations and quite knowledgeable on the early history, but it was just as we were leaving that he made a remark that left me gasping.

"We're raising money to replace the organ", he said.

"It's a problem being poor, but that's the only way we an get things done, by going round with the begging bowl."

I made some inane comment about it probably being good for the soul and then asked whether the organ was beyond repair. I said that I had heard of organs being repaired and rebuilt, and suggested that this might be less expensive.

"Oh no, it's not that. It's actually in very good condition, but it came from a non-conformist chapel in Frontown some years ago and I really can't stand the thing. Every time I hear it I expect it to start playing the Hallelujah Chorus."

"Is that bad?" I asked.

"It's not proper Church music is it? No, it will have to go. And so will I. I've got a meeting shortly. Look forward to seeing you on Monday Mr Curtis. I'll pop in and see that everything's all right."

"And that's an ambiguous statement if ever I heard one," I thought to myself as I drove away. "You are going to have to tread cannily, Ken old lad."

And tread cannily I did. There were two lady members of staff who gave the impression of having taken up their duties shortly after the departure of the Romans and one young man, Rodger Metcalf, who was just a year out of college. In addition to my Headmasterly duties I was required, as usual, to teach the top class full time with the luxury of an efficient female who appeared for a few hours each week to sort out the diner money and do such other clerical duties as I hadn't time to attend to. The children, whose parents were either genuine locals or commuters into Frontown or Shilby, were a pleasant bunch with no noticeable vices and plenty of enthusiasm, features they shared with Mr Metcalfe. His consuming passion was the World of Nature and, as he had been the official ornithologist or entomologist on a few minor expeditions to remote parts, I assumed that he was also knowledgeable. The two maiden ladies had long since run out of consuming passion, if indeed they had ever had any, but were reliable and conscientious which can, at times, be less wearing.

It became evident before many days had passed that Rodger and the Rector were not in complete accord. The latter did not get excited by flora and fauna, unless it happened to be edible and he considered that too much time was being spent by the children on studying such things instead of on Maths and English. By the time he broached this matter to me it wasn't unexpected and I had assembled my facts in readiness. I pointed out that, in addition to the valuable scientific observation and reasoning required, the study of the natural world around the school involved much work in practical mathematics and description English and showed him the children's books to prove it. He conceded the point with some reluctance but continued to harass poor Rodger in other ways. It seemed that this was more of a personal vendetta than a concern over the children's education and both the Rev and Mrs Uppingham did their best to make life unpleasant for Rodger in a number of petty ways. It was only their own fault, therefore, that I did not keep them informed on the subject of the Metcalfe's Plot Project.

The builders, having completed the new extension to the school had started to turn their attention to the grounds. These, the plans showed, had to be made level and then grassed for use as playing fields and as stage one of this activity the place suddenly became alive with bulldozers and men with picks and chain saws and shovels. To the delight of the children large machines started noisily removing hills, tearing down trees and filling ditches. Rodger was not amused.

"Don't let them do it, Mr Curtis!" he implored. "They must stop it. They're ruining an important natural habitat that can never be replaced. It's murder, Mr Curtis! Don't you realise there's all-the-year-round project material there for the children. For goodness sake stop them before it's too late!"

"Calm down a bit and let's be horribly practical," I said. "First of all, I take your point and I think you're right but there's more to it than that. Most of the ground will have to be levelled like it shows on the plan, but we might be able to rescue a corner of it. After all, it's plenty big enough for both. You have a good look round, select which bit you think is the best for your purpose or to retain as a nature reserve or whatever you want to call it. Make out a case for it and I promise I'll get on to the D E O as soon as you let me have it."

"It will be on your desk first thing in the morning," said Rodger, "or these vandals will have flattened the lot."

Mentioning this to Peter that evening over a simple meal of baked beans on burned toast, he came down, as I would have expected on the side of the angels.

I don't suppose you would call me a big church man," he started. "Agreed so far. I wouldn't," I said.

"Don't interrupt when I'm giving you a bloody good service. Like I say, I'm not always in agreement with these church people, but on this occasion there's no doubt at all that this Rector or whatever you call him, is right."

"How do you come to that conclusion, then?"

"Because there's too much of this stupid bloody mucking about at school nowadays. We never did it, did we? We didn't indulge in luxuries like crawling down rabbit holes and grubbing up bugs and weeds and things. If we'd wasted our time like that we'd never have been able to learn all that useful stuff about Pythagoras and how to find square roots and things like that. Next thing you'll be wanting a flaming lake with swans...."

"Hey! Stop a minute! You've just given me an idea. I seem to think there's a bit of a beck somewhere on the edge of our land. We might be able to use that you know. It would mean diverting it on to this Metcalfe's Plot, but if that's not too difficult it could be worth thinking about. I'll have a look at that first thing in the morning.

"Hell's bells, that brings back memories! Do you remember when we dammed that stream up in Fairy Wood so that it would make a waterfall over that bit of a cliff? Took us days. Pity we hadn't paid too much attention about where it was going to go when it hit the bottom. That chap didn't seem any too pleased when the waves started rolling in through his back door."

"That's right. It was good fun doing that wasn't it?"

"Good fun! We were bloody hooligans. I tell you what; it's a nice evening, let's have a run over to Sandwick Monkton and look at this river of yours and then we can call in at that nice pub they've got there. What's it called?"

"The Tranter Arms. Good idea. But we're not sloshing about in Wellies you know. This has to be done, if I may coin a phrase, through the proper channels."

"God, you get worse. Come on, we'll use my car or we shan't be there before closing time."

I was right about there being a stream, but what I hadn't realised was that at some time in the past it had actually flowed through Metcalfe's Plot but had been diverted to make a sinuous loop through a scenic bit of the Rector's garden complete with a rotting rustic bridge in the willow pattern mode.

"All we need to do," said Peter, who had assumed control, "is to dig out where it was dammed up. You can still see the old course through those bushes. The water'll divide, half going through his garden and the other half through your bit and then it'll join up again down there. Piece of cake. You could do it in no time with half a dozen big lads with spades."

Rodger was ecstatic when he heard about the plan next morning, and was all for starting work then and there. I counselled caution however, and we made a carefully worded addition to the persuasive report he had prepared. As soon as school was over we charged over to the office in Shilby and presented our case to the D E O. I was in for another surprise. We had unwittingly touched a cord in his soul for he was, he admitted, a butterfly man himself. Before long I was forgotten as the two of them nattered away about fritillaries and swallowtails and disappearing habitats and such like technical details. During a momentary lull I managed to get in a word about the Metcalfe's Plot Project.

"Yes, yes! Excellent idea! I'll come round in the morning and have a look myself. Don't worry about the contractors; I'll see to them. Now, Mr Metcalfe, have you ever been to Italy, up in the Dolomites? No? Well, I remember...."

I made my excuses and crept away.

A week or two later, after clearing out the original channel, the dam was breached with the bribed assistance of a couple of the workmen, and water flowed again through Metcalfe's Plot. Unfortunately it didn't do much flowing through the gap into the Rector's garden and when I peered over the hedge all I could see was the old rustic bridge spanning a sinuous stretch of mud. I feared for the future.

Curiously we never heard a thing about it. Whilst admitting that neither the Rector nor his wife spent much time in the garden and particularly that part of it away from the house, they were not the kind to miss much and it couldn't really be expected that they would fail to notice that they no longer had a river. I inclined to the view that the Rev. had by-passed the normal complaints procedure and gone straight to the D E O with his story. Rumour had it that his standing wasn't all that high in that direction and it could be that he had left with a flea in his ear.

It was beyond mere rumour that the anti-Rodger campaign was stepped up, but always manifesting itself out of school and after school hours. He rented a couple of rooms from a widow with a cottage in the main street. She was a kindly soul and was grateful for the help he gave her in the garden, carting coal buckets and so forth. One evening the Rector and his wife called on him there. Would he mind if they gave him a little advice, they asked? They then proceeded to do so, purely for his own good, as they pointed out in some depth. It had come to their ears from an elderly ad respectable lady of the village that she had been subjected to a very distressing experience on the previous evening. Returning home down the village street her eyes had been attracted towards a window – a bedroom window, where the curtains had not been fully pulled together and in the full glare of the electric light she had seen Mr Metcalfe in his underwear!

"You know what village people are like," continued the Rector, "and with you being a teacher this sort of thing could get the school a bad name. We wouldn't want that, would we?"

"No, of course we wouldn't want that," said Rodger, looking straight at the sour- faced Mrs Uppingham who, he was prepared to bet, was the elderly and respectable lady referred to and who, he was prepared to wager even more, would have climbed a tree to get a better view if she had been agile enough.

A few nights later the double act appeared again at the cottage. They had just happened to notice, said the Rector, that two boys from the school had visited Mr Metcalfe earlier that evening, arriving at about 22 minutes past five and staying until twenty six minutes to seven, or thereabouts.

"That's right," said Rodger, "John Haniman and Dennis Paley. Nothing's happened to them, I hope."

"I hope not, indeed," answered the Rector, "do you mind telling us why they were here?"

"No, of course not. They are a couple of bright lads and they are very keen on some nature work we have been doing so I invited them to look at some slides of an expedition I have been on. But what is all this about?"

"Do you think it is wise to invite them here?" asked the Rector evasively.

"As they are eager to learn, yes, I think it was very wise," said Rodger who was beginning to lose his temper at the inquisition.

"That's as maybe, but you know what people are like in the village. They might put the wrong interpretation on such visits and that would not be a good thing for the school or for yourself, would it?"

Rodger told me that when eventually the penny dropped and he realised what they were getting at he was almost sick over the two of them. He then invited them to leave and suggested that if they ever called on him again he would take pleasure in slinging them both in the village pond.

Unpleasant as they were, there was little I could do about these incidents except give my unstinted support to Rodger and all his works whenever his name cropped up in conversation with either of the Uppinghams. Then, one day towards the end of my appointment at the school, Rodger informed me that he was entertaining a young and attractive female visitor on the Saturday and expected some sort of demonstration from the Village Watch Committee.

"Hang on a minute, Rodger," I said, "this sounds as though it could be a situation with distinct possibilities. I can't tell you what to do, of course, but it might be worth while thinking about it for a minute or two."

We did so and I heard no more about it until, early on Monday morning, we had a visit from the holy duo, looking smug, and the D E O looking tight-lipped.

"This is important," he said peremptorily, "Make arrangements for your class and Mr Metcalf's and then I would like to see you both in your office please."

"Now, Mr Metcalfe," he said when we were assembled, "I have just had a serious complaint laid against you by the Rev. Uppingham. It concerns a matter, which occurred out of school premises and out of school time so, strictly speaking, it is not my concern. Nevertheless, as you are a teacher at a small village school with connections with the church, and as you also live in the same village, I believe I am justified in expecting certain moral standards. Furthermore, in connection with this incident, I am told that you were, er.. insolent, is the word I was given... to Mrs Uppingham and later to the Rector who, as you well know, is the chairman of the School Governors. I have heard their story. I would now like to hear yours."

Rodger cleared his throat. "Yes, sir," he said "I assume you are alluding to the visitor who came to see me this weekend?"

The D E O nodded impatiently.

"Well, sir, this young lady called here by prior arrangement, arriving on the 10.30 am bus from Frontown. We had a drink and a sandwich at the Tranter Arms where we chatted with several local inhabitants of my acquaintance. As the young lady had not been in the neighbourhood before, I then took her for a walk round the places of interest. Do you wish to know where we went, sir?"

"No, I do not," snarled the D E O, "just get on with it."

I managed to give Rodger a warning scowl. I thought he was rather overdoing his imitation of PC Plod giving evidence in court.

"Right, sir. We returned to my rooms in Mrs Bland's cottage where we prepared an evening meal together. After that we sat and talked until I had a telephone call at approximately 10.27pm. it was from Mrs Uppingham. She said she was aware that a young lady had been with me all day. I said she was correct. She then asked me whether I thought it was time the young lady should be leaving. I replied that I did not think so at all. Mrs Uppingham then asked me when I intended the young lady to leave. I replied as far as I could tell at the moment it would be by the 3.20 bus on the following, to wit, Sunday."

The D E O had stopped growling and eating his pen and was beginning to look at Rodger with new interest.

"Then what happened?" he asked quietly.

"The Rector came on the phone, sir. He asked whether Mrs Uppingham had heard correctly. Did I intend the young lady to stay the night with me at Mrs Bland's cottage? I said that she had heard correctly, and I might have added a phrase indicating that I considered it to be none of her business. The Rector then said that I would hear more about the matter and that he would be reporting it to the highest authority. I took that to mean you, sir, and not the Almighty. I believe the exact phrase I used to the rector was that he could please his bloody self. It was perhaps less polite than it might have been.

The D E O looked at him pensively for a moment and then asked him quietly, "Mr Metcalfe; do you mind telling me the identity of this young lady?"

"Not at all, sir," said Rodger, "I'm surprised nobody has asked me before. It was my sister."

"Thank you, Mr Metcalfe," said the D E O, "there's nothing further to be said." Without a word to the rest of the company he picked up his brief case and went.

We must get back to the children, Mr Metcalfe" I said before there was time for any recriminations and that was more or less the last time I had anything to do with the regrettable Uppinghams.

There was just one thing I would have liked to happen before I left. I would have liked one of my talented musical friends to sneak into the church some warm night when the rectory bedroom windows were open and all was peaceful and quiet. Then, at about 2am I would have liked him to stoke up that non-conformist chapel organ to it's maximum output and, with all stops out, roar into the Hallelujah Chorus.

A pity all my talented musical friends are so law abiding.

CHAPTER TWELVE

As far as discussing my affairs were concerned, Peter became even more useless as time went on. Having decided that Joan was to be his soul mate, he discarded his old life in the manner of a lizard sloughing it skin, and then rushed headlong into matrimony with typical panache. The engagement ring had to be the biggest and rarest piece of jewellery outside the Tower of London, and the party to celebrate its presentation was based on Hollywood's most expansive period. After these necessary frivolities, there had been the serious business of persuading a reluctant Building Society that, in spite of stories to the contrary, he was a good risk and was actually doing them a favour by offering them the chance to lend him money. In the matter of selecting a house on which to spend the Society's gold, there was some divergence of opinion between what Peter could afford and what Peter thought appropriate to his prospects in life. Joan became quite skilful in steering him away from moated granges and what the agents called 'gentlemen's residences'.

In view of all this activity he evinced no wild enthusiasm when I told him I was to return to Shipham, but this time as Head of a Junior School.

"Bloody good show" he said, "they couldn't make a better choice. Joan went to see a super place today. Not quite in the same class as that haunted manor with fifteen acres that I told you about, but a fabulous place just the same. Two-bedroom bungalow, just a mile or two from here in Rookhope. Fabulous garden with three rose bushes and some big sort of purple things. Where did you say you were going?"

I was very patient and resisted the temptation to clump his head with something heavy.

"Shipham", I said.

A flicker of interest passed over his face.

"That's where you were at the dotty school, isn't it? There was a nice girl taught there, name of Pansy or something. Don't look so gormless you silly devil, you know very well whom I'm talking about. She came here for tea one day and then we saw her in that music shop in Bankford."

"Yes, I remember her very well, as a matter of fact. Her name was Penny." "That's right. That's what I said. You'll probably come across her again. I seem to remember that you were a bit keen on her, but you let some little thing stand in your way, apart from that daft anti-girl-friend attitude that you put on, I mean. What was it, now? It seems that you behaved very commendably for once," he concluded, suddenly recalling his future commitments.

"Nonsense. If anyone was keen, it was you with that nasty lascivious mind you seem to have forgotten you once had. Anyway, there are loads of schools in Shipham, even assuming she is still in the neighbourhood. It's a long time ago. The probability is that she's raising a family of her own in New York or London or some such foreign part."

I was wrong, though. As usual I went to chat up the local Divisional Education Officer before taking over. His name, James Jamieson, had a familiar ring and there was immediate mutual recognition when I was ushered into his office. In the far-off days when I had been going my uncomplicated way at the school from which I had been transferred on to the Supply Staff, Jim Jamieson had been a minor clerk at the local office and our paths had crossed fairly frequently. Now here he was, looking larger and more prosperous and very important but still, I was pleased to see, the same cheerful down-to- earth character I remembered.

"Hello, Ken" he smiled; I've been wondering whether it was you ever since I heard from County. It's good to see you after all these years. Sit down and we'll have a cup of coffee."

We chatted for some time about the old days with a sort of semi-formal friendliness and then came the business of the school.

"There's no point beating about the bush," said the D.E.O., "Bentown School is in the worst area in Shipham. Practically the whole intake comes from one estate and, although the housing people tell me they don't put problem families there as a matter of policy, nobody else will accept a house there, so it comes to the same thing."

I asked what sort of problems he was talking about.

"The lot. Broken homes, low I.Q.'s, truancy, father in the nick.... you name it. There are some good families, of course, and some very worthy people, but it wouldn't be fair to you to pretend they were the majority."

"What about the staff?" I asked.

"A pretty good lot – mixture of experience with some very keen younger ones. Your deputy is Stan Evens. He wanted the Headship but I wasn't too sure. Anyway, you'll see for yourself and make your own mind up whether he has more about him than it seems. Then there's Mrs MacDonald and Miss Metcalf. They have been taking the younger ones and I think it's probably what they're best at. Mrs Worth and Mr Green were both appointed last year and then there's Mrs Hawthorne who's been there longer than anyone.'

"This Mrs Worth – would it be the same one who was at Carlton Royd a year or two back?"

"Yes, that's right. A very useful person is Mrs Worth, though she'd be the last person to let anyone know, or even to think so herself. She's a music expert, you know, and that's her main role at Bentown. She does some remedial work, but it's the music that's really outstanding. I went to their Christmas concert last year and I really don't think I've ever heard children sing so well. Quite something."

When I left some time later it was with the feeling that if I did my job properly, I had not only an ally but a friend, in high places. I knew, too, that this would not mean favouritism in any shape or form and I much preferred it that way.

My next call was to the school. It was slap in the middle of this housing estate, which was itself cut in two by the main road, the railway and canal, running parallel with each other along the valley floor. A walk round the streets was not encouraging. There was the odd house which looked cared for, but by and large it was scruffy with smashed windows, peeling paint, and gardens of untended grass, weeds, derelict bicycles, prams and old iron. There were some pre-council estate buildings on the main road; pubs, shops, a blackened Victorian church and the school, a pretentious, asymmetrical edifice with the date 1870 over the door. It formed the meat in the sandwich of the road on one side and the canal on the other with the railway just beyond that. It wasn't exactly a restful place. The front playground was minute so that the traffic rattled past with the same mind-clogging effect as at Crickley Main Road Boys Secondary and Friars Chapel Junior.

Except in the front classroom the noise wasn't quite so bad once inside. It was in some ways an interesting building, showing signs of having been added to on several occasions during its lifetime by people who had no intentions of being inhibited by what had gone before. My office and the store room had originally been the bedrooms of the school house, the living room now serving as the staffroom. Apart from this it was a single storey construction but, because of the slope of the land from the road down to the canal, on several different levels with the staircases in unlikely places.

I liked it and I told Peter so that evening. He didn't show any great excitement until I mentioned that Mrs Worth was on the staff.

"I bloody told you, didn't I?" he asked, "I knew you'd come across Brenda Worth again as soon as you told me where you were going. Kismet – that's what it is."

"Kismet my foot," I said, "it's a coincidence, that's all, and of no great significance anyway. Mind you, I must admit it surprised me when Jimmy told me she was a music expert. Fancy me not knowing that."

"It all goes to show what a flaming ninny you are. How you can work with someone for months, practically side-by-side, without finding out all their likes and dislikes I really don't know. I knew all about Joan after three weeks."

"She knew all about you in ten minutes. Now stop talking rubbish and give me your share of the fish and chip money. I'll go and get something to eat. I know that the idea of such a gross thing as food appals you at the moment, but before you get back on to cloud nine, get the vinegar out and cut a couple of slices of bread."

The next morning when I arrived at school, I was so anxious to avoid any suggestion of favouritism that I introduced myself to everyone else before going in search of Mrs Worth. She had, unusually I gathered, gone straight to the music room instead of calling in at the staff room first and it was there that I eventually found her. She was messing around with some recorders when I popped my head round the door and she hadn't changed a bit. Wearing a bright blue dress and a matching headband in her brown hair she looked just as slim and fresh as I had imagined.

"Good morning, Mrs Worth," I said, "surprise, surprise!"

She looked up from the table and gave me the same attractive, shy little smile. "Hello Mr Curtis," she said, "It's nice to see you."

"And nice to see you, too. I was really surprised when I heard you were here. Pleased, too. It's a funny thing, you know, but Peter said I'd meet you. You remember Peter?"

"Of course. How is he?"

"Fine, fine. Sends his regards and all that. There's another funny thing, too. I never knew you were a music expert."

"I don't know who told you that, but I'm no expert. I love music and I enjoy teaching it, but that's a different thing altogether. I seem to remember that you're a musician."

"That's another exaggeration. I enjoy it, too, and if you have no great objection I'd like to sit around when you have the choir and the orchestra." "Of course I've no objections. I'll be glad of your help."

"Yes, well, must be off I suppose. There seem to be a few things need doing. See you later then."

"Yes, see you later."

It was not, even by my standards, brilliant conversation. Some years had passed since we last met and even then, although friendly, we had never been on confidence exchanging terms – witness my ignorance as to her musical interests. Now we had met again but under different circumstances and, although I had no illusions about being the big boss, I could see that it was going to make any resumption of our 'all pals together' attitude a little difficult. In so many little ways, I realised, our minds worked on the same wavelength. Like me, she had an ingrained respect for authority, however minor and however little deserved, and this was going to mean a certain amount of formality in our relationship, which had not been there before.

This saddened me and, for a moment, made me resentful. Then reason told me that we had never been on any more than friendly terms, that this was all I ever wished it to be, and that now I could get on with the task of running the school.

It soon became apparent that, as so often on previous occasions, the picture of masses of undisciplined hooligans tearing the place apart was grossly exaggerated. Many of the children, it was true, gave little evidence of processing more than an irreducible minimum of brain power, and their speech, not dialect but sloppy 'towny talk', would have been incomprehensible to anyone not already attuned. Because of their experience of life, many were lacking in confidence and security and needed constant reassurance. Yet, when it all boiled down, they were children like any others. Anyone who could not enjoy their company had no right to be in the teaching profession to start with.

I found that there was a small but enthusiastic parents' association, the twenty or so members of which were eager to organise social events and to raise money for which they pressed me to find a worth cause. We seemed to have all the usual things which were, at that time, regarded as desirable extras in a Junior school, like tape recorders, a typewriter and so on, so I cast around for something more exotic. A cooker I had already persuaded the D.E.O. to hire for us from the electricity board and it was due any day. I stood in the hall, looking out of the back window on to the canal, and then I had my brainwave. We would have a boat!

It was possible to, and the children frequently did, chuck stones into the canal from the playground. It was navigable as far as the Mersey in one direction and the Humber in the other. Particularly to the west towards, across and through the Pennines, there was pleasant, sometimes spectacular scenery and plenty of open spaces ideal for camping. A boat would enable our estate-bound children to explore a new environment, to learn to live together, to accept a challenge, to become self-reliant. Standing there in the hall I was quite carried away with the idea and could see no arguments against such a scheme, which were worth considering. Local firms, I felt sure, would chip in with donations if the case were presented to them properly, and I was equally confident that personal enquiries and maybe some letters to the press would bring a suitable craft to light.

In the next few days I carefully documented my case and presented it, with some trepidation, to the next P.T.A. committee meeting. Not only they, but the staff to whom I had broached the idea previously, were unanimously enthusiastic. It was agreed that the teachers would start making enquiries about a boat. The terms of reference were simple enough – as big as possible and as cheap as possible.

In the meantime, the everyday running of the school had to be attended to and I was delighted that everybody, from the lady who dished out the dinners to the deputy Head, was so competent and so helpful that the thing went like clockwork. There were the occasional spanners in the works, of course, such as the time when I had cause to remonstrate rather forcibly with one Roger Grainger. He was a large boy for eleven, with a tendency for redistributing other people's property. After a series of incidents concerning missing toys and small amounts of cash in which his involvement was suspected, he was caught red-handed one day helping himself to money from the purse of a small girl in the first year. The error of his ways was pointed out to him and he was told that a letter would be written, inviting his father to call at school and discuss his son's future. He looked belligerent as he left my room, but went back to his class quietly enough. At twelve o'clock, three excited girls came to tell me that they had been looking across the canal to the railway and seen Grainger and three other boys climbing on to a train. Not being given to logical thought, it was difficult getting any sort of coherent story out of them.

"Are you sure it was Roger Grainger you saw?" I asked the chief speaker, one Rosy Dent by name.

"Ooh yes, sir, because that coloured thing sir. It's red, isn't it Dolores?" she appealed to a skinny girl who was having difficulty unstacking her teeth from some revolting toffee like substance. We all waited anxiously for her pronouncement.

"Ay," she said at last.

"There, sir", said Rosy proudly, her word placed beyond doubt.

Dolores (pronounced to rhyme with 'applause') returned to poking around inside her mouth with her fingers.

"Yes, but what is this red thing and what has it to do with Grainger?" I asked. "It's that bag thing 'e 'as. And Jackie Sidebottom and Gary Whatever 'is name is an' that daft lad from Missawthorn's class."

"They were with him, were they? Did they get on the train too?" "Ay, Dolores ses to me, 'Hey," she ses, 'that's that daft lad from...'"

"Yes, yes, alright, Rosy. Now tell me how they were able to get on a train." "They sort of put one foot up like this, sir, an' then..."

"I don't really mean that, Rosy. I mean, was the train going slowly and what kind of a train was it? You tell me, Crystal."

Crystal, who had been simpering quietly to herself during these verbal exchanges pulled herself together and prepared to bend her mind to the problem.

"Well, it were one o' them funny trains – sorter round like, wa'n't it, Rosy?" she said.

"Never mind Rosy for a minute. What do you mean by a sort of round train?" "Well, it's sorter long and round an' it 'as steps up."

"It says 'Shell' on the side," said Dolores, who had succeeded in stuffing whatever delicacy she had in her mouth into one cheek, giving her the appearance of an asymmetrical hamster.

"Oh, I see. You mean it was a tanker?"

"Ay, I suppose so," said Dolores doubtfully.

"They climb up that ladder at the back. I saw 'em," said Rosy, anxious at seeing her role as chief narrator slipping away.

"So it was going slowly, was it?"

"Nay, it wa'n't goin' at all. It 'ad stopped at them signal things. Then, when they'd got on, it started again."

"Right. Thank you very much, girls. I'm pleased you came to tell me this. Now run along and play and I'll see to it."

By now my imagination was, as usual, working overtime and I could see a picture in my mind's eye of a train roaring into a tunnel and children being swept off like flies. For the next half hour the telephone was red hot.

I told the police. I told the people at Shipham station and I told the welfare officer to tell the boys' parents. Then I rang up the D.E.O. and told them what I had told everybody and, rejecting the idea of chasing the train in the Wolseley, I sat and waited. After about half an hour the phone rang. It was the railway people.

"The train you were talking about is a through tanker to Heysham," said the man. "It didn't have a stop at Shipham, but they always go through slowly. Nobody here saw anything unusual and neither did the chap in the signal box, but I'll have it stopped, just in case. I'll let you know as soon as I hear anything."

There were calls from the police who had patrolled the area slowly, and the welfare officer who had called at the homes without seeing any signs of the miscreants. Then the railway man came on again.

"We stopped the train three miles the other side of Crossleigh and had it searched," he said, "but there was no one there. Wherever they are, you can take it they're not on the train now."

I thanked him profusely and wondered what to do next. Commonsense eventually won and, after leaving my phone number with all sorts of people, I went home and sat by the telephone biting my fingernails. Round about ten o'clock I had a call from the police. The boys had been picked up, tired and hungry in Crossleigh, a small town ten miles away. They had jumped down from the train as it slowed near Shipham station, having travelled only about half a mile. Grainger had apparently persuaded his three weak-minded accomplices that he was leading them to London where they would be free of parental and educational tyranny. They set off walking in the wrong direction, arriving in Crossleigh some three hours later with blistered feet and, in the hearts of three of them, a growing conviction that Grainger was not the dashing hero he had appeared in the past. They had the sense not to break into a sweet shop as he suggested and eventually the daft lad from Missawthorne's class showed that he wasn't so daft after all by going up to a policeman and telling him he wanted to go home.

A week or two later the police and social services people called to see me about an entirely different matter and the same afternoon friend Grainger disappeared from amongst us. It was a regrettable fact that nobody, not even one of his pals, was sorry to see him go, for he had reached the stage where his personal problems had become less important than the effect he was having on others. He came to see me once or twice on his days off from the residential establishment whence he had been sent, apparently under the impression that we were old pals. I showed interest, but it would have been hypocritical to do more. There were still plenty of children in need of help and attention and they had to be my first concern. There were, of course, moments, too of real pleasure when it was possible to forget for a while the seamier side of life.

I was beginning to look forward to those sessions with the choir and what we call the orchestra – actually recorders and percussion, augmented by a tall, thin lad whose father was teaching him the trombone. There isn't all that much music written for descant and treble recorders, triangles, drums, glockenspiel, chime bars and trombone, so Mrs Worth and I had fun writing out our own arrangements.

She was not only a very fair pianist and knowledgeable theoretically, but she also had the sort of delightfully unforced soprano voice which I could listen to indefinitely. In addition she had the rare ability to be able to pass on her own quietly intense love of music to the children so that they sang with a smile and the sound was a joy to hear.

My contribution was to pipe in with the recorder, at which I was becoming quite adept, or beat a drum when anything tricky was required in the rhythm department. Apart from being very jolly, I convinced myself that it was all educationally sound.

Meanwhile the search for a suitable canal boat proved to be more difficult than I had imagined. Anything of the cabin cruiser type was priced out of our reach and, in any case, most of them were too small for our purpose. Then, wandering around the boatyard area of Frontown one evening, I saw it. It was about the size of the Q.E.2 and was moored against the dockside bearing a notice advising interested parties to see the dock keeper about its selling price etc. It had about it an unfinished look, which suggested to me that it might not be all that expensive.

There was no mistaking the lock keeper's cottage. Situated as it was, in the very centre of a busy city, immediately behind a main line railway station, it was the only dwelling place within shouting distance. Hampered by a network of waterways and railways, the developers had left this area to the boatyards and a few crumbling buildings used as stables and storage space by businessmen of the rag and bone type. It was by no stretch of the imagination beautiful, but you could walk round without being knocked over by traffic, there were two interesting locks and a gracefully arched bridge with that attractive ninety degree turn on to the towpath which is characteristic of some canal bridges.

Standing on this, I looked down on to the cottage, stone built and with shining black and white paint work to match the lock gates, and a garden in tubs and boxes and barrels which was a riot of colour. Standing by the open door was a small, ancient man wearing a collarless white shirt and navy blue waistcoat and trousers. He was puffing in a contemplative way at a short, stumpy pipe. I descended the stairs to the towpath and approached the cottage.

"Good evening," I said, "This is a surprising place to find in the middle of Frontown!"

"Aye," he said, inspecting me carefully, "It's not so bad. It were better when it were busy, though. It were hard work but you didn't get no vandals in them days."

"Yes, you're very much on your own down here, aren't you? Do you get much bother?"

"Youngsters mostly, but the bobbies are very good. They always pop round here and see there's nowt wrong. I saw you looking at old Ada Simpkins just now. Are you thinking of buying her then?"

"Ada Simpkins? Who's.... Oh, I see what you mean. I thought it was called Cressida."

"She was Ada Simpkins for years when she were working between here and Liverpool but this chap 'at bought here gave her this little foreign name instead. Ay, she's an old Leeds Liverpool boat – biggest you can get on this canal."

"Really? Well, I am interested in a way." I said, and went on to tell him about the school and why we wanted a boat.

"That's a right good idea. Whether Ada Simpkins is the boat you want is a different thing. She's a bit of a handful through the locks for anyone who's not used to it.

This chap as bought her, 'e's spent a lot of time and a lot of brass on doing her up. Been at it for a year or more and she's still only half finished, but he's got fed up or summat and now he wants to sell her. Hold on a minute and I'll get the keys and we'll go and have a look round."

Once on board I was even more impressed by the sheer size of the thing, particularly when holding the huge lump of timber which was the tiller and looking for'ard to what would normally be the sharp end but which was, on Cressida, only slightly less than square. A professional looking superstructure had been built on, with windows along the sides and leaving just a small deck space fore and aft. In the centre was a hatchway opening on to the stairs, which led down to a corridor. Towards the stern this gave access via folding doors to bedrooms, a bathroom and a kitchen, all in a partially finished state. Forwards, the corridor led straight into a big lounge the full width of the vessel. Through the clutter of paint pots and boxes of nails and empty milk bottles I could see this as a luxury cruiser par excellence. Not only that, I could see it developing as a project for the children – finishing the woodwork, painting, making furnishings and so on.

I went aloft again and gazed round with misty eyes and visions of tall sailing ships and tropical islands and me as Captain Hornblower. Then, suddenly, I had a horrible thought. I turned to the lock keeper.

"What makes it go?" I asked. "Pardon?" he said.

"What makes it go? Do you row it or pull it with a horse or jump in the water and push it, or what?"

"Oh, I see. Nay – there's that arrangement over the stern. He puts an outboard motor on that. He reckons he wants extra for the motor."

I realised that my dreams had got in the way of asking about such mundane things as prices.

"What is he asking for it?" I asked.

The little man spat carefully into the canal.

"A lot more nor it's worth," he said. "Five hundred pounds he told me. I'll not deny he's put some good timber into her, but she's not finished and it's what she's worth to other folk that matters."

"And what do you think she's worth?"

"Nay, I can't really say that, can I? If I were offering, it'd be a lot less than half, but that's up to you. She's only costing him money in mooring fees now, and he's getting no pleasure out of her. I reckon anyone'd be doing a favour to take her off 'is hands."

I reported back to my colleagues and one evening the following week a deputation consisting of Stan Evens, Arthur Green, Joan Metcalfe, Penny Worth and myself went to inspect Cressida. All were impressed, Stan cautiously, Penny and myself enthusiastically, Arthur and Joan all for leaving a deposit and pulling the thing back to Shipham there and then. All this was duly told to the parents' committee and I was instructed to open negotiations with the owner and, at the same time, find out about insurance, arrange for an independent inspection, look around for moorings near the school, find out the official attitude, and so on.

In and amongst the school routine, all these matters were attended to. After some haggling a sum of two hundred pounds was agreed on, subject to a satisfactory trial run and inspection; I arranged with a marine engineer acquaintance to give it the one over; a nearby firm generously gave us permission to moor up to their premises, and officialdom gave guarded approval. Arrangements were made to meet for a trial run early one Saturday morning and the same five members of our party duly turned up at the dockside. There was the rapid chuffing of a small motor from somewhere inside Cressida and a smell of petrol fumes.

"What's happening?" I asked the lock keeper who had come out to greet us. "Pumping her out," he said.

"Pumping her out!" I echoed, "why does she need pumping out?"

"Wooden boats always take in water. Gets in between the planking. She'd have been full up only it's shallow here. She's been sitting on the bottom for months."

Before we had time to digest this, a bearded young man dressed like a deep sea fisherman appeared from the hatch and hailed us cheerfully.

"Ahoy there!" he bellowed, "come aboard. We need a few extra hands."

We clambered up, feeling inadequate in our more formal clothing and, in my case at least, worried about this pumping business.

"I'm Jim Crawshaw," said the young man, "and this," referring to a hair covered face which had just popped up, coughing and choking, from below, "is Daphne. What's up old girl – getting a bit thick down there, is it?"

As she was rapidly disappearing in a swirling fog of exhaust fumes which were pouring out of the hatchway, the question seemed a bit frivolous but he appeared not to notice.

"Arnold's sorry he couldn't come along himself. Business and all that, you know, but no need to worry. Daphne and I'll look after you. That's it – cough it up old girl. It is getting a bit smelly. Oh, damn. It's stopped again."

The thumping from below had, indeed, ceased and the mists began to thin slowly.

"Tell me," I asked, "what's the need for all this pumping? We knew nothing about this."

"Wooden boat, old boy. Standard practice. Has to be done regularly, you know. Arnold asked me to tell you, by the by – you can have the pump if you like for an extra twenty-five quid. I'd say it's worth it. Saves a lot of hard labour. Now, what we have to do is to fix up the outboard and then, when we've dried her out, we're ready for off. Pop down and get that blasted pump going again will you, Daphne, old thing? Can't do everything y'know."

He strode purposefully to the stern whilst Daphne's head disappeared below the hatch.

"Well, I suppose we'd better lend a hand," I said, "does anyone fancy going below?"

Penny and Stan eventually sort of volunteered. I suggested that the rest of us should form a choir and sing excerpts from 'Orpheus in the Underworld' as they lowered themselves out of sight, but Penny said some of the less cheerful parts of 'Faust' would be more appropriate. When they had gone, the remaining three followed the skipper to see what we could do. He was looking thoughtfully at a mass of khaki and rust coloured machinery lying on deck.

"Ex-American Navy, this y'know. Damn good motor when it goes, but a bit on the temperamental side and cumbersome, too. Now, let's think of the best way to tackle it."

Some two hours later, dirty, dishevelled and bad tempered, we had our first chance to stand back and observe what progress had been made. The outboard, surely the heaviest and most sharp-cornered ever made, was mounted none too securely on the metal grid thing stuck out over the stern. The dense smoke screen surrounding us would have been useful had there been enemy submarines in the vicinity. The pathetic little motor bounced about downstairs, causing a pulsating dribble of water to alternately spurt and die away out of a pipe and into the canal whence, presumably, it percolated through the gaps in our hull and back inside again. Various figures lay around in attitudes of exhaustion or asphyxia or both and the deck was strewn with empty Elastoplast tins.

Only the bearded Crawshaw retained the powers of movement and thought. He walked over to the hatch and yelled inside.

"Ahoy there, Daphne. How is she?" he called.

After a brief interval the head appeared over the top of the hatch and this time the long hair was swept aside to reveal a surprisingly young and pretty face liberally smeared with engine oil and what appeared to be soot.

"Fine," said Daphne, "she's just about clear."

"Good girl. We'll have a go at getting the outboard started then. Open us a few bottles of beer while we do the work, will you, love?"

"O.K. Skipper," she said, put out her tongue at him, grinned and went below.

An hour later, with the aide of some sandwiches and strong drink, and helped by the switching off of the pump motor, we were regaining something of our enthusiasm. After only a further half hour the outboard coughed into life, we cast off hurriedly before it had time to die on us and, slowly, the boat began to move. It was a wonderful feeling, this coming to life of an inanimate object and I was prepared to forget the perils of the immediate past and concentrate on the present. I dangled my legs over the cabin side and watched the bank sliding slowly past. The day was fine and everything was as I had imagined it would be – calm, quiet, peaceful and unhurried. I slowly turned my head to look up front and shot to my feet. We were streaking towards a closed gate, about half the width of Cressida, at a speed which I reckoned to be a lot of knots too many.

312

"Hey – look at that!" I squeaked to Penny who had been sharing my blissful unconcern.

"We'll never make it," she murmured, "I knew I should never have been a sailor."

"Not to worry, old girl," shouted our skipper, who was controlling our progress with considerable skills, "we'll make it all right. At least a couple of inches to spare all round when we get in the lock."

The trouble was getting into the lock. We stopped and tied up and Daphne came on shore with us to show us how to work the gates and sluices. Unfortunately, due to our size, nothing less than maximum opening of the gates would do, but there was so much rubbish about that this was by no means easy to attain. We spent half an hour with boat hooks and things clearing stuff away until at last we could scrape our way in. Then there was the exciting business of watching Cressida slowly lift herself whilst we anxiously checked that she wasn't going to be caught on any projections. Then, of course, we had the same pantomime getting her out at the top. There was added interest this time as Joan Metcalfe, in retrieving part of a bicycle from behind the gate, fell in.

As everybody was busy at the time, the incident passed unnoticed until her head appeared over the side.

"Man overboard!" she said.

"Good Lord, you're all wet. What are you doing there?" asked Arthur in surprise.

"I am hanging on to a rope and shouting 'Man overboard'," she explained. "Which man would that be?"

"The man would be me and I'm cold and I need help, so hurry up please."

We pulled her aboard, wringing wet and smelling of pollution. Fortunately the contingency was not unforeseen and the girls took her below and ministered to her needs, a process which included fairly stiff libations for all from the whisky bottle. They explained that this was to frighten away the germs and not, in any way, for pleasure.

It was now getting on for early evening and I thought that, in view of the time it had taken to travel about two miles, it would be as well to ask our skipper what his plans were. I suggested to him that it might be a good idea to think in terms of turning back.

"Turning back, old boy. Whatever for?" he asked.

"Well, it's getting a bit late, isn't it, and we have a pretty good idea by now of what it's all about."

"Some misunderstanding, old boy. Arnold said to take it to Shipham. In any case we can't turn a thing like this round when we feel like it, can we, eh?" He laughed uproariously at the very idea.

"But we'll never make it to Shipham tonight," I said, "with all the locks and swing bridges and so on."

"Not to worry, old boy. We'll moor at Charfield and Daphne and I'll kip onboard. You get a bus back to Frontown and pick up your cars and then you can join us again tomorrow."

It surprised us all, in view of what had gone before, that this forecast of what could happen did, in fact, come to pass, and at about half past ten we were making our separate ways home. I gave Penny a lift and, talking over the day's happenings, we decided that, because everything was so new and strange, we had enjoyed ourselves. Whether this meant that it was going to be of any use for the children as a matter on which we were beginning to have doubts.

"There wouldn't be much use saying to a class that we were going to take them for a trip up the canal and then make them sit still for four hours until we were ready to go," said Penny.

"An that lock gate business is a pest. It might be better away from the towns but we've no guarantee. I'm beginning to think that the thing is just too big and awkward to be any use."

"Yes, I'm sure you're right. It's a pity though. It seemed to have such great possibilities."

"Never mind. We'll think it over. I'm pleased you came, Penny. In a peculiar sort of way I've enjoyed today."

"I see you haven't lost your gift for paying strange compliments – if that's what it was intended to be. I've enjoyed it, too, Mr Curtis. Thanks for the lift home. I'm sorry I can't be with you again tomorrow, but you do understand about the church choir, don't you?"

"Yes of course. Our loss is their gain and all that sort of thing. As a matter of fact I'm surprised your husband lets you out of his sight for as long as he does."

She leaned back against the car door and looked at me and smiled.

"You really are out of date, Mr Curtis," she said, "My husband disappeared two years ago and I'm expecting my divorce at any time. I really should have told you I suppose, but I thought everyone knew. Which just shows how self-centred I have become. There's no earthly reason why you should know."

"Oh, really – I am an idiot. I'm sorry..." I began, but she interrupted me. "There's no need to be sorry, Mr Curtis. Even when I knew you before, he was hardly ever at home and, really, I'm much better off without him."

"Well, well. You'll have to give me time to get used to this. But I have been a prize clot, haven't I? In the meantime, thanks for your company, Penny. Good night."

"Good night, Mr Curtis," she said.

I dreamed that night of guiding Cressida, shrouded in exhaust fumes, into the lagoon of a palm fringed island where Penny Worth, dressed like Dorothy Lamour, was playing the piano on the beach and singing 'Old Macdonald had a Farm'.

Before setting out in the morning I rang my marine engineer friend who, after recovering from being awakened in the early hours of Sunday morning, agreed to be at our moorings that evening.

Now that we no longer expected to be able to leap aboard, press a knob or two and move off, as one would with a car, the delay in starting caused no dismay. I was unhappy, it is true, at hearing the pump engine going again when I arrived and it seemed to me to take a very long time to get rid of the surplus water.

"She hasn't been mobile for a couple of years, you see," explained Jim Crawshaw, "The timbers dry out and then she shoves her way through the water and in it comes. Perfectly natural."

Being an easily convincible sort of person, this sounded reasonable to me, but I still couldn't help thinking that a couple of hours pumping before undertaking even the shortest voyage was a bit much. However, we eventually chugged slowly along, clearing out the canal as we went at no expense to the Inland Waterways Board, and accompanied by groups of small children who threw words of encouragement and other things as we passed. The fishermen were not so pleased. As we took up most of the available water space, they had to wake up and haul in their lines, and some of their comments had little to do with the quietly contemplative pastime beloved of Isaac Walton.

Late afternoon saw us tying up at our own private moorings at Shipham, all of ten miles from our starting point the previous morning and feeling like Christopher

Columbus. Adamant that they had been given no instructions about returning Cressida to her home in Frontown, our skipper and Daphne were anxious to be on their way so we thanked them and showed them where to find a bus. When they had gone we sat on the cabin roof and looked at each other.

"You know, I could get used to this life," said Joan, whose enthusiasm was in no way dampened by her immersion.

"Me too," said Arthur, "I'm all for it."

"The thing that's worrying me," I said, "is that all we asked for was a trial run. Now we seem to be in full possession."

"And owing two hundred quid plus whatever it takes to finish and not being at all sure that it's any use to us," said Stan.

We were a bit sombre when Tony, my boat expert friend, arrived and took a quick cursory glance.

"Lord," he said, "you didn't tell me it was an ocean liner. This thing would fetch a fortune on the Thames that's no use to you, though. Right – let's get inside and have a look."

He gathered together his technical equipment consisting of an electric torch, a screwdriver and a boy-scout's penknife and went below. We followed in silence.

"Making a bloody good job of the conversion, as far as they've got," he said, "but that's not what you want to know. Let's have these boards up."

In a few minutes the flooring from various parts of the vessel was propped up against the cabin walls and we were peering into the wet depths beneath.

"A bit damp, isn't she?" said Tony, "has she collected all this today?" We admitted that this was so.

"That doesn't look so good to me," he said, and started crawling on hands and knees, shining his torch into remote corners and probing with his knife. After a couple of minutes he sat up.

"What do you think of that?" he asked, and handed me a fistful of thick, pulpy material.

"Actually, I'm not mad about it," I said, "what is it?"

"It's a bit of one of the bottom timbers. If I tried really hard I reckon I could go right through. Hang on a while and I'll see how much more there is."

We went aloft and sat around gloomily waiting for the inevitable verdict. It wasn't long before he emerged.

"Pity," he said, "great pity. Someone's wasted an awful lot of money here. If you'll pardon the expression, I wouldn't touch it with a barge pole. The hull is rotten in several places and that's where the water is coming in – not between the planks."

"And what's the cure?" I asked.

"Only one thing, Ken. Have her in dry dock and put new timbers in, and that'll cost a bomb. In any case, I think she's too big for you to cope with round here."

"So, as far as we are concerned she's useless?"

"Just that. Don't spend a penny on her. Now, where's the nearest pub?"

The idea seemed sound, so we went with him to drown our sorrows. The boat had been such a good idea and it seemed such a pity that nothing was going to come of it, that we concentrated hard on overcoming our grief and ended up singing sea shanties in the moonlight by the canal and watching Cressida slowly settle on to the bottom.

It took a number of letters and a touch of acrimony to sort matters out but, eventually, someone else bought her and one morning I noticed she had gone. We were all relieved, but sad too.

It wasn't the end of our canal ventures, though, for I managed to make arrangements with a secondary school at Sheepton, fifteen miles further into the Pennine country, to borrow a little outboard motor cruiser they had built themselves and hardly ever used. We had a few trips with it, taking half a dozen children and a couple of staff each time. After Cressida it was like driving a Mini instead of an articulated lorry, getting away from the quayside within five minutes and slipping in and out of locks with no bother at all.

The children learned to leap ashore and run on to the next lock or swing bridge so there was no unnecessary waiting. Occasionally they jumped in the water or ran through cow-claps or started to open bridges when cars were still on them, but there were no disasters and we had a lot of fun. It made us regret even more not having been able to own a craft ourselves, but at a school new things are happening all the time and we didn't have time to weep too much.

CHAPTER THIRTEEN

At school, the new cooker had arrived in a large cardboard box, which was left in a corner of the hall until such time as we could find a use for it. The old schoolhouse kitchen was pressed into service as a domestic science room and a succession of boys and girls made their first experiments in the culinary art under the guidance of Mrs Hawthorne. There was a steady flow of chocolate buns, ginger biscuits and such like delicacies, some of which were donated to the staff for their mid-morning break. The relish with which these were disposed of varied according to the known behaviour pattern of the child who had, literally, had a hand in the preparation.

One day Stan Evans came to me with a puzzled expression on his face. "Barry Ford's disappeared," he said.

"You mean there was a puff of blue smoke and there he was, gone?"

"Except for the blue smoke, yes. He was in my class until break time. He was playing with the others and he came back into school with them when the bell went. That's the last anyone has seen of him."

This Barry Ford was a child who was never going to embarrass his parents by his academic achievements. He was, in fact, as we educationalists say, thick. He did not realise that he knew nothing and was, therefore, saved the disappointment of trying to learn. He was cheerfully ignorant and, although his behaviour at times was a little odd, everyone liked him. He had moments when, like

321

anyone else, he was pleased to be able to demonstrate some small skill and receive his quota of praise. I remembered one day when he came up to me in the hall and said, "Hey, sir, see what I can do." He then hurled himself upwards into the air and, curling over like a spent rocket at the end of its trajectory, landed on the parquet floor on the top of his head. He stood up, looking slightly cross-eyed, and beamed.

"Is that it?" I asked.

"Ay, sir," he said.

"Then don't do it again. You'll either smash the floor or kill yourself and neither of those would be a good idea."

On the present occasion we sent out scouts to search the odd corners, or to see whether he had got stuck down the toilet, but there was no sign of him. The children were certain that he had come up the stairs from the back playground and into the hall after break.

"It's ridiculous," said Stan, "you can't disappear in the hall here."

I was just about to agree with him when, as if by a magnet, we both turned and looked at the cooker box in the corner.

"Is it possible?" I asked.

"With Barry Ford anything's possible. Let's go and have a look."

We walked over, lifted the flap at the top and peered in. There, curled up at the bottom, fast asleep, was Barry.

Stan had been prepared to murder him, but his expression softened.

"Poor little sod," he said. I'll leave him 'til dinnertime and then belt the box with the blackboard ruler. That should wake him up."

During this first term the D.E.O. was a fairly frequent visitor, partly because he considered it an important part of his duty to visit all schools regularly, and partly to ensure that I didn't let the place got to rack and ruin. I asked him one day how long I was likely to be in occupation because, as far as I knew, no move had been made to make a permanent appointment.

"Well," he said, "you know that your predecessor left to go to a bigger school and I suppose you've heard rumours that a new school is going to be built. Actually it's more than just a rumour. There is going to be a new building to take the place of this one and Cooper Street Infants. What is speculation is when a start is going to be made and, frankly, I don't know. One thing is settled, though, and that is that the Headship of the new place will go to Miss Stopton who, as you know, is Head of Cooper Street now. It comes under reorganisation, you see, so we can make a direct appointment."

"And where does that leave me?"

"In possession, for the time being. No one is likely to apply for this job if we advertise it, knowing that it's for a very limited time and with no prospects at the end of it."

"So that means I could be here until the new school is built, presumably. How long is that likely to be?"

"Minimum eighteen months, maximum three years. I just can't be any more definite than that at this stage. I'm hoping that there'll be more information at the end of this week when the committee has met again, but if you were to press me, I'd say two years at least."

This news opened up all sorts of possibilities. For the first time I would be able to think and plan ahead, not for a couple of weeks, but for a couple of terms or even years. It was a prospect I enjoyed but, in the meantime, there was the present to think about and, as far as out-of-the-routine events were concerned that meant sports day. I had already found out that there was a considerable amount of tradition connected with this affair, which I would flout at my peril.

Not having a field of our own, the sports day was held on the grounds of the secondary modern school about a quarter of a mile away and the big event of the afternoon was always the one-mile race. For this, a cup had been presented by the chap who had, at one time, been the big landowner hereabouts and was now chairman of the school managers. This Sir Edward Mills-Crofton lived about fifteen miles away in his last mansion and expected to be asked to present his cup at the sports day each year. I, personally, thought that a mile was too long for eleven year olds but was told quite clearly that non-inclusion of this event would result in lynching by the citizenry, if the squire didn't have me bricked up in the wall of his house first.

The other thing was a staff and parents three-legged race, which, I gathered, was always good for a laugh, particularly at the expense of the Head who was, apparently expected to fall about in untidy heaps with his partner. Grown men and women with memories of canings and detentions and tellings-off came from miles around to see this spectacle and enjoy a bit of good, clean fun.

So the programme was made out, entries were received, with or without coercion; Sir Edward accepted the kind invitation to attend and present his cup and this object itself was taken from its hiding place in the stock room and given a polish. It was an imposing if unlovely thing, gaining in sheer size what it lacked in subtlety of line. Engraved on it in a sort of tomb-stone makers Gothic was the name of our benefactor and the event for which it was to be awarded, the names of the winners appearing on a miniature shields which were nailed on to the plinth. The polishers, suitably impressed with the importance of their task, had to be told to go easy on the abrasives as the plating was wearing thin in one or two places.

On the morning of the day itself the weather looked reasonably promising as Arthur Green and I went along to the field armed with tape measures and stakes and string and one of those little trundling machines that is supposed to make white lines. Most of the measuring had been done on the previous evening so, with our helpers from Arthur's class not getting in the way too much, we completed the preparations in good time. There was a straight track, half delineated by white lines and half by bits of string, and with an irregular white patch in the middle where Arthur, in his fury at having to go over every line six times, had flung the machine from him. The two boys who had been helping him at the time had taken notes home explaining that it was a mechanical fault, which had led to their immersion in a solution of whitewash. There was a circuit of two hundred and twenty yards, or thereabouts, and in the centre was a table on which the cup would be displayed and a royal box in the form of two staffroom chairs for our guests.

After dinner the children, by now wildly excited, crocodiled up the road to the field and went to their appointed stations. It was always a great surprise to me that, although they never listened to instructions, chattered constantly about irrelevancies and could not answer simple questions yet, when the moment arrived, they – or most of them – did the right thing.

It was the same with music. I often went into the music room where the choir was supposed to be rehearsing, only to be met by the most hideous din. The choristers would all be snarling at each other in voices which were not merely loud, but coarse and strained to an unbelievable degree.

"Gerofferme 'and, yer stupid nit," a little blonde girl would be screeching.

"Get lost. I'll beat yer 'ead in if yer don't shurrup" her best friend would riposte wittily.

All over the room this was happening and then Penny would play a chord on the piano, smile sweetly, and there would be silence. She would play the opening bars and out of those mouths would come,

"Say, ye who borrow, Love's magic spell...." In sweet heavenly voices that would have enchanted Mozart himself.

I came, in time, not to understand, but to accept and be thankful for this remarkable facility.

On the present occasion I was pleasantly surprised to find the children going into the spectators' or competitors' enclosures of the appropriate age groups without requiring more than the necessary minimum of shepherding so that, dead on time, we were ready for the first race. This was a forty yard dash for the seven year old girls who were lined up facing in approximately the right direction of travel. Although we were quite happy, I doubt if it would have done for the White City. One child was balanced on one leg like a stork, her hands clasped over the head, another was jumping up and down and waving delightedly to her mother who reciprocated from the middle of the track, and two more were deep in conversation. Only one no doubt under the influence of a relative who knew about these things, was leaning forward eagerly awaiting the signal to start.

Arthur, wanting to do the thing properly, had borrowed a starting pistol from somewhere and, holding this aloft, chanted the approved formula.

"On your marks!" he said, and, although nobody actually moved, one or two glanced at him to see what he was on about.

"Get set!" he intoned after a suitable interval, whereupon the stork imitator noticed the pistol for the first time and began to cry quietly to herself.

Then he fired and there was an almighty crack and a cloud of smoke. The girl with the eager stance was flat on her face in the grass, the jumping up and down one was breaking all known records in fleeing to her mother and the others were gazing at Arthur with expressions of wonder tinged with admiration. It was decided that, for the younger ones at any rate, it would be better to say one, two, three, go, and hide the firearm somewhere where the older boys couldn't get at it.

So, apart from some confusion during the first relay, events progressed uneventfully as Mrs MacDonald remarked. The reason for the relay difficulty was that, as practice had been done in the confines of the school yard it had been necessary for the lead person to dash to the opposite wall where number two would take the baton, run back to number three and so on. This to-and-from action had impressed itself on the minds of the participants to such an extent that the wide open spaces of a continuous circuit baffled them. The number ones set off all right and handed over to the number twos who paused irresolutely and then had a discussion as to what to do next. Having sorted it out to their own satisfaction they dashed back to the start where, of course, nobody was waiting to receive the batons, so they turned round and ran back again. The number ones, seeing nobody else available, prepared to take the batons and go back yet again. This could have gone on all afternoon had it not been for the number threes and fours who, tired of waiting for their turns, charged across the field, tripped up those who were still shuttling backwards and forwards like batsmen in some crazy cricket match, and started thumping them.

After this heavy stuff the light relief came in the form of the notorious three- legged race. It was possible to tell when this was due because the spectators all began to look happy and to stop talking and to move towards the track as you see happening on the films when the preliminaries are over and the Derby is about to start. I don't know how the pairs had been arranged but I found myself partnered by Penny, which pleased me. Indeed, when I realised that in order to make any sort of progress it would be necessary to put our arms round each other I found the sports day taking on a completely different meaning.

"We are not going to be made to look ridiculous," I said to her just before the start, "it is really quite simple. Just a matter of timing. If I count so that we have a matched stride, we shall not only keep upright, we might even win."

"Yes, Mr Curtis," she said meekly.

It didn't quite happen that way, of course. We set off all right and whether it was the unevenness of the ground or the disturbing roaring of the crowd I don't know, but about half way down the course things started to go awry. We ended up in the usual untidy heap after one or two involuntary somersaults to the intense gratification of all and sundry. We sat there on the grass untying the handkerchief that held us together.

"I think the trouble was that you were in four-four time and I was in six-eight," said Penny.

"In that case we were heading for trouble from the start," I said, "everyone knows that six-eight is for marching, not for running."

"At least we've proved one thing." "And what would that be?"

"We don't need pogo sticks to bring us to the ground. We can do it unaided.

We picked ourselves up, waved to the cheering multitude and prepared to be dignified again ready for the arrival of Sir Edward. This thought made me glance towards the central table and comedy immediately turned to tragedy. The cup was not in its place of honour and, what was more, a dark green Bentley that could only belong to the great man himself, was driving into the ground.

I hurried over to Stan Evans and hissed, "Find those two morons who are supposed to be in charge of the flaming cup, will you?" And then moved over to greet Sir Edward and his Lady. I bumbled a bit as I always had a tendency to do under such circumstances. I told myself very firmly that I was probably brainier than he, that I certainly knew much more about education, that it was ten to one he couldn't play a saxophone and the recorder as well as I could. There were other similar arguments like the often recalled advice of the policeman before my first interview outside County Hall, but I still felt awkward and inferior, just because he was what he was. There was one thing I had learned over the years, though; I could now hide my feelings a lot better than I used to do, and I doubt if anyone on the field suspected that I was anything but at ease.

"Welcome, Sir Edward," I said with a sort of off-hand gaiety suitable to the occasion, "how nice to see you. It really is good of you to spend your valuable time with us in this way."

This was pure hypocrisy, as I knew for a fact that he spent all his waking hours sitting in a corner of his mansion watching the telly. He took it all in, however, and introduced me to his wife, a pale, elderly shadow of a woman, and we strolled together towards the centre of the field chatting amiably enough. As we neared the table he started peering here and there in an anxious fashion like a hen that has lost its chicks. "Haven't got the cup on display this year, eh?" he asked.

"No. Well, not yet. We've been giving it a special clean, you know. Two very reliable girls looking after it most carefully, of course. Mr Evans has just gone to get it from them. Should be here now, really. I can't think what's keeping him.

There was, in fact, nothing keeping him for, at that moment he came through the gate looking rather red in the face and headed straight over to where we were standing. One hand, I noticed, was behind his back. He looked as though he would prefer not to be noticed but as Sir Edward was staring straight at him this was going to be difficult.

"Its Mr Evans, isn't it?" said our distinguished guest, "Remember seeing you before, eh?" Got the old cup safe and sound then?"

"Well, sir, I'm afraid there's been a little accident. It's.... er...." he gulped and revealed what it was he had been holding behind his back.

It was a flat, metallic object, roughly the shape of the sort of cup one would one would present to someone on a sports day but looking as though it had been cut out of a sheet of cardboard. It was also coated in dried mud and bits of gravel.

"Good God! What the devil is that?" asked Sir Edward.

"It's the cup, Sir" mumbled Stan.

"What in God's name has happened to it, man? It looks as though it's been under a damned steam roller, eh?"

"And so it has," said Stan, recovering a little of his customary calm, "the two girls who were supposed to be bringing it here were crying rather a lot and weren't very coherent, but as far as I can gather they set off all right. Then the one who was doing the carrying was pushed playfully by the other one, the cup flew out of her hand and that was it. You may have noticed they're doing the road outside the school. A road roller happened to be passing at that moment."

Sir Edward was a man of naturally rubicund countenance but his face took on an even deeper hue as the rest of us watched him with bated breath. I felt sure that I was about to have a new experience – that of watching a baronet, have a heart attack. He looked at each of us in turn, his already prominent eyes protruding further and further from his head as unearthly rumbling sounds started to emanate from somewhere inside and he began to shake uncontrollably. I was on the point of dispatching Stan to make a 999 call when I realised that Sir Edward was not dying – he was laughing. He laughed until tears ran down his purple cheeks and, somewhat tentatively, we all began to join in. Eventually he wiped his eyes and blew his nose.

"God," he said, "That was better than T.V., just looking at your faces. Thank the Lord I shall never have to give that wretched thing away again. I hated the sight of it. Don't worry, I'll get you something else. My goodness, Emily, I enjoyed that!"

As this high drama was drawing to a close I noticed Arthur hovering around and looking concerned. He came over and murmured, "Ready for the mile, Mr Curtis. Can I start 'em?"

I sat my guests down, excused myself and went off with Arthur to the starting line. There was a large, enthusiastic and completely inexperienced entry ranging from the dullest to the brightest and including almost every known form of wearing apparel. There was Chris Dewhirst looking every inch the expert in shorts, singlet and spiked shoes whereas Willie March, having been told that a mile was a long way, had come prepared in a donkey jacket, corduroy trousers and wellington boots. Some said that he had sandwiches and a thermos flask in his pockets.

Then there was Kevin Camp, a lad whose birth certificate confirmed that he was eleven years old and who was, indeed, well developed physically. Unfortunately, his brain had found it hard work keeping pace with his body and had given up the struggle a long time previously. He had asked one of his more literate contemporaries to put his name down for any appropriate event and so found himself in the classic mile. The fact that this distance held about as much meaning to him as infinity worried him not at all.

"Remember it's eight laps, Kevin," I said to him as he went to line up.

He grinned his acknowledgement of this information without, I was sure, knowing what laps were and probably not being all that certain about the meaning of 'eight' either.

Arthur went through the starting routine for the last time that afternoon and fired his pistol. Fifteen boys ambled away at the sort of pace one might expect in what was, for them, a very long distance race, and Kevin shot off into the distance like a hare escaping from the hounds. Inevitably he came in at the end of a lap, grinning broadly, streets ahead of the field and under the impression that he had won. Joan Metcalf pointed him in the right direction and gave him a push. The realisation dawned on him that there was more in this than met the eye and, accelerating like a rocket, he galloped in pursuit of the rear end of the file in front of him, still well in the lead. Seven times this happened. Seven times he slowed to a stop and seven times he was restarted. At the end of the eighth lap he had got the hang of the thing and had to be forcibly restrained from setting off again. In spite of his erratic progress he won by half a lap from Dewhirst who had paced himself carefully according to a pre-arranged plan and seemed very cross about it.

Kevin was a popular boy and received a standing ovation when he went up to receive the flattened cup from Sir Edward who said he had shown a fine example of the tenacity of purpose which had made England a great nation.

Everyone said it had been a good day and I was inclined to think they were right.

There was just one more ceremony that term which was new to me. Being the time of year when the top class children left to go to secondary schools I had to say my farewells to them at a final assembly. I felt the solemnity of the occasion very keenly. When we sang "Lord dismiss us with they blessing," and there were those who wept. I gave them a little chat in which I told them, sincerely, that I was going to miss their company and that they would be welcome to come and see us at any time. In other words the same old stuff that had been said year after year in thousands of school all over the country but, to the children, and to me, it was important. I reflected that, for the first time for many years, it was the children who were leaving and not I.

The staff had organised a little fuddle in a neighbouring restaurant a few evenings previously so that, once the children had gone, it was only necessary to wish everyone a happy holiday and then, for five weeks, turn my back on it all.

For some reason it turned out that Mrs Worth and I were once again the last to leave.

"Going anywhere exotic?" I asked her.

"I'm afraid not. Finances don't' run to anything more than a week this year, so I'm going to a farm I know in Wensleydale."

"Are you really? Do you know, it's my favourite part of the world – maybe because I've been going up there for years now and it seems almost like going home? I suppose you would really prefer somewhere more glamorous, though."

"No. I like seeing new places, of course, but I love the Dales, too. Somehow when I get up there everything seems just right. My idea of Heaven would be to teach in a little school somewhere between Leyburn and Hawes and if I had any sort of determination I suppose I would be doing just that. It's only the thought of leaving friends and relations that stops me I suppose."

"Well, I'm staggered. Do you know, I thought I was the only person on earth who had ideas like that? Well, well, well. I tell you what, Penny – I shall be having as much time up there as I can get myself. I'll look out for you. We might bump into each other, don't you think?"

"We keep doing it, don't we? It would be nice. Anyway, have a good holiday, Mr Curtis."

"Thanks, Penny, and the same to you."

I didn't really expect to see her, of course, but I thought it would be pleasant for once to share the pleasures of a much-loved part of the world. Not that I really expected anyone to feel about it as I did. It was all, no doubt, just the usual polite conversation.

When I reached home Peter was looking through the evening paper.

"Hey!" he greeted me, "you've talked about this chap. One of your bosses."

"There are thousands of those. Which one are you on about?"

"Obediah Smith. Stupid bloody name. Fancy going through life called Obediah!"

"What about him?"

"He's dead. Had a stroke yesterday and snuffed it straight away. Not all that surprising, I suppose. He was eighty three."

So that was it, I thought. My sympathies were, at that moment, entirely with me. What right had he to go and die like that? I felt he had done me a mean trick and I resented it deeply.

"There's no need to look so flaming miserable," said Peter, "you didn't' know him all that well, did you?"

"No, I hardly knew him at all," I said, "but he was a character, you know. Cute as a barrow load of monkeys, they used to say. He'll be missed."

"Well, if that's all, you'd better see if that bloody rattletrap of yours will start. We've just got time to call and see Wilf for half an hour and then you can run me over to Joan's. I took Lizzie in for a service this afternoon and you can't expect me to walk, can you?"

"Of course not, Pete," I said, and we locked the door and went out.

CHAPTER FOURTEEN

EPILOGUE AND PROLOGUE

Peter broke the news to me one day that the date was fixed for the last week in July. There was no need to ask the date for what, as little else had been spoken about for months.

"We all had a get-together last night", he told me on evening, "and got down to details. You're going to be best man".

"It didn't occur to you to ask whether I would like to be best man?" I asked. He looked at me in surprise.

"What the bloody hell for?" he asked, "it's all been fixed". "In that case I accept".

"Of course you do. It's going to be a proper affair with toppers and all that, so you'd better get yourself rigged out. The service is going to be at Dorlan Church. Joan's mum likes a bit of ceremony so we're having it there – it's high church".

"You mean it has a tall spire".

"I knew you'd say that, you silly devil. You know very well what it means. They get dressed up in fancy robes and things, and they chant, and they burn that smelly stuff. What's it called?"

"Incest?" I suggested.

"That's right. Incense. I think it's damned silly, personally, but we've got to keep Joan's mum happy".

This was very true. Joan's mum was a charming person for ninety percent of the time, but if she took it into her head to be displeased, strong men quailed.

337

"The reception's going to be at the Dorlan Arms. Everyone's been invited. You'll make a speech, of course".

"Of course. Seriously Pete, you're going to have to tell me a lot more aren't you? I know nothing about high church services for a start".

"Oh hell, I'd forgotten. You're one of those non-conformist people aren't you? All tambourines and hallelujahs. There won't be any of that, I can tell you".

"What a pity. I was looking forward to bashing my tambourine and shouting hallelujah when his vicarage said "do you take this chap for better or worse?" Now you've disappointed me".

Later on we did go into minute detail, of course, until everything was arranged to Peter's satisfaction. The only real problem was with the cars, which, he insisted should all be Rolls Royce's. He was so adamant, that he took over the organisation of this part himself, although it really had nothing to do with him.

"I don't want two Rolls-Royces and two Daimlers", he said to the representative of one firm, "I want four Rolls-Royces or nothing".

"In that case sir", said the man, I shall make arrangements with another company to let us have two more Rolls-Royces. That will of course, make it a little more expensive".

"Who mentioned money?" demanded Peter grandly, knowing that it wouldn't be his.

Being Peter, an agreement about the weather had been negotiated with the Almighty, and the wedding day was one of unbroken blue skies and hot sunshine. Joan looked incredibly beautiful in her white dress with a long train and Peter contrived to look smug and self-conscious and nervous all at the same time, which was unusual for him.

Whether I looked smug, I don't know, but I was certainly nervous. However, the ring was not forgotten, the parson was paid, the Rolls-Royces whispered to and fro, and the speech went down well, as it should to an audience of people who had been stoked up with food and fine wines. The bride and groom reappeared in their holiday clothes, there was much cheering and laughing and off they went to a secret rendezvous in Perpignan called the Hotel de Anglais. Things fell a bit flat after that, except in the case of a coterie of distant relatives who, determined to take full advantage of the free booze, had long since forgotten what occasion it was they were celebrating.

Eventually it was all over and I went back to the flat and changed out of my Moss Bros outfit and sat down and looked around. It felt very empty and lonely and I wondered what I was going to do with all my evenings.

This mood did not last for long, of course, I was shopping around for a new car for one thing and as this was to be the first new vehicle I had ever owned, it was occupying my mind for a great deal of the time. The old Wolseley really was past it by now and I had realised for months that it would have to go. I felt quite sad about it, even though its performance was now negligible, it demanded sympathetic fiddling to get it to start in the mornings, and its tyres, brakes, battery and exhaust system were all in need of expensive attentions. After spending hours trailing round the garages in the area, where my suggestion that they should allow money on the Wolseley was greeted with either laughter or incredulity, I had a ridiculously generous part-exchange offer against a new Morris Minor from a place that went bankrupt almost immediately afterwards.

My feelings about this new acquisition were mixed. I had loved that Wolseley and nursed it through its illnesses and coaxed it in its awkwardness as one would a wayward son. On the other hand I now had a brand new, shining car on which everything worked the first time of asking, and which was watertight, comfortable and warm. I was, of course, frightened to death in case anyone put a dirty hand on the paintwork. Loose gravel on the roads brought me down to walking pace and I would only park where other people, all of whom would be less skilful than I, would have plenty of room to get by without scraping the wings.

It was perfectly natural that the first journey of any length, taken at the recommended running-in speed, should be to Wensleydale. In deference to the newness of everything I even went the easy way through Ripon and Middleham instead of by one of the exciting passes over the top from Wharfedale. This really was the start of the holiday. No words could do justice to the calm, peaceful loveliness, which meant so much to me. It was pleasant, too, to saunter along at a gentle pace, knowing that if I pressed the brake pedal the car would stop, that if I changed gear I would not finish up holding the unattached lever in my hand and that the horn button, if depressed, would produce a tooting sound instead of cutting of the ignition.

I looked out for Mrs Worth, of course, but realised that I hadn't thought to ask where she was staying. As I reckoned there was about a hundred and twenty square miles where she might be, the chances were pretty slim and yet I somehow felt aggrieved when I didn't see her, as though she were deliberately avoiding me.

So the days passed rather purposelessly by. I had my outings; I saw the four rainless days of a test match at Headingley; I visited one or two old pals and I practice the saxophone and the recorder. Then, one afternoon about a week before the end of the holiday, I was sitting in the flat facing up to the idea that I felt miserable. I couldn't finish the Guardian crossword, I didn't want to have anything to do with music, the idea of riding around in the car held no appeal and I saw no pleasure in going for a drink on my own. Then I realised that I had hit the nail on the head – I just could see no pleasure in the prospect of doing any of these things by myself.

"Curtis, you fool," I said aloud – a habit which was causing me some concern. "You want your head examining. You are not the self sufficient creature you imagined yourself to be. You will, this very evening don some respectable clothes, try to remember where Penny Worth lives and go and ask her out for a ride or a drink or something".

With something approaching joie de vivre I made myself some baked beans on toast and then went into the routine I had mapped out. I shaved with more than usual care, squirted myself with some aftershave stuff which had been lying around unopened since three Christmases before and arrayed myself in my best slacks and a snazzy new sports jacket. When all was ready I sat in the Morris going through all the symptoms of having a relapse.

"You're a fool", I told myself, "getting all worked up like this. You know nothing ever goes the way you expect it. Be logical for once and look at it this way: – Point one; it's a hundred to one she won't be home. Point two; if she is, there's sure to be someone with her – you don't even know if she has a boyfriend, do you? Point three; assuming she is in, what gives you the idea she will want to see you? Point four; she's quite a bit younger than you are, so stop kidding yourself.

I sat for a moment and thought it over.

"Accepting the fact that you are a fool", I said, "at least having got yourself tarted up, you may as well see the thing through now. If she's out, she's out and if she's in and doesn't want to see you, then she'll say no and that will be the end of it. You weren't doing anything else, were you?"

I agreed that I wasn't doing anything else, started the Morris and turned down the road to Shipham. On the way I rehearsed my excuse for calling. I considered I needed an excuse, mainly to explain my presence if someone else should happen to be there, but also because I couldn't see myself charging straight into the house and whizzing out again with her under my arm like Young Lochinvar, without a word of explanation.

In twenty minutes I was taping on the door, feeling a complete fool and knowing nothing would go as planned. Then the door opened and there she was. Her face broke into that smile as she opened the door wider.

"Why Mr Curtis. This is a nice surprise. Do come in".

"Thanks. I hope you don't mind my calling. Shan't keep you a minute, really. I was just passing and..."

"Yes, of course, I understand. You'll be in a hurry, but can I make you a cup of coffee or anything? I'm sorry I haven't anything stronger to offer. Do sit down, please".

I perched on the edge of a settee and groped in my pocket for my excuse.

"No hurry at all and I really don't want anything just at the moment, thanks. I was passing, you see and I brought this along. Bought it the other day to try out. It's music for the recorder and piano and I wondered if you could have a look over the piano parts and then maybe we could have a go at it later. I just thought I'd bring it. Had to come past, you see", I ended, anxious that she shouldn't miss this bit of the story.

"Yes, of course, I'd love to", she said, flicking over the pages. "It looks a bit beyond my sight reading capabilities, I'm afraid. Could you leave it with me?" She put the music on top of the piano and looked at me and smiled. "You know, I've been on my own for days. I am glad to see you!"

"I suppose I feel the same way, really. Peter got himself married you know, so I've had about as much as I can stand of my own company. It palls after a while, doesn't it?"

"It does indeed," she looked around as though wandering what to do next. "I am sorry I can't offer you a drink. Are you sure you won't..."

"No, I won't" I interrupted her, "but I've a better idea. Why don't you come out for half an hour or so and I'll buy you a drink instead".

"That would be marvellous! Are you sure I'm not taking up your time? I really would love to get away for a little while if you're sure you don't mind".

"My evening is at your disposal and, anyway I want to show off with my new car, I haven't had the chance yet".

"A new car, too! This is an evening of surprises. Would you mind waiting a minute while I do something with my hair? I shan't be long. Put a record on, or help yourself to a book or something".

She disappeared upstairs and left me thinking that this could not be happening to me. Everything I had planned was working just as I had planned and that had never been known to happen before. Not only that, but I was feeling a kind of pleasure which was way beyond the sort of thing one might expect at the prospect of taking a young lady for a drink.

True to her word, it seemed only a few minutes before Penny was back, looking, young and slim and fresh and happy.

343

She was gratifyingly impressed with the new car and I was self-deprecatingly modest about it as though I'd made it myself.

"Do you know", I said, as we moved off, "no one has sat in that seat before. I hope it's adjusted all right. Have you any choice where to go?"

"The seat is heaven," she said, "and I don't mind in the least where we go. I'm happy just to it here and be driven around".

"Right then, we'll go to Ma Brown's. Always assuming I can find the way, of course".

This Ma Brown's is a hostelry on the edge of the moors, famous at one time for providing sustenance to walkers and cyclists, but now more of a motorists' evening run out from town.

"That'll be nice," Penny said "I've never been in there, and yet I've always known it as a landmark".

"Same here, I'm not really a pub expert, you know. At least it will be something new for both of us".

So we trundled slowly along, chatting more and more freely as the few short miles went by until we saw the rather dark, square building with its background of heather and rocks. I parked the car with something less than my usual fuss and we went inside together.

"You know, Mr Curtis, I feel a fraud. I don't really like drinking – alcohol type drinking, I mean. It makes me ill. I'm sorry, but do you mind if I have an orange juice?"

"Mr dear Mrs Worth, I don't know why you think you have to apologise. An orange juice you shall have. I'm not exactly the last of the big drinkers, you know. Two small glasses and I spend the rest of the night asking to go to the toilet. There's just one grumble, though. If you keep calling me Mr Curtis, I shall make you pay the bill".

We went and sat down in a quiet corner and she told me why she had left ESN teaching, and about her sort of music and about the Dales, and I told her about the Supply Staff and about my sort of music and about the Dales. Then we started to branch out into more abstract philosophical fields and spoke of attitudes towards people and the arts and money and of what life was all about. I found myself putting into words secret things, which I had never mentioned to another soul and the time flowed by and we agreed on everything. It was only the landlord calling time that brought us back to earth, and we went out to the car and the clouds were flickering across the face of the moon. We drove slowly out of the car park and on to the moorland road.

"You know, Penny", I said, looking straight ahead, "we seem to have agreed on just about everything, don't we? I can't remember when I've enjoyed an evening so much".

"I feel just the same, Ken," said Penny quietly, "it's such a change to talk to someone who isn't always worried about how to be better than someone else. I'm sorry I put things so badly, but do you know what I mean?"

"Of course I know what you mean. It's nice just to be able to be yourself, isn't it? Without putting on an act, I mean. You're not putting on an act, are you Penny"?

"Oh no. Please don't think that. Everything has been so easy tonight and I really have enjoyed every minute."

We travelled awhile in silence – not a strained silence, but peaceful and happy and not needing to talk all the time.

"I've a confession to make", I said eventually, "I didn't have to pass your house at all tonight. I just wanted to see you. There you are – not much of a confession, really".

"I'm so glad", she whispered.

"And now I shall sing a comic song for a bit of light relief", I said.

When we arrived back at her house, Penny asked whether I would like to have a coffee, but I declined.

"We've done nothing special, but I've had a marvellous time" I said, "maybe I've said too much already, but I meant every word of it. Thanks, Penny, and goodnight".

"Goodnight, Ken, and thank you ever so much", Penny said and waved as she closed the door behind her.

I must have driven back to the flat, but I don't remember much about it. I have a feeling that I sang and laughed rather immoderately and when I got in I just stood in the middle of the room and beamed. Then I had an idea. I went to the telephone and dialled Penny's number. It had only buzzed twice when I heard her voice.

"It's only me", I said, "am I being a nuisance?"

"Hello, Ken. Of course you're not being a nuisance. It's lovely to hear you". "It's just that it occurred to me, I didn't ask you if you would see me again some time. Will you, perhaps?"

"Of course I will. I'd love to".

"How about tomorrow then? Can I call for you again?"

"Yes please. Thanks again for a lovely evening, Ken, and now I've got something to look forward to as well".

"And me. Goodnight, again, Penny – I'll see you tomorrow, then." "Yes, see you tomorrow. Goodnight".

I sat back and grinned inanely at the wall.

Thoughts of a kind were racing through my head, though I made no attempt to put them into any sort of logical order. I thought of how certain causes had the most unlikely effects; of how being in a certain place at a certain time would start a chain reaction which no one could foresee, and of how disappointments and compensations seemed to be in the habit of going closely together. I thought of how the demise of Alderman Smith, though regrettable, had no bearing on my life for I was capable of doing anything. There was, at that very moment, somewhere underneath the sideboard, a copy of the Times Educational Supplement in which was an advertisement for a Headship which only that morning I had dismissed as beyond my reach but now realised was mine for the asking. I had a feeling that I was beginning to get my values right again and I felt just simply, ridiculously, happy.

"And that", I announced loudly to a poor reproduction of Van Gogh's Sunflowers which happened to be in my line of vision, "Is What Life Is All About".

Ken Griffin was born in 1916 and the events in this book take place the 1950's, 60's and 70's.

Ken was an extremely talented and yet modest man. He did indeed marry 'Penny' in 1980 and they had a happy life together in Wensleydale until Ken's death at the age of 95.

During this Wensleydale period Ken was retired and 'Penny' was appointed head of three different village schools. Ken supported her in this and became an unpaid extra staff member. He also found time to entertain locally on his Saxophone and Clarinet, at one time with 'The Octogenarians' a group of five 80+ year olds who also featured on television as the oldest band in the country.

He continued to explore Wensleydale on foot and on his beloved motorcycle, painted water colours, cartoons and wrote.

Although the teaching anecdotes in this book are basically true he took a certain amount of poetic licence with personal details. Both Ken and 'Penny' had been previously married, Ken with a son and daughter and 'Penny' with a son, Robert who lived with them in Wensleydale.

To Kens delight there were frequent visits from his much loved and increasing family of grandchildren and great grandchildren.

Not long before Ken died we met up with his old friends Joan and Peter. Joan still beautiful and lively in her 90's and Peter as forthright and loveable as ever. Peter died peacefully in 2013.

I owe a tremendous debt of love and gratitude to Robert and Carol Merrett, my son and daughter in law, who, through the wonders of technology have typed, edited, and assembled this work for me and to Ken's memory from their home in Australia.

Wendy Griffin (Penny) Wensleydale 2013

Visit the Facebook page
http://www.facebook.com/educatingyorkshirepostwar for more information and to share with your friends.

From left to right – Peter, Penny, Joan and Ken

Ken and Peter with three more friends